REVOLUTION
AND CHINESE
FOREIGN
POLICY

REVOLUTION AND CHINESE FOREIGN POLICY

PEKING'S SUPPORT FOR WARS OF
NATIONAL LIBERATION

Peter Van Ness

UNIVERSITY OF CALIFORNIA PRESS
BERKELEY, LOS ANGELES AND LONDON 1971

UNIVERSITY OF CALIFORNIA PRESS
BERKELEY AND LOS ANGELES, CALIFORNIA

UNIVERSITY OF CALIFORNIA PRESS, LTD.
LONDON, ENGLAND

COPYRIGHT © 1970, BY PETER VAN NESS

FIRST PAPERBACK PRINTING 1971

ISBN: 0-520-02055-3
LIBRARY OF CONGRESS CATALOG CARD NUMBER: 73-89893

PRINTED IN THE UNITED STATES OF AMERICA

FOR ELLEN

CONTENTS

LIST OF TABLES

ACKNOWLEDGMENTS

In my search for a better understanding of the foreign relations of the People's Republic of China, I have received assistance from many quarters. It is my pleasure to acknowledge these debts.

Several institutions generously provided financial support for this project. At the University of California at Berkeley, the Center for Chinese Studies, the Department of Political Science, the Graduate Division, and the President's Office all helped finance my research; and the Graduate School of International Studies at the University of Denver also generously contributed its support. The Center for Chinese Studies and the Universities Service Center in Hong Kong kindly made their research facilities available to me, and I am particularly grateful to the people on the staffs of these two institutions for the help they willingly gave me, especially James C. Y. Soong, formerly at Berkeley, for his extremely competent research assistance.

Many colleagues and friends, not always agreeing completely with my approach or conclusions, made extensive comments and criticisms on drafts of the manuscript. Richard Baum, Joseph W. Esherick, Edward Friedman, Michel Oksenberg, and Richard H. Solomon particularly made major contributions to the improvement of the study. My wife, Ellen, edited the many drafts, and Mrs. Grace O'Connell expertly typed the lot. Their help has been indispensable.

Finally, special thanks are due Chalmers Johnson who provided the continuing support and encouragement so vital to sustain an extended research effort such as this has been.

Needless to say, I alone am responsible for what appears on the following pages. Any shortcomings or mistakes in the study are my own.

ABBREVIATIONS

CQ	*China Quarterly*
CSM	*Christian Science Monitor*
HC	*Hung-ch'i*
JMJP	*Jen-min jih-pao*
MR	*Monthly Review*
NCNA	*New China News Agency*
NYT	*New York Times*
PR	*Peking Review*
SCCS	*Shih-chieh chih-shih*
SCMP	*Survey of the Mainland China Press*

INTRODUCTION

After long delay and following three years of cultural-revolution violence, the Ninth Congress of the Chinese Communist Party was convened in Peking on April 1, 1969. A new leadership was chosen, and new domestic and foreign policies were enunciated in a report to the congress by Vice-Chairman Lin Piao. Although Lin warned that the cultural revolution was not yet over and might continue for decades, his report spoke of "decisive victory"; and the convening of the congress appeared at least to signal an end to the domestic turmoil that had characterized Chairman Mao's Great Proletarian Cultural Revolution since it had been proclaimed in the spring of 1966.

Several months before the congress was convened, Maoists with the assistance of the Chinese Army had begun to consolidate their power throughout the country. By September 1968, "revolutionary committees" had been established as the new political authority in all of China's twenty-nine major administrative districts; and on October 31, a plenary session of the CCP Central Committee condemned and expelled from the party the most prominent individual target of the cultural revolution, Liu Shao-ch'i, "the No. 1 Party person in authority taking the capitalist road."

Nevertheless, it was as yet unclear precisely how successful the Maoists had been in purging their "revisionist" opponents from positions of power within the country, and Lin Piao's report to the party congress provided only vague indications as to what directions new domestic and foreign policies would take.

Clearly, as the Maoists say, the future of China is at stake in the cultural revolution, and its outcome will have a profound effect on the subsequent development of the People's Republic of China. The Maoists further claim that, even more important, the future of the world is also at stake, as Chairman Mao charts a course that all societies may ultimately follow. The present period in history, they assert, is the era of Mao Tse-tung's thought, a time when Mao, "the Lenin of the present era," is showing the way forward to communism.[1]

The principle significance of Mao's thought, say the Maoists, lies in its contribution to developing a successful revolutionary strategy and tactics, as well as to solving problems of postrevolutionary development. In other words, Mao claims to have made major theoretical innovations in dealing with two central problems: the first, how a revolutionary movement overthrows the existing government and wins state power; and the second, how the movement then consolidates its newly won power and uses it to build toward the communist ideal society. Before the Great Proletarian Cultural Revolution, Mao's reputation as a political theorist rested mainly on his work concerning the strategy and tactics of rural insurrection as a means of gaining state power. However, since the cultural revolution—as Mao and his followers have become overwhelmingly preoccupied with problems of

[1] Since the Ninth Party Congress, the term "Mao Tse-tung's thought" (*Mao Tse-tung szu-hsiang*) in official English language translations has been rendered "Mao Tsetung Thought," and official party statements have spoken of "Marxism-Leninism-Mao Tsetung Thought." In this study, however, the earlier usage, more appropriate to the time period under consideration, is employed.

postrevolutionary development—the Chinese press has described Chairman Mao more as a postrevolutionary theorist. Moreover, in both areas of Mao's theoretical interest, his adherents claim that he has developed theory which is applicable not merely to China and its unique situation, but, what is more, theory which has universal relevance and applicability. Thus, Mao's works contain implicit and often explicit systematic generalizations, or conceptual models, relative to both problem areas—to both successful revolutionary strategy and postrevolutionary development.

This study focuses on the former of the two central problems to which Mao has addressed himself, making revolution in order to gain state power; but in a special sense. This is not a study of the history of the CCP's experience in making revolution in China from 1921 to 1949, but rather it is an analysis of how the Maoists have interpreted that experience for the purpose of dealing with foreign revolutionary efforts, or wars of national liberation, in the years since the CCP won power on the Chinese mainland. This, then, is a study of Chinese foreign policy and how support for foreign revolutions fits into that policy.

Much has been written in a general way about Communist China's foreign policy, but little as yet has been done in the way of systematic comparison of China's relations with different countries. This study attempts to move toward a more systematic approach by comparing and analyzing Chinese policy toward all countries of Asia, Africa, and Latin America with regard to the specific question of Peking's support for wars of national liberation. There is, however, no attempt made here to analyze Mao Tse-tung's military strategy or to write a sociology of revolution; this has been ably done by others.[2] Rather than focus on Mao's contribution to the

2 For a particularly thoughtful sociology of revolution, see Chalmers Johnson, *Revolutionary Change* (Boston: Little, Brown, 1966). For Maoist military strategy and tactics, see Tang Tsou and Morton H. Halperin, "Mao Tse-tung's Revolutionary Strategy and Peking's International Behavior," *American Political Science Review*, March 1965, pp. 80–99; Samuel B. Griffith (trans.), *Mao Tse-tung On Guerrilla Warfare* (New York: Praeger, 1961); and Mao Tse-tung's own *Selected Military Writings* (Peking: Foreign Languages Press, 1963).

tactics of guerrilla warfare or even on the general question of implementing a revolutionary strategy in overseas areas, this study is primarily concerned with the analysis of principles of Chinese foreign policy and, more specifically, with the use of revolution as an instrument of that foreign policy.

In its broadest form, the question this study seeks to answer is, What function does Peking's attempt to foment revolutions abroad perform within the general framework of China's total approach to world politics? Analyzing and comparing both stated foreign policy and actual Chinese behavior, the study further seeks to answer such specific questions as, What is the theoretical or ideological foundation of Chinese revolutionary policy? How are Chinese endorsement and support of revolutions made manifest? What kinds of foreign revolutionary organizations do the Chinese Communists support? What factors determine their choice of specific individual countries as targets for revolution?

It should be made clear at the outset, however, that this study deals with but one of several aspects of Chinese foreign policy: public support for foreign wars of national liberation. As do other sovereign states, the People's Republic of China carries on conventional diplomatic relations with many foreign governments and currently maintains official missions in forty-six foreign countries.[3] Also, Peking has actively sought to develop closer ties with countries with which it does not have official ties; a good example is Japan, a country that has in recent years become China's most important trading partner in spite of the fact that Tokyo continues to refuse officially to recognize Peking. Thus, only with respect to certain countries and colonial areas (some twenty-three during 1965, for

[3] As of spring 1969, the People's Republic of China maintained diplomatic relations with all 13 of the other countries of the communist world (including Yugoslavia and Cuba), 8 Western European countries, 12 non-communist Asian countries, and 13 African countries—a total of 46. However, no country in the American hemisphere except Cuba had yet recognized Communist China; and six countries (Burundi, Central African Republic, Dahomey, Ghana, Indonesia, and Tunisia) had either broken or suspended diplomatic relations with Peking.

example) do the Chinese Communists call for violent "armed struggle"[4] against the established government.

Operationally, Chinese foreign policy is implemented on three levels: official, semiofficial, and communist party levels. At the official, government-to-government level, Peking pursues foreign relations through diplomatic channels much as any other state does. These relations include establishment of diplomatic relations, negotiation of treaties and international agreements, development of official trade relations, granting of technical and economic aid, and so forth. At the semiofficial level, China seeks to make contact with a variety of groups and individuals in virtually all countries in the world (communist and non-communist), whether or not the government of the particular country maintains diplomatic relations with Peking. Often the objective of such relations is the development of trade (if no official trade relations exist) or the cultivation of contacts with local groups sympathetic to China or with the objectives of Chinese policy. Sometimes called cultural or "people's" diplomacy, semiofficial diplomacy is perhaps a more accurate term; because although the individual Chinese sponsors of this sort of international intercourse are nominally nongovernmental organizations, there is little question that they come under official government, and ultimately party, direction. In many cases these organizations obviously have been established solely for the purpose of making unofficial contacts in foreign countries, often after Chinese offers of official ties have been refused. A final operational level of Chinese foreign policy involves relations between the CCP and other communist parties. It is at this level, as well as at the semiofficial level, that the Chinese seek to establish and maintain contact with individuals and organiza-

---

4 "Armed struggle" (wu-chuang tou-cheng) is the term commonly used by Peking to denote political activity that reaches the point of violence. Technically, national liberation struggles may be either violent or nonviolent, e.g., revolutionaries may resort to guerrilla warfare and a military strategy, or they may choose to confine their tactics to peaceful protest and political agitation. This study focuses on Chinese support for violent national liberation efforts, those engaged in revolutionary "armed struggle" against established authority.

tions that are actively attempting to overthrow established foreign governments.[5]

Furthermore, this study deals only with those attempts to overthrow established governments that are publicly endorsed by Peking. For the purposes of this analysis, Chinese support for foreign revolutions is defined minimally as *public endorsement in the official Chinese press of the armed struggle of any group or organization that is publicly committed to and actively pursuing the overthrow by force of the established government of any foreign country or territory.* The three most important aspects of this definition are public endorsement by Peking, overthrow of the government as the revolutionary movement's objective, and armed insurrection as the means to that end.

This does not deny that China, like many major powers, may at times seek to encourage secret coup attempts against unfriendly governments, nor does it deny that the Chinese have been, and apparently continue to be, involved in undercover arms smuggling, bribery of officials, and possibly even attempts at political assassination. The question is not one of methods employed in carrying out opposition activities (these same methods may be used in support of overt revolutionary

[5] One additional point should be made with regard to levels of Chinese foreign policy. The three levels of foreign policy operations do not operate exclusive of one another, nor without central coordination. If China has established diplomatic relations with a country, the two countries will almost inevitably have semiofficial relations also, and perhaps communist party relations as well. If diplomatic relations have not been established, semiofficial relations and communist party relations (and even public support for revolution) may operate concurrently. The primary advantage for the conduct of foreign affairs of having contacts on several levels with a single country is that it gives Peking the opportunity to exert considerably more influence on the internal affairs of that country than would be provided by a conventional diplomatic relationship alone. While these levels represent separate interests in most countries with which China has relations, their counterparts in China, though nominally representatives of different groups, are all theoretically responsive to the direction of the Chinese Communist Party. Hence, by means of the central direction of representatives operating at various levels abroad, Peking has the opportunity to gain more operational flexibility and can potentially exert more influence in the affairs of foreign countries than would normally be the case.

movements), but whether the movement attempting to overthrow the government by force is publicly endorsed by Peking.

To have conceptualized the study so as to include Chinese
covert as well as public support for revolutionary movements
would have made the project impracticable. Even after con-
sulting the complete police files of all the countries concerned
plus the records of the United States Central Intelligence
Agency—none of which, of course, is accessible to the private
researcher—one could still not be confident that he had a complete and accurate picture of Peking's covert international
contacts.

The fact of the matter, however, is that for good, practical
reasons in addition to ideological ones the Chinese Communists rely very little on covert attempts to overthrow foreign
governments. When they are actively seeking to overthrow a
foreign government, they generally make their position quite
public and explicit. For from a practical point of view, there
is little evidence to show that Peking actually sees much hope
for secretly organized coup attempts led by communists or
even other left-wing organizations in the countries of the
Third World. If such a coup d'etat were successful, the Chinese would probably welcome it; but to be successful any coup
would have to subvert the local army, and there are few if any
cases of armies in Asia, Africa, and Latin America showing
much sympathy for local communist parties or left-wing revolutionary movements. Even if the army were subverted, agreeing to remain passive or even to join the coup, the Chinese
appear to recognize the extreme likelihood of Western intervention to suppress leftist-led insurrections.[6] British intervention to put down the army mutinies in East Africa in 1964,
American intervention in the Dominican Republic in the
spring of 1965, and French commitment to intervene to fore-

6 For an example of a non-Chinese, but still communist, view of the difficulty
of carrying out revolution because of the danger of foreign intervention to
suppress the revolution, see the article by a Guatemalan Communist, José
Manuel Fortuny, "Has the Revolution Become More Difficult in Latin
America?" *Peace, Freedom, and Socialism*, August 1965, pp. 26–32.

stall possible changes of government in many of its former African colonies[7] are all relevant cases in point.

Moreover, in ideological terms, Peking is committed to support openly operating revolutionary movements that actively seek popular support and legitimacy and that pursue military tactics based on a concept of protracted war against established authority rather than overnight coup d'etat. This commitment is founded, among other considerations, on an assessment that only a truly mass-based and popular revolutionary movement would have a good chance of both defeating the local army and providing a sufficiently powerful military force either to forestall foreign intervention or to have some chance of defeating foreign intervention if it occurred.[8]

Finally, it is clear that the decision to support the violent overthrow of a foreign government is not taken lightly by the Chinese. To encourage mass demonstrations and agitation against a foreign government is one thing, but to support a revolution against a foreign power is an act of great consequence, particularly for a government that claims to seek relations of "peaceful coexistence" with its fellow independent Afro-Asian states. Peking distinguishes carefully between two different types of opposition policy in its relations with the countries of Asia, Africa, and Latin America: the one, a public, ideologically conceptualized support for violent insurrectionary movements that seek to overthrow established authority; the other, support of relatively peaceful political agitation, often encouraged by Chinese overseas representatives, which generally has as its objective the modification of

[7] See *NYT*, November 17, 1967, p. 1; and *CSM*, April 5, 1968, p. 11.

[8] For example, the fall of the left-of-center Goulart government in Brazil in April 1964 is attributed by a New China News Agency report to a "US-engineered military coup d'etat" which succeeded, the report says, because the Goulart regime "did not resolutely rely on the people and did not have control of the armed forces."*PR* 1965, no. 3, p. 22. See also the analysis put forward in the American Marxist magazine, *Monthly Review*, which argues in effect that in Latin America only truly mass-based movements built on an alliance of the peasants and the workers can make a durable revolution, one that can defeat the kind of intervention which overthrew the Arbenz government in Guatemala. "The Breakthrough in Guatemala," *MR*, May 1965, pp. 1–8.

government policy or at most a change of personnel holding public office.[9] The distinction between these two policies is clearly seen, for example, in the difference in China's policy over the past few years toward Kenya and the Congo (Kinshasa). Peking's activities in Kenya, with which China has established diplomatic relations, have been politically involved to the point of drawing official Kenyan criticism on several occasions and even provoking the deportation of official Chinese representatives. However, this is a very different policy from that pursued by the Chinese in the Congo only a few miles away, where Peking has provided military support and political encouragement to armed revolutionaries engaged in a violent and protracted struggle to overthrow the Kinshasa government. The question of what criteria seem to determine the Chinese decision to support revolution in one country and maintain relatively peaceful relations with another will be one of the more important questions to be answered in the following analysis.

In form, this study is an analysis of both the theory and practice of Chinese support for wars of national liberation. It begins with a section on the Maoist ideology of the national liberation struggle (Part I), which is followed by an empirical analysis of actual Chinese support for wars of national liberation during 1965 (Part II) just prior to the outbreak of the Great Proletarian Cultural Revolution. The final section (Part III) deals with both the theory and practice of Chinese support for wars of national liberation during two years of the cultural revolution, 1966 and 1967. Since the concept of national liberation concerns colonialism and gaining independence from colonial domination, the scope of the study is limited geographically to China's relations with the three most colonized continents during recent history: Asia, Africa, and Latin America. It should be noted in passing, however, that

---

[9] Maps and articles in the Chinese press dealing with political movements in Asia, Africa, and Latin America draw sharp distinctions between armed struggles and other kinds of political activity. For examples, see the map of Africa in *JMJP*, April 15, 1964, p. 4; and the article in *Shih-shih shou-ts'e*, February 4, 1965, pp. 2–5.

Peking has also been keenly aware of different kinds of revolutionary potentialities in other areas of the world—for example, showing a continuing interest in the American Negro movement and, during the spring of 1968, offering vocal encouragement to the student-led uprisings in Western Europe.

CHINESE FOREIGN POLICY, 1949–1969

Since the study focuses somewhat narrowly on foreign policy during the middle 1960s, it seems appropriate to conclude this introduction with at least a brief description of the history of China's foreign relations since the establishment of the People's Republic in 1949, in order to put the analysis which follows in suitable perspective.

No scheme of periodizing the history of Communist China's foreign policy is completely satisfactory, mainly because many different factors determine Chinese policy toward each of the many countries of the world, and these factors do not vary consistently over time. Nevertheless, it seems to me that we can think usefully about the development of Chinese foreign policy in terms of at least four broad periods that might be designated generally as follows: 1949–1952, communist internationalism; 1953–1957, peaceful coexistence; 1958–1965, militant anti-imperialism and the emergence of antirevisionism; and 1966–1969, the Great Proletarian Cultural Revolution.

Both domestic needs and the tenor of contemporary world politics had much to do with shaping the CCP's initial policies toward the outside world. By 1949 the antifascist alliance of World War II had broken apart, and the Cold War between the United States and the Soviet Union was well under way. The two superpowers and their respective allies were faced off across Europe; and in Asia, established governments, some colonial and others newly independent, battled communist party-led wars of national liberation. In a matter of months, international politics had taken on a bipolar power configuration with the United States and the Soviet Union at swords' points around the world.

Yet, it was not international politics but domestic concerns that held first priority for the Chinese leadership during the first period, 1949–1952. The CCP had just come to power in a country that comprised one-fourth of the population of the world, a nation beset by a century of social revolution, foreign invasion, and political turmoil. During this initial period in the history of the People's Republic of China, the new leadership was looking inward, focusing its attention on consolidating its power throughout the country and laying the social foundations for the new China. Aside from an obvious concern with national defense, the Peking government's interest in foreign affairs seemed limited in scope primarily to the communist world, the countries on China's borders, and other colonial and semicolonial countries of Asia. Two statements by China's leaders appeared to set the tone for this period. The first was Mao Tse-tung's essay, "On the People's Democratic Dictatorship,"[10] in which he put forward an essentially black and white—with us or against us—view of world politics and spoke of "leaning to one side," toward the communist countries and away from the non-communist ones. The second was Liu Shao-ch'i's opening address to the Asian and Australian Trade Union Conference held in Peking in November 1949,[11] which he devoted exclusively to the national liberation struggle, discussing the major elements of the successful Chinese strategy and calling on the delegates to take the Chinese road to liberation from colonialism in their own countries.

The principal foreign policy concerns during the first three years of the Republic were to unify the country and defend China's borders, to build a close alliance with the communist world, and to encourage the communist party-led national liberation struggles in the neighboring countries of Asia (a policy that had been part of the Soviet-sponsored general line in operation since 1948). The Chinese Army's march into Tibet and its intervention in the Korean War, both begun vir-

[10] *Selected Readings from the Works of Mao Tse-tung* (Peking: Foreign Languages Press, 1967), pp. 302–315.
[11] *Hsin-hua yueh-pao*, December 15, 1949, pp. 440–441.

tually at the same time in the autumn of 1950, can best be understood in terms of these concerns. Tibet had long been viewed by Chinese Communists and Nationalists alike as part of Chinese territory; and the Chinese intervention against the Allied offensive north of the 38th parallel in Korea was prompted by fears for China's territorial integrity, commitments to Moscow, and a conviction that the "progressive" tide running in Asia should not be reversed by "imperialist" intervention.[12] In early 1950 the Chinese Army had been preparing to invade Taiwan as well in an effort to win final victory in the civil war with Chiang Kai-shek's Nationalists; but President Truman's ordering of the US Seventh Fleet into the Taiwan Straits on June 27 after the outbreak of the Korean War made the invasion plans unfeasible and involved the United States in Chinese domestic affairs in a manner which continues down to the present.

In the second period, 1953–1957, Peking emphasized peaceful coexistence between communist and non-communist countries; this period produced the so-called Spirit of Bandung. In the development of foreign relations Chinese policy shifted gradually away from attempting to drive Western influence out of Asia by direct confrontation or unequivocal support for revolutionary wars, and toward efforts to win Asian neighbors away from alliances with the West through offers of peaceful coexistence.[13]

By 1953 the foundations of the new society on the Chinese mainland had been laid; a firm alliance with Moscow had been negotiated; and the "imperialists" had been thrown back from the Manchurian border by the Chinese intervention in Korea—albeit at heavy cost to the Chinese "volun-

12 For an analysis of factors relating to the Chinese intervention in Korea, see Allen S. Whiting, *China Crosses the Yalu: The Decision to Enter the Korean War* (New York: Macmillan, 1960).

13 For an analysis of the peaceful coexistence period in Sino-Thai relations, for example, see David A. Wilson, "China, Thailand and the Spirit of Bandung," *CQ*, April–June 1967, pp. 149–169 (part 1); and July–September 1967, pp. 96–127 (part 2).

teers." This accomplished, China began to make overtures to many of the non-communist countries of the world, especially the new countries of Asia and Africa. The earlier national liberation emphasis was replaced by a willingness to deal constructively with non-communist countries at a government-to-government level, on the basis of mutual respect and at least a temporary live-and-let-live approach by the Chinese.

Peking became more outward-looking during this period, even activist in its diplomacy, and symbolic of the time was the Afro-Asian conference of heads of governments held in Bandung, Indonesia, in April 1955, at which the Chinese delegate, Premier Chou En-lai, discussed measures for the promotion of world peace and international cooperation with leaders of the independent countries of Asia and Africa (several of which had been designated by the Chinese as proper targets for wars of national liberation only a few years earlier). However, the Chinese peaceful coexistence line began to merge into a more militantly anti-imperialist policy soon after the Bandung Conference, as the Chinese drew sharper distinctions between enemies and friends, pressing friendly governments to take firmer stands against the West and seeking to increase pressure on those governments that would not. The period closed with the first signs of the Sino-Soviet dispute becoming evident following Khrushchev's denunciation of Stalin at the 20th Congress of the Communist Party of the Soviet Union held in February 1956.

The third period in the history of Chinese foreign policy, 1958–1965, began with the Chinese clearly striking out on their own, innovating in domestic policy (the communes and the Great Leap Forward) in a search for an independent Chinese road to economic and social development, and adopting an assertive new foreign policy divergent from, and increasingly in opposition to, that of the Soviet Union. Progressively more doubtful of the wisdom of Soviet policy, Peking began to stake out its own geographical areas of interest on the international scene—among the communist parties and communist governments of Asia and the non-communist countries of the Third World—and to seek closer economic relations with the industrialized countries of Europe and Japan.

This new departure in Chinese foreign relations stemmed perhaps from a combination of frustration and confidence. The Bandung peaceful coexistence policy had failed to break the line of American military power and alliances in East Asia. In fact, there is evidence that the United States had begun to take the initiative by expanding its influence in Southeast Asia during these years, and that the Chinese were pressed to adopt new, more vigorous tactics to counter it.[14] On the other hand, Peking enjoyed some sense of security and pride in the successes of China's domestic development to date (the relative ease with which the CCP had collectivized agriculture, the substantial economic growth rates which had been registered through 1957, and the new industry built), and the Chinese evidenced a growing optimism in their assessment of the opportunity for new initiatives in international politics, especially after the successful orbiting of the first two Soviet earth satellites in the autumn of 1957. These clear indications of Soviet superiority in rocket technology led the Chinese to conclude that Soviet strength was sufficient to deter the US from attempting "nuclear blackmail" against communist bloc foreign policy initiatives, and as a result, the time had come to make the most of the improved power relationship. This was the era of the East Wind prevailing over the West Wind, a time when communists should press the attack on the world status quo. However, the Soviets did not agree. Fully aware of the destructive capability of their own weapons, Moscow grew increasingly less willing to take the kind of risks in international politics that could possibly lead to a nuclear holocaust.

By 1960 Chinese initiatives had received sharp setbacks, both at home and abroad. The failures of the Great Leap Forward and the commune experiment (in combination with

[14] David Mozingo makes a particularly compelling argument to this effect in his essay in *China Briefing* (Chicago: University of Chicago Center for Policy Study, 1968), pp. 23–51.

natural disasters) had cost China, in the opinion of some economists, as much as a decade of economic development;[15] and the Soviet Union had administered clear rebuffs to China's attempts to urge the communist world into a more activist international posture, especially, during the offshore islands crisis of late summer and early autumn 1958. Moreover, an earlier Soviet commitment to help the Chinese develop nuclear weapons had apparently been revoked in 1959,[16] and in 1960 Soviet support for Chinese economic development was abruptly terminated when Russian technical advisers in China were ordered to pack up and return home.

Following these initial reverses and the sharpening of the Sino-Soviet dispute, Peking made a carefully conceived effort to create a new force in world politics to be comprised primarily of the colonial or newly independent countries of Asia, Africa, and Latin America. Competing with both American and Soviet influence in the Third World, Peking sought to form an alliance no longer on the basis of peaceful coexistence but of militant anti-imperialism. A foreign policy of simple non-alignment was now barely acceptable to Peking, as the Chinese pressed foreign countries to adopt a more radical position with respect to the world status quo. The principal objective of the alliance was to oppose "US imperialism," but soon "Soviet revisionism" was also singled out for attack.

The Chinese apparently saw the Third World as the area of greatest political opportunity on the contemporary world scene. It was a world in flux, one in which old political orders and alliances were crumbling and new ones being formed—an area where new friends could be won, old balances of power upset, and powerful new alliances established. Capitalizing on the various appeals of the Chinese revolutionary experience before and after 1949, the Peking government saw in the volatile conditions of Asia, Africa, and Latin America its best chance to influence world politics and to apply most fruitfully

15 For example, see Alexander Eckstein, *Communist China's Economic Growth and Foreign Trade* (New York: McGraw-Hill, 1966), pp. 84–86.
16 *PR*, 1963, no. 33, p. 14.

China's limited resources toward the attainment of foreign policy objectives. A measure of Chinese confidence in the political potential of Asia, Africa, and Latin America is the now familiar global concept put forward by Chinese Defense Minister Lin Piao in September 1965, which viewed North America and Western Europe as "the cities of the world," and Asia, Africa, and Latin America as "the rural areas of the world" which must ultimately encircle "the cities" with world revolution.

In pressing their anti-imperialist offensive in the Third World, the Chinese strategy was profoundly radical, but their tactics remained astutely pragmatic. Seeking to undermine the power and influence of the West in the developing world, the Chinese hoped to alter the entire world power structure; however, to attain this objective, Peking did not revert to a dogmatic reliance on revolutionary tactics alone but sought to build a broad alliance on several levels. For example, this period was the time of the greatest Chinese success in winning formal diplomatic recognition by non-communist governments: twenty-two new countries established diplomatic relations with Communist China between 1958 and 1965, seventeen of them from Africa.[17] Government-to-government relations, the granting of economic and technical assistance, forming new trade relations, the use of "people's diplomacy," as well as support for wars of national liberation—all played a part in Peking's vigorous new diplomatic offensive.

This was also a time of deep dissension within the CCP leadership, caused by differences primarily over matters of domestic policy which led ultimately to a public dispute and finally to the violence and chaos of the cultural revolution. Paradoxically, after the failure of the Great Leap Forward in 1959, Chinese domestic policy tended toward moderation as China's planners sought to minimize the economic setbacks of 1959–1961; but Chinese foreign policy during the same

[17] For the names of the countries and the dates of the establishment of relations, see A. M. Halpern, ed., *Policies Toward China: Views from Six Continents* (New York: McGraw-Hill, 1965), Appendix A; and *PR*, 1965, no. 31, p. 20.

time became increasingly radical, both in the hardening of Peking's anti-imperialist line in relations with the countries of the Third World and in the explicitness and bitterness of China's denunciations of the Soviet Union. The Soviets were moving progressively toward detente with the United States and the world status quo, while China ever more actively sought to unite and direct the opposition.

This third period of Chinese foreign policy culminated in the abortive attempt to hold a second Afro-Asian summit conference in June 1965. The Chinese spoke of a "Second Bandung," but the Spirit of Bandung was singularly absent from Chinese policy statements. Instead of peaceful coexistence, Peking was pressing for a clear-cut denunciation of the United States, especially on the issue of the Vietnam War, and exclusion of the Soviets from the conference. It will never be known what would have happened had Algeria's President Ben Bella, host for the proposed conference, not been overthrown by his Defense Minister Houari Boumedienne just ten days before the meeting was scheduled to convene, since the coup d'etat and subsequent violence at the conference site ultimately served as sufficient cause to postpone the conference (which was later postponed indefinitely). Nevertheless, China's position on substantive issues before the conference and its insistence even after the coup that the meeting still be held as scheduled are good examples of Chinese policy at the time. As Richard Lowenthal has pointed out,[18] Chinese attempts to press the countries of the Third World into an alliance simultaneously against the world's two superpowers (principal sources of much-needed development aid) were clearly unrealistic. Forced by Peking to take a stand, the majority of the countries of the developing areas simply would not go so far as to endanger their relations with both the US and the USSR.

In the fourth and final period to date of Chinese foreign policy, 1966–1969, the dispute within the CCP leadership of

[18] Tang Tsou, ed., *China in Crisis* (Chicago: University of Chicago Press, 1968), 2:13.

several years' standing boiled to the surface, and for many long months chaos reigned on the Chinese mainland. Diplomatic representatives from communist as well as non-communist countries suffered bitter attacks from demonstrating Red Guards, as China seemed to be lashing out indiscriminately at the outside world. Clearly, China's leaders were preoccupied with the internal struggle, and foreign relations became only a secondary concern. What is more, during the anarchy that ensued, the dominant faction, the Maoists, apparently lost control for a time of the operation of the Foreign Ministry, and leftist extremists within their own faction took actions against foreign countries and their representatives which even Chairman Mao could not sanction. The general feeling of foreigners, communist and non-communist alike, as they viewed the events of the cultural revolution was that China had turned inward on herself, and there was no predicting which country might next be chosen for insult or assault. Singled out as the special target for Maoist hostility was the Soviet Union. The "revisionism" that ruled in the Soviet Union, the Maoists felt, served as a pernicious example for other communist party states, and its counterrevolutionary doctrine had to be expunged before it gained control even over the Maoist homeland.

The particular time span covered in the present study, then, bridges two periods of Chinese foreign policy, the last years of the period characterized by militant anti-imperialism and the emergence of the Sino-Soviet dispute, and the first two years of the cultural revolution. The subject for analysis is a single aspect of Chinese policy, support for wars of national liberation, and the part it played in Peking's foreign relations during that time.

PART I
REVOLUTION IN THEORY:
THE IDEOLOGY OF THE
NATIONAL LIBERATION
STRUGGLE

Marxist-Leninist ideological treatises usually comprise two major parts: an analysis and evaluation of the current situation, and a prescription for action to be taken on the basis of that analysis.[1] Part I of this study adopts this general framework of exposition. Chapter 1, Peking's View of the World, and chapter 2, Facing the Enemy, describe the Maoist view of the problem confronting national liberation movements in the developing areas. Chapter 3, China's Program for Revolution, concerns Peking's proposals for political and military action to be taken to deal with that problem.

From another point of view, the three chapters can also be seen as separate commentaries on some of the major functions of a revolutionary ideology. When used to aid in the mobilization and organization of popular support for a revolutionary movement, a revolutionary ideology generally performs at least three major functions: (1) to analyze and explain existing

---

1 This distinction corresponds roughly with the distinction made by Franz Schurmann between "pure ideology" and "practical ideology." He writes, "Pure ideology is a set of ideas designed to give the individual a unified and conscious world view; practical ideology is a set of ideas designed to give the individual rational instruments for action." *Ideology and Organization in Communist China* (Berkeley and Los Angeles: University of California Press, 1966), p. 22.

conditions so as to demonstrate their unjust character and to point to a source of the injustice, the potential enemy; (2) to analyze the nature of the enemy in such a way as to point up both his viciousness (to emphasize the immediate need to take action against him) and also his weaknesses (to encourage confidence among the people to oppose him); and finally, (3) to propose an alternative to the status quo, a program for the organization of a revolutionary movement that can take effective political and military action against the enemy, and that incorporates in its policies widely accepted values and popular economic and social objectives. All three functions involve an attempt to create for the revolutionary movement an "awakened," politically conscious mass support which, in the Chinese view, is perhaps the most important single prerequisite for the success of a revolution. As Mao Tse-tung has put it, "The revolutionary war is a war of the masses; it can be waged only by mobilizing the masses and relying on them."[2]

The material presented in Part I is drawn primarily from the writings of Chairman Mao and from official policy statements published during 1960–1965, the years of greatest emphasis on relations with the Third World. Obviously, foreign policy did not remain constant during this time. The greatest change occurred in Peking's relations with Moscow, which became progressively more strained during the period. Also, during 1965 and the early part of 1966, Chinese leaders engaged in a heated "debate" over foreign policy questions (particularly with regard to Vietnam, the Soviet Union, and the strategy for defending China in the event of war with the United States); as a result, official policy statements were published during that time which took different positions on certain important issues, varying in accord with the views of the author.[3]

Nevertheless, the Chinese view of the national liberation

[2] Mao Tse-tung, *Selected Works* (Peking: Foreign Languages Press, 1964), 1:147.

[3] For analyses of the issues and the parties to this debate, see the contributions by Uri Ra'anan and Donald Zagoria in Tang Tsou, ed., *China in Crisis* (Chicago: University of Chicago Press, 1968), vol. 2.

struggle has remained fairly consistent over the years. Where significant changes have occurred as the result of changing Chinese foreign policy or policy differences among China's leaders, these changes are indicated in the text and notes.

A final injunction. The discussion in the next three chapters will at different times relate to three different political arenas: the history of the Chinese revolutionary experience; contemporary international affairs and the requirements of Chinese foreign policy; and the domestic political situation in the individual countries of Asia, Africa, and Latin America. Peking often draws analogies between the first and third; and Lin Piao in his article of September 3, 1965 (in which he writes of "the rural areas of the world" encircling "the cities of the world") has drawn an analogy between the first and second.[4] The reader should beware. Historical analogies are full of pitfalls—especially when they are stretched so far as to compare domestic political strategy with that used in international affairs. What is of particular importance is to note the role and the interests of the CCP in each of the three different situations, and not, by analogy, to confuse them.

[4] *PR*, 1965, no. 36, p. 24.

1

PEKING'S VIEW
OF THE WORLD

"Since World War II, US imperialism has taken the place of German, Italian and Japanese fascism, and become the principal enemy of the people of the world," declared P'eng Chen,[1] member of the Chinese Communist Party's Political Bureau and Secretariat, in a speech in Indonesia on May 25, 1965. He continued:

Throughout the postwar period, repeated and intense struggles have been going on between the people of the world on the one side and US imperialism and its lackeys on the other. The vast areas of Asia, Africa, and Latin America are the main battlefields of these struggles.

Taking the world situation as a whole, the contradiction between the oppressed nations of Asia, Africa, and Latin America and imperialism headed by the United States is the most prominent and most acute of all the fundamental contradictions and is the principal contradiction in the contemporary world.[2]

[1] P'eng Chen was subsequently to become one of the first of China's more prominent leaders to fall victim to the Great Proletarian Cultural Revolution. Interpretations of why he was purged differ, but there seems to be agreement that on *foreign* policy issues P'eng's position did not differ importantly from that of the Mao-Lin group.

[2] *HC*, 1965, no. 6, p. 4.

P'eng Chen's speech was important for several reasons. It took a hard, new slap at Moscow and developed new theoretical formulations on which Lin Piao would later base his essay on people's war, and it also introduced a discussion of present world "contradictions." Understanding the Chinese use of contradictions theory is particularly important because it provides an insight into the way Peking looks at both its domestic situation and the world.

CONTRADICTIONS THEORY

The Chinese Communists analyze both domestic and international political affairs within a conceptual framework of "contradictions," which is based on the theory of dialectical materialism as interpreted by Mao Tse-tung. Mao's exposition of dialectics includes both natural and human phenomena and conceives of a world in the process of constant change, propelled by the continual posing and resolving of the contradictions that are inherent in all things.[3]

For those who believe in the theory of dialetical materialism and use it to determine policy, being able to distinguish the major contradictions in a given situation at a particular point in time has a very practical significance. Distinguishing and rating in importance the major contradictions in contemporary domestic or world affairs supposedly enables political leaders to determine which political force in terms of its fundamental economic interests is the principal opponent of the leadership at any point in time; which other political forces can be relied on for support against the opposition; and finally, what the strengths and weaknesses of the opposition are and which strategy and tactics might be most successfully used to defeat it.

Mao Tse-tung, in his theoretical treatise "On Contradiction," writes that essential to the practical application of the

[3] For a brief discussion of the role of contradictions in Maoist philosophy, see John Lewis, *Leadership in Communist China* (Ithaca: Cornell University Press, 1963), pp. 47–52.

contradictions analysis is the determination of a principal contradiction:

> There are many contradictions in the process of development of a complex thing, and one of them is necessarily the principal contradiction whose existence and development determine or influence the existence and development of the other contradictions. . . .
>
> Hence, if in any process there are a number of contradictions, one of them must be the principal contradiction playing the leading and decisive role, while the rest occupy a secondary and subordinate position. Therefore, in studying any complex process in which there are two or more contradictions, we must devote every effort to finding its principal contradiction. Once this principal contradiction is grasped, all problems can be readily solved.[4]

The principal contradiction determines which is the most pressing problem facing the leadership; this contradiction must be resolved (the problem solved, the opposition defeated) before it is possible to move on to a higher stage of development. Among examples of the principal contradiction, Mao cites the Sino-Japanese War (1937–1945), a time, he says, when the contradiction between the Chinese people and Japanese imperialism became much more important than the class contradictions dividing China; therefore, domestic contradictions became subordinate ("nonprincipal") contradictions, while the fight for survival between the Chinese people as a whole and the Japanese invaders became the principal contradiction and the focus of the CCP's attention and activity.[5]

For several years before 1965, however, official Chinese analyses of the contemporary world situation had avoided pointing out a principal contradiction, and had instead put forward an alternative formulation which distinguished four major "fundamental contradictions" (in Chinese, *chi-pen mao-tun* as compared with principal contradiction, *chu-yao mao-*

---

4 Mao Tse-tung, *Selected Works*, 1:331–332.

5 *Ibid.* For a good example of contradictions theory applied to contemporary Chinese society, see "Grasp the Principal Contradiction, Hold to the General Orientation of Struggle," translated from *HC* in *PR*, 1967, no. 22, pp. 43–46, an article which analyzes Chinese society during the cultural revolution.

tun). The four were said to be the contradictions between the
socialist and imperialist camps, between the proletariat and
the bourgeoisie in capitalist countries, between the so-called
oppressed nations and imperialism, and among the imperialist
countries themselves.[6] Although Peking had apparently been
reluctant to designate any of the four as the principal contradiction or even to rate the four contradictions in any explicit
order of priority, the Chinese did indicate a particular emphasis on certain geographical areas of the world (Asia, Africa,
and Latin America) by the use of a concept of the "concentration" or "focus" (*chi-chung*) of contradictions:

> The various tyes of contradictions in the contemporary world
> are concentrated in the vast areas of Asia, Africa, and Latin Amer-
> ica; these are the most vulnerable areas under imperialist rule and
> the storm-centres of world revolution dealing direct blows at im-
> perialism. . . .
> The anti-imperialist revolutionary struggles of the people in
> Asia, Africa, and Latin America are pounding and undermining
> the foundations of the rule of imperialism and colonialism, old
> and new. . . .
> In a sense, therefore, the whole cause of the international pro-
> letarian revolution hinges on the outcome of the revolutionary
> struggles of the people of these areas.[7]

In emphasizing revolutionary struggles in the developing
areas, Peking had apparently come to believe that, compared
with the relative political stability of the industrialized countries of the West at that time, the conflicting political and
economic forces so evident in the new nations of Asia, Africa,
and Latin America provided a vastly greater potential for revolutionary change. Propelled into modernity by the trauma of
World War II and rising nationalistic and economic aspirations, Asia (and later Africa) had become the scene of the most
profound postwar political changes.

Moreover, the people of Asia, Africa, and Latin America

6 The classic statement of this position is in the CCP Central Committee letter of June 14, 1963, to the Central Committee of the Communist Party of the
Soviet Union, *The Polemic on the General Line of the International Communist Movement* (Peking: Foreign Languages Press, 1965), pp. 6–7.

7 *Ibid.*, p. 13.

comprise over two-thirds of the world's population; and, the Chinese argue, their resources and markets provide the economic foundation for the prosperity of the industrialized countries of America and Europe. The Third World nations are the "strategic rear areas" on which Western imperialism depends, but which Peking hopes to turn into "front lines of fiery struggles" against "US imperialism."[8]

In the spring of 1965, the Chinese altered their view of major world contradictions so as to place even greater emphasis on the "anti-imperialist struggle" in Asia, Africa, and Latin America. In May 1965, P'eng Chen, attending the Indonesian Communist Party's anniversary celebrations, declared in a major policy speech that the contradiction between the "oppressed nations" of Asia, Africa, and Latin America, on the one hand, and "imperialism headed by the United States," on the other, had now become the principal contradiction. Having for years avoided pointing out one of the four fundamental contradictions as the principal contradiction, official Chinese policy now stated, in effect, that the battle against imperialism (and especially American imperialism) was the most important single aspect of the worldwide communist struggle, and that the primary responsibility for bringing about world revolution had shifted away from the working class movements of the industrialized countries in the West to the national liberation movements of the backward areas of the Third World. Defense Minister Lin Piao, four months later in his article "Long Live the Victory of People's War," repeated P'eng Chen's analysis of the principal contradiction and spelled out in greater detail some of the theoretical implications of the new official position:

Taking the entire globe, if North America and Western Europe can be called "the cities of the world," then Asia, Africa and Latin America constitute "the rural areas of the world." Since World War II, the proletarian revolutionary movement has for various reasons been temporarily held back in the North American and West European capitalist countries, while the people's

8 See, for example, *SCCS*, 1965, no. 11, p. 2.

revolutionary movement in Asia, Africa and Latin America has been growing vigorously. In a sense, the contemporary world revolution [as compared with domestic revolutions in developing countries] also presents a picture of the encirclement of cities by the rural areas. *In the final analysis, the whole cause of world revolution hinges on the revolutionary struggles of the Asian, African and Latin American peoples* who make up the overwhelming majority of the world's population.[9]

Hence, the new principal-contradiction analysis as first enunciated by P'eng Chen, and the theoretical implications of this analysis for Chinese foreign policy articulated in lengthy detail by Lin Piao, unequivocally placed the full focus of Chinese foreign policy on the anti-imperialist movement of Asia, Africa, and Latin America. "Imperialism headed by the United States" was the foremost world enemy in Peking's view; and the struggle of the people of Asia, Africa, and Latin America against imperialism and the US was the essence of the current stage of development of world revolution. Only when this contradiction had been successfully resolved could the process of world development advance. Hence, primary responsibility for the success or failure of the current stage of the world revolution depended on the outcome of the national liberation struggles of the peoples of the Third World.[10]

[9] *PR*, 1965, no. 36, p. 24 (emphasis added). The idea of an international strategy analogous to the domestic strategy implemented during the Chinese Revolution had long been implicit in Chinese foreign policy and had been noted by at least one scholar; see Robert A. Scalapino's analysis in Joseph E. Black and Kenneth W. Thompson, eds., *Foreign Policies in a World of Change* (New York: Harper & Row, 1963), pp. 549–588, and especially p. 559. Also, earlier Chinese statements, such as P'eng Chen's in May 1965 (*HC*, 1965, no. 6, p. 5) had quoted an analysis made by the Indonesian Communist Party chairman, D. N. Aidit, which argued essentially the same thing.

[10] There were obvious implications in this new analysis of the principal contradiction for China's ideological dispute with the Russians. Whereas the earlier Chinese formulation, which distinguished four "fundamental contradictions" in the contemporary world, could be seen as relatively conciliatory with regard to Soviet policy, the new formulation broke sharply with the Soviet view. The new Chinese position on the principal contradiction was apparently intended to provide the ideological foundation for fresh attacks on both of China's major enemies. It appeared to be intended as a sort of double-edged sword, to be wielded in ideological battle against American "imperialists" on the one hand, and especially against Soviet "revisionists" on the other. After explaining in his Indonesian speech that it was the responsibility of all

US IMPERIALISM—THE ENEMY

The Chinese Communists base their view of imperialism on Lenin, who saw it as "the highest stage of capitalism."[11] In terms of this analysis, Lenin meant that imperialism was the zenith of capitalist economic development, a stage when competition among many business enterprises would, by a process of survival of the fittest, lead ultimately to the domination of the economies of the most advanced capitalist countries by monopolies and cartels. These monopolies would no longer be controlled by individual managers but by the few men who controlled capital, the financiers. Imperialism, Lenin said, was characterized by the "super-abundance of capital" which caused monopoly enterprises (enjoying an excess of capital generated by the success of domestic economic ventures) not only to export goods, but also to begin to export capital as well in an effort to exploit the resources of other less developed areas of the world in order to derive even greater profits.

It is this quest for resources to exploit, Lenin argued, that was the motivating force behind imperialism and the expansion of European empires into the areas of Asia, Africa, and the Americas. Survival of the capitalist economic system, he wrote, depends on the acquisition of overseas territories to exploit; and so intense and aggressive is the search for resources to feed the capitalist machine that competition among the major imperial powers influences the politics of the entire globe.

The Leninist view of imperialism provided not only the theoretical foundation for Mao Tse-tung's own theories of the Chinese Revolution, but also the framework for the contemporary Chinese analysis of the nature of imperialism and the

---

true Marxist-Leninists to single out this contradiction and resolutely support the anti-imperialist struggles of the developing areas, P'eng Chen concluded, "The attitude one takes on this question constitutes the most important criterion for distinguishing between Marxist-Leninists and modern revisionists, between revolutionaries and counter-revolutionaries, and between real revolutionaries and sham revolutionaries" (*HC*, 1965, no. 6, p. 6).

11 V. I. Lenin, "Imperialism, the Highest Stage of Capitalism," *Selected Works* (Moscow: Foreign Languages Publishing House, 1952), vol. 1, pt. 2, pp. 433–568.

character of the current world situation. Underlying Peking's ideological position concerning the principal contradiction—that the struggle of the colonial peoples of Asia, Africa, and Latin America against imperialist control was the primary factor in the current world scene—are the Leninist arguments about the innate aggressiveness of imperialism and its vulnerability to being deprived of overseas resources. Imperialism, the Chinese argue, is ever seeking new areas to take over; to remain idle or to relinquish foreign holdings would initiate an economic decline, possibly ending in the collapse of the imperial power. Focusing its foreign policy on the colonial and formerly colonial areas of the world, Peking saw the outcome of the battles in Asia, Africa, and Latin America against imperialism not only as resulting in the creation of new, possibly anti-Western states in those areas, but also as bringing about the eventual collapse of the capitalist economic system itself by depriving the capitalist countries of the foreign resources and markets they require.

In November 1948, even before he had won control of the Chinese mainland, Mao Tse-tung proclaimed the United States to be the most formidable of the remaining imperialist powers and the greatest present threat to world peace. Having survived the onslaught of Japanese imperialism and then battling the Kuomintang government for control of China, Mao declared, "Since the victory of World War II, US imperialism and its running dogs in various countries have taken the place of fascist Germany, Italy and Japan and are frantically preparing a new world war and menacing the whole world."[12]

As Mao saw the world in 1949, only one major imperialist power, the United States, had emerged unweakened from the shambles of World War II. Taking advantage of its world preeminence, the US sought to "enslave the whole world." Like all imperialists, Mao argued, American imperialism was by nature aggressive; the class contradictions in capitalist society

12 Mao, *Selected Works*, 4:284–285.

propel imperialism ever onward to new aggressive adventures, leaving war and chaos in its trail; war and misery in the world will never cease until the capitalist system itself has been defeated. Mao wrote,

How different is the logic of the imperialists from that of the people! Make trouble, fail, make trouble again, fail again . . . till their doom; that is the logic of the imperialists and all reactionaries the world over in dealing with the people's cause, and they will never go against this logic. This is a Marxist law. When we say "imperialism is ferocious," we mean that its nature will never change, that the imperialists will never lay down their butcher knives, that they will never become Buddhas, till their doom.[13]

More recently, Peking's view of imperialism, and specifically the American variety, has if anything become more antagonistic. For example, in their comprehensive policy statement in the summer of 1963, "A Proposal Concerning the General Line of the International Communist Movement," the Chinese described the aims of US imperialism as

trying to erect a huge world empire such as has never been known before. The strategic objectives of US imperialism have been to grab and dominate the intermediate zone lying between the United States and the socialist camp, put down the revolutions of the oppressed peoples and nations, proceed to destroy the socialist countries, and thus to subject all the peoples and countries of the world, including its allies, to domination and enslavement by US monopoly capital.[14]

In the Chinese view, imperialism is the source of war between nations, and the threat of war will exist as long as imperialism remains. Past world wars "originated in the contradictions inherent in the capitalist world and in the conflict of interests between the imperialist powers"; but, of course, communist countries have no such "antagonistic social contradictions," and "no world war can ever be started by a socialist country."[15]

13 *Ibid.*, p. 428.
14 *PR*, 1963, no. 25, p. 9.
15 *PR*, 1963, nos. 10 and 11, p. 24. Actually, the Maoists have contradicted themselves on the question of whether or not "antagonistic contradictions" can exist in socialist societies. In *On the Correct Handling of Contradictions*

Only when imperialism is defeated and the capitalist system overthrown can lasting peace be attained.

ARMED STRUGGLE—THE STRATEGY

Confronted by such a vicious enemy as the United States, Peking argues, the people of the whole world—all of whom are threatened by the US—must use force to protect themselves. If imperialism, currently manifested in the immense military power of the United States, is by nature aggressive and hence will brutalize the people of the world until they finally rise up and defeat it, then the various nations must unite to defend themselves, take up arms, and carry forward the struggle against "US imperialism" and its "lackeys." "War, this monster of mutual slaughter among men, will be finally eliminated by the progress of human society," Mao has said, "but there is only one way to eliminate it and that is to oppose war with war."[16]

The Chinese argue that in the individual countries of Asia, Africa, and Latin America where the battle against imperialism led by the United States is focused, the problem of state power is uppermost (as it is, according to Marxist-Leninists,

---

Among the People (Peking: Foreign Languages Press, 1960), Mao himself wrote that antagonistic contradictions might indeed develop in a socialist society, between "the people" and "enemies of the people" (pp. 8–9). The implication of his argument, however, was that the communist party dictatorship would control these antagonistic contradictions and resolve them in favor of "the people." Yet, more recently, the idea of antagonistic contradictions in a socialist society has played an important role in theoretical treatments of the cultural revolution. See, for example, *PR*, 1967, no. 22, pp. 43–46. The question of whether or not a socialist country could possibly start a war also raises theoretical difficulties in the contemporary political context. For example, Chou En-lai has charged the Soviet Union with "fascist aggression" for its invasion and occupation of Czechoslovakia in August 1968 (*PR*, 1968, no. 36, pp. 6–7). The implication of this charge, plus other recent Chinese statements with regard to Soviet policy (accusing the Soviet Union of carrying out imperialist and colonialist policies in the Third World, for instance), is that a socialist country in which a "revisionist" leadership takes power becomes something else. As the revisionists restore capitalism, apparently the state begins, in the Chinese view, to behave in both domestic and foreign affairs like a capitalist rather than a socialist state.

16 Mao, *Selected Military Writings* (Peking: Foreign Languages Press, 1963), p. 78.

in any revolutionary situation). Basing their argument on Lenin's thesis in *The State and Revolution,* the Chinese hold that those who have power will not relinquish it peacefully, and that, generally speaking, the imperialists and local reactionaries must ultimately be overthrown by revolutionary war.

Debating with Moscow on the question of the inevitability of war and seeking to refute Soviet charges that the Chinese were oblivious to the dangers of igniting World War III through their militancy and were unmoved by the human cost of a possible atomic holocaust, Peking argued that, although wars of national liberation were in many cases inevitable, this did not mean that wars between states need also be inevitable. The Chinese claimed that a distinction should be made between revolutionary war and world war. The first is inevitable; the second can be avoided. Moreover, they said, "the spark" of revolutionary wars need not lead, and has not led, to world war.[17]

The Chinese regard the Soviets as being primarily concerned with how to maintain the status quo and avoid nuclear war. The Chinese respond that, according to Marxism-Leninism, real peace can never come until imperialism is dead. Therefore, revolutionary wars are not only an effective and necessary weapon against the imperialist enemy, but also are the best means of attaining a true and lasting peace. The Soviets, Peking says, are selling out the people of the backward areas in the name of preserving peace and are scheming with the U.S.—"the most ferocious and most arrogant aggressors in the history of mankind"—to dominate the world.[18]

Until quite recently, the Chinese did not deny the possibility of so-called peaceful transition, taking power by peaceful means rather than violent.[19] But they cited Lenin and

[17] See *Two Different Lines on the Question of War and Peace* (Peking: Foreign Languages Press, 1963), especially the discussion on pp. 14–20.

[18] *The Leaders of the CPSU Are the Greatest Splitters of Our Times* (Peking: Foreign Languages Press, 1964), pp. 20–21.

[19] "The Differences Between Comrade Togliatti and Us," *PR,* 1963, no. 1, pp. 16–18.

years of experience to demonstrate that the chance of non-violent transformation was very slim. Moreover, with regard to "peaceful co-existence," Peking declared that such a policy might be a very suitable one for relations *between states* (and Peking did indeed advocate peaceful coexistence with countries having different social systems); but the Chinese insisted that there could be no peaceful coexistence between oppressed peoples and their oppressors.[20]

From a theoretical point of view, then, the Chinese argued that the conditions for revolution in Asia, Africa, and Latin America, produced by the concentration of contradictions in those areas, were excellent. They should be seized upon, the Chinese said, to advance the cause of progress and world peace. The enemy, imperialism, appears fierce but is actually weak. He is vulnerable in his "strategic rear"—in the areas of Asia, Africa, and Latin America—and he can be defeated by a forcefully pursued strategy of armed struggle.

[20] "The principle of peaceful co-existence can apply only to relations between countries with different social systems, not to relations between oppressed and oppressor nations, nor to relations between oppressed and oppressing classes. For an oppressed nation or people the question is one of waging a revolutionary struggle to overthrow the rule of imperialism and the reactionaries; it is not, and cannot be, a question of peaceful co-existence with imperialism and the reactionaries." *Ibid.*, p. 15.

2

FACING THE ENEMY

Returning to China after a long trip through ten African countries in late 1963 and early 1964, Premier Chou En-lai gave the following report concerning the changes he had seen in the attitudes of the African people:

During our visit to the new emerging African countries, we were most deeply impressed by the profound change in the mental outlook of the African people. Their courage and enthusiasm, energy and vigour, bespeak the mettle of a people who have become independent and have stood up on their own feet. They dare to be the masters of their own house and to manage their own state affairs; they dare to despise their enemies and to fight all oppressors, old and new. This fighting spirit constitutes the fundamental strength for the establishment of all the new emerging states. With this fighting spirit, a people can defeat all schemes and plots of the imperialists and old and new colonialists and overcome all difficulties and obstacles on their road of advance. Africa today is no longer what it was in the late 19th and early 20th centuries. It has become an awakened, militant and advanced continent.[1]

Chou En-lai's analysis of contemporary African political conditions in terms of mass political attitudes is very much in the tradition of the Maoist view of politics. The ideological orientation of the CCP as it emerged from the victorious Chi-

nese Revolution places great emphasis on "awakening" the
political sensibilities of the masses and on fostering "correct"
mass political attitudes. In an important sense, much of Mao's
writing on revolution and Peking's contemporary policy statements with regard to wars of national liberation can be seen
as a sort of psychology of revolution for potential revolutionaries in Asia, Africa, and Latin America—a guide to inculcat-
ing the mass political attitudes necessary to face up to the
enemy and dare to make revolution.

The strategic situation that Mao Tse-tung and the CCP confronted in their struggle for power in China is one which
virtually all revolutionaries face: an objectively weaker force
(the revolutionaries) confronts an objectively much stronger
force (established authority) which they seek to overthrow and
destroy. The established government controls the legal instruments of violence, primarily the army and the police, and its
power appears to be much superior to that of any competing
organization in the society. Hence, the central problem for
would-be revolutionaries is to conceive of a method of using
their weaker force to overthrow the stronger, government authority. They require both a workable military strategy and
an ideological conceptualization of present social conditions
that can credibly demonstrate to the populace the evils of the
existing system and pose an attractive alternative to it. One
of the major objectives of such a conceptualization is to aid in
structuring social discontent into hostility toward established
authority, and thereby to win popular support for the revolutionary alternative. Another objective is to build confidence
among potential revolutionaries by analyzing the relative
power positions of the revolutionaries and their enemies in
such a way as to demonstrate the vulnerability of the enemy
and to point out a clear road to victory for the revolution.

DESPISE THE ENEMY STRATEGICALLY; TAKE FULL ACCOUNT OF HIM TACTICALLY

At the heart of the Chinese strategic view of revolution (developed out of the Chinese Revolution but equally applicable,

they feel, to revolutions in other countries) is the principle, "despise the enemy strategically; take full account of him tactically":

To despise the enemy strategically means to perceive that the class enemy, viewed in its essence and in the long run, is bound to perish in the end, no matter how powerful he may be for a time; and that the revolutionary forces will eventually win, no matter how weak they may be for a time. In the last analysis, it is the masses of the people who are really powerful, and not imperialism and the reactionaries. That is why we should dare to struggle against the enemy, dare to overthrow the rule of imperialism and the reactionaries and dare to seize victory. . . .

To take full account of the enemy tactically means that with regard to any given part of the whole, and in each specific struggle, it is necessary to take the enemy seriously, to be prudent, to pay careful attention to the art of struggle and to adopt forms of struggle suited to different times, places, and conditions in order to isolate and wipe out the enemy step by step.[2]

By "tactically taking full account of the enemy," the Chinese mean that one should never underestimate the enemy or his capacity to maintain himself in power. Citing Lenin as authority, the Chinese argue that domestic reactionaries and foreign imperialists are persistent and vicious enemies who will spare no effort to suppress their opponents and stamp out the fires of revolution. Imperialism may be "parasitic, decaying and moribund capitalism" as Lenin argued; but until it is completely defeated by the armed struggle of the masses, it is not only capable of, but fully prepared to, suppress violently those who rise against it.

On the other hand, Peking argues, revolutionaries should "strategically despise the enemy" and should not overestimate his strength. Those who seek to overthrow reactionary regimes should carefully analyze the foundations of their enemy's power to see how strong he actually is and where his greatest weaknesses lie. Such an analysis, the Chinese say, will conclude that in the long run it is the revolutionaries, not the reactionaries, who are truly powerful, because real power resides in

2 Shao Tieh-chen, "Revolutionary Dialectics and How to Appraise Imperialism," PR, 1963, no. 2, pp. 14–15. Translated from HC, 1963, no. 1.

the people and no reactionary government can keep the support or even the acquiescence of the people once they have become politically conscious. Reactionary regimes are by nature oppressive, Peking claims, and their exploitation of the great majority of the people will ultimately fill the ranks of the revolution and bring about the regime's own downfall.

Therefore, in the long range Chinese view, the governments of all non-communist societies are only apparently powerful. They are still capable of sustained resistance and even of causing great casualties among the revolutionary forces (especially when revolutionary leaders make mistakes); but in the long run and from a strategic point of view, they can and will be beaten. "The people,"[3] on the other hand, are seen to be truly powerful; they comprise a potential revolutionary force of some 90 percent of the population, which, when sufficiently awakened to political realities, will rise up against the reactionary minority and sweep them into oblivion.

OF POWER AND "PAPER TIGERS"

Mao Tse-tung's paper tiger thesis is probably the best known version of this Chinese view of world power realities.[4] Over

---

[3] All those who take up the "progressive" cause and oppose the "reactionaries" become, by definition, "the people." Mao demonstrated the flexibility of this concept of "the people" in his essay, *On the Correct Handling of Contradictions Among the People* (Peking: Foreign Languages Press, 1960). pp. 8–9: "The term 'the people' has different meanings in different countries, and in different historical periods in each country. Take our country for example. During the War of Resistance to Japanese Aggression, all those classes, strata and social groups which opposed Japanese aggression belonged to the category of the people, while the Japanese imperialists, Chinese traitors and the pro-Japanese elements belonged to the category of enemies of the people. During the War of Liberation, the United States imperialists and their henchmen—the bureaucrat-capitalists and landlord class—and the Kuomintang reactionaries, who represented these two classes, were the enemies of the people, while all other classes, strata and social groups which opposed these enemies, belonged to the category of the people. At this stage of building socialism, all classes, strata and social groups which approve, support and work for the cause of socialist construction belong to the category of the people, while those social forces and groups which resist the socialist revolution, and are hostile to and try to wreck socialist construction, are enemies of the people."

[4] For a somewhat similar exposition of Mao's paper tiger theory, see Ralph Powell, "Great Powers and Atomic Bombs Are 'Paper Tigers,'" *CQ*, July–September, 1965, pp. 55–63.

twenty years ago, in the summer of 1946, Mao first put forward
this thesis in an interview with an American friend of the
CCP, Anna Louise Strong. World War II was over, and the
stage was set for the final battle between the Chinese Communists and Chiang Kai-shek's Nationalist government for control of the Chinese mainland. Soviet Russia had discouraged
the CCP from attempting to take power by force,[5] but Mao,
looking into the future, gave the following account of the
power situation of that time:

> The atom bomb is a paper tiger which the US reactionaries use
> to scare people. It looks terrible, but in fact it isn't. Of course, the
> atom bomb is a weapon of mass slaughter, but the outcome of a
> war is decided by the people, not by one or two new types of
> weapon.
> All reactionaries are paper tigers. In appearance, the reaction-
> aries are terrifying, but in reality they are not so powerful. From a
> long-term point of view, it is not the reactionaries but the people
> who are really powerful. In Russia, before the February Revolu-
> tion in 1917, which side was really strong? On the surface the tsar
> was strong but he was swept away by a single gust of wind in the
> February Revolution. In the final analysis, the strength in Russia
> was on the side of the Soviets of Workers, Peasants and Soldiers.
> The tsar was just a paper tiger. Wasn't Hitler once considered very
> strong? But history proved that he was a paper tiger. So was Mus-
> solini, so was Japanese imperialism. . . .
> Take the case of China. We have only millet plus rifles to rely
> on, but history will finally prove that our millet plus rifles is more
> powerful than Chiang Kai-shek's aeroplanes plus tanks. Although
> the Chinese people still face many difficulties and will long suffer
> hardships from the joint attacks of US imperialism and the Chi-
> nese reactionaries, the day will come when these reactionaries are
> defeated and we are victorious. The reason is simply this: the reac-
> tionaries represent reaction, we represent progress.[6]

According to Mao's Marxist historicism, therefore, those on
the side of "progress" and "the people" will ultimately triumph against all odds. Their enemies, who today may appear

[5] Milovan Djilas, *Conversations with Stalin* (New York: Harcourt, Brace and
World, 1962), pp. 182–183.
[6] Mao, *Selected Works*, 4:100–101.

strong and fierce, are only paper tigers destined for the dustbin of history.

Mao's paper tiger theory, which is very similar in meaning and political purpose to Lenin's earlier characterization of imperialism as a "colossus with feet of clay," is probably the most graphic example of the Chinese concept of despising the enemy strategically but taking full account of him tactically.[7] China's enemies and the enemies of "the people" of the world are said to have a dual nature; they are both real tigers and paper tigers at the same time. Seen from the long-term strategic point of view, they are isolated from the people, and their frantic attempts to maintain themselves in power run contrary to the progress of history; therefore they are paper tigers. Seen from the short-run tactical view, however, they "have eaten millions and tens of millions of people and will continue to eat people in the future" and are therefore ferocious, real tigers which must be taken very seriously. Hence, a good revolutionary should derive confidence in ultimate victory from his knowledge that the enemy is strategically weak, but he must also be prepared to fight persistently and tenaciously against an enemy who is tactically still very strong.

The first aspect of this two-sided nature—strategically despising the paper tiger—is probably the most important for the Chinese and the major reason Mao put forward the argument at all. When he first spoke of paper tigers in 1946, he was face to face with an enemy, the Chinese Nationalist government, which was aided and supplied from the vast resources of the most powerful country in the world, the United States. Confronting what appeared to be a vastly superior enemy, Mao Tse-tung no doubt felt the need of a concept or slogan that would help to undermine the intimidating influence of the Nationalist superiority in armaments and materiel and enable him to inspire confidence among his own troops to fight the apparently more powerful enemy. This was not a

[7] The Chinese Communists have also used fear of ghosts and the analysis of traditional Chinese ghost stories to make the same point. See *Stories About Not Being Afraid of Ghosts* (Peking: Foreign Languages Press, 1961).

new approach, however, but one very much in tune with the Maoist view that the most important force in history is an organized, politicized mass of people. One of the major emphases in Mao's thought has continually been on a sort of "where there's a will, there's a way" assumption, a determination that a sufficiently motivated and mobilized populace can surmount almost any obstacle.[8]

However, the second aspect of the paper tiger–real tiger view of imperialism and reaction is almost equally important. Having shown through an examination of the first aspect that the enemy is weak at the core and having shown why the revolutionary forces should be confident of ultimate victory, emphasis on the second aspect sets the frame of reference for a long, bloody battle and argues in effect that the people have no choice but to take up arms against a vicious, aggressive enemy.

THE DEFENSIVE POSTURE

Fundamental to the Chinese conception of wars of national liberation is an attempt to portray the struggle as a defensive one being waged against a persistently aggressive enemy. The utility of such a defensive posture soon becomes clear.

The first postulate of this view is that the enemy—imperialism and local reactionaries—is ever aggressive and can in no way be convinced to change his vicious nature (see the discussion on pp. 30–33). Given such an enemy, obviously the only thing the people can do is to join together, arm themselves, and make war against him.

[8] Of course, this approach to laying the foundations for a revolutionary movement has a history of success to reinforce Mao in his convictions. In fact, it seems that once again during the Great Proletarian Cultural Revolution of 1966–1969, one important reason for Mao's persistence in battling against the so-called revisionists in the CCP leadership was his conviction that they were opportunistically leading China to long-run failure by wanting to emphasize material work incentives and individual self-interest in an effort to increase economic production in the short run. Mao knew from the experience of the years before 1949 that it was not self-interest or the hope of higher salaries which motivated the troops of the People's Liberation Army to fight against overwhelming odds to ultimate victory; and he seemed to be saying that if China was ever to attain the greatness which it sought, the new China as well would have to be based on this kind of selfless dedication.

From the Chinese point of view, all wars are seen to be either just or unjust. In his "Problems of Strategy in China's Revolutionary War," Mao wrote, "We support just wars and oppose unjust wars. All counter-revolutionary wars are unjust, all revolutionary wars are just."[9] A different way of putting Mao's point is to say that most wars are both just *and* unjust depending on what side of the battle one looks at. Wars among reactionaries may have no just aspect at all; but wars of national liberation are obviously just wars when seen from the view of the revolutionaries, and unjust wars when viewed from the side of the enemy imperialists and local reactionaries. The distinction between just and unjust has the effect of wrapping the revolution in a cloak of legitimacy.

Moreover, a just war is almost always viewed as a defensive war; thus the revolutionaries are not only seen to be fighting a righteous battle, but also one in which they have been set upon by local and foreign aggressors and are fighting for their very survival. The hoped-for result of such a formulation is to win greatly increased popular support for the revolution,[10] as well as the other benefits that legitimacy bestows: increased fighting spirit among revolutionary troops, international support for the revolution, a determination to overcome all obstacles to see that justice prevails, and so forth.

The revolutionary response to such an aggressive enemy intent on waging an unjust war, the Chinese say, should be a tit-for-tat struggle against the oppressors. For each enemy aggression the revolutionary forces should respond in kind, returning violence with violence. If the population is unresponsive to the revolutionaries' call to battle or unconvinced of the aggressive intent of the government, Chinese policy is not above recommending the managing of a "negative example" —that is, provoking the government or a foreign power into making a violent reaction against the revolution which in-

9 Mao, *Selected Military Writings,* p. 79.
10 As Mao has said of the Chinese Revolution: "Patriotic, just and revolutionary in character, the war waged by the People's Liberation Army was bound to win the support of the people of the whole country. That was the political foundation for victory over Chiang Kai-shek." *Selected Works,* 4:160.

volves an attack on the civilian population to prove that what the revolutionaries have said about the aggressive nature of the government and the foreigners is true. Lacking the capacity to provoke a negative example, often a simple lie—repeated over and over again until it becomes believable—suffices. For example, Peking continues to argue that the North Korean invasion of South Korea in June 1950 was actually a defensive operation mounted in response to a southern invasion of the North.

One of the many lessons learned by the CCP from the traumatic years of the Chinese Revolution is apparently that violence is one of the most rapid and effective methods of mobilizing an apathetic population, and that violence by foreign troops is probably the most effective mobilizer of all. It would perhaps be going too far to say that Peking welcomes massive foreign intervention in revolutionary situations in Asia, Africa, and Latin America (such as those in Vietnam and the Dominican Republic); but it is clear that the Chinese see great advantages resulting from such foreign intervention, not only in mobilizing indigenous popular support for revolutionary movements, but also in strengthening world-wide anti-Western sentiment.[11]

MEN VERSUS MACHINES

But what of the enemy's fearful weapons? Even when convinced that history is on their side, that their cause is just, and that they must fight or be slaughtered by an aggressive enemy, how can a mobilized people dare to attack an opponent armed with tanks, machine guns, and helicopters, not to speak of atomic bombs, jet airplanes, and missiles?

The leadership of the CCP faced this problem throughout the Chinese Revolution and during the war with Japan. As early as 1938, in the first year of the anti-Japanese war, Mao Tse-tung attacked those who argued that ultimately it was armaments that determined the outcome of a war:

11 On this point, see, for example, Mao's interview with Edgar Snow reported in the *New Republic*, February 27, 1965, pp. 17–23.

This is the so-called theory that "weapons decide everything," which constitutes a mechanical approach to the question of war and a subjective and one-sided view. Our view is opposed to this; we see not only weapons but also people. Weapons are an important factor in war, but not the decisive factor; it is people, not things, that are decisive. The contest of strength is not only a contest of military and economic power, but also a contest of human power and morale.[12]

Peking's view on the question of men *versus* machines is founded essentially on Marxist historicism which sees men as ultimately overcoming all obstacles (human and material) to carry history forward to its final culmination in communism. More specifically, however, the Chinese argument rests on the postulate that in almost any non-communist society, roughly 90 percent of the population is oppressed by a ruling 10 percent of the population, which exploits the great majority for its own selfish ends. The Chinese, therefore, see the 90 percent —once it has been awakened to political realities and has become aware of its real political interests—as potential supporters of a revolution to overthrow the exploiting 10 percent.

Peking argues further that machines, and more specifically weapons, must obviously be operated by men. To keep order in a society and certainly to wage war against a revolution, the ruling 10 percent of the society must have the acquiescence and the cooperation of a large percentage of the people. If, however, the vast majority of the population refuses to cooperate—refuses to become policemen and soldiers and man the weapons turned against the revolution—then the ruling classes cannot long maintain themselves in power; and in spite of their vast superiority in weapons, they will ultimately go down to defeat at the hands of the revolutionaries. Hence, men not machines, Peking argues, are decisive.

In the context of the Atomic Age and the era of weapons of mass destruction, it becomes even more important for the Chinese to defend men as the decisive factor in history, as opposed to machines and the terrifying products of advanced weapons

12 Mao, *Selected Military Writings*, pp. 217–218.

technology. In this connection, a significant aspect of the Sino-Soviet dispute has centered on the question of how to evaluate the significance of atomic weapons and has revolved around the issue of "nuclear blackmail." Peking charges that the Soviets overemphasize the influence of atomic weapons to the point of claiming that "the laws of social development have ceased to operate and the fundamental Marxist-Leninist theory concerning war and peace is outmoded."[13] The Chinese see Soviet policy as a sort of united front against all kinds of war, atomic and revolutionary. They see it as a policy that the Soviets put forward ostensibly in the name of peace and saving mankind from nuclear annihilation, but which is in fact an attempt to preserve the status quo and prevent the peoples of Asia, Africa, and Latin America from making revolution.

The Chinese agree that atomic weapons have a terrifying destructive capacity and should not be underestimated, but they do not agree that "local wars" or revolutions will necessarily lead to atomic wars. Nor do they agree that nuclear technology has changed the laws of historical development, and that revolutionaries, therefore, must join hands with reactionaries to work together to prevent the extermination of mankind by nuclear holocaust.

The significant point is that China, a have-not power clearly interested in seeing radical change in many areas of the world, cannot readily agree with the Soviet formulation which the Chinese interpret to mean, don't start anything anywhere, because even the smallest conflict in the most faraway land may bring on the cataclysm that will destroy us all. If the Chinese were to accept this view, which they denounce as "nuclear blackmail," they would be afraid to support revolution to bring about the political change which they seek and would fall victim, they argue, to the reactionaries who try to use atomic weapons to intimidate the people and prevent them from making revolution.

However, rather than being intimidated by atomic weapons

[13] "More on the Differences between Comrade Togliatti and Us," *PR*, 1963, nos. 10 and 11, p. 25.

or the fear of the annihilation of mankind, Peking suggests that a weapon from its own arsenal, "the spiritual atom bomb," will actually prove to be the most influential one:

However highly developed modern weapons and technical equipment may be and however complicated the methods of modern warfare, in the final analysis the outcome of a war will be decided by the sustained fighting of the ground forces, by the fighting at close quarters on battlefields, by the political consciousness of men, by their courage and spirit of sacrifice. . . . The reactionary troops of US imperialism cannot possibly be endowed with the courage and the spirit of sacrifice possessed by the revolutionary people. The spiritual atom bomb which the revolutionary people possess is a far more powerful and useful weapon than the physical atom bomb.[14]

This revolutionary heroism—"the political consciousness of the people, their courage and readiness to make sacrifices and defy hardships and death"—is the substance of real power, the Chinese argue, and it provides a revolutionary people with the most formidable of weapons, one which they alone can possess, and with the means to overthrow their reactionary enemies.[15]

THE PSYCHOLOGY OF "DARING TO STRUGGLE"

To many, the arguments described in this chapter may appear to be little more than a fairly transparent rationalization by

[14] Lin Piao, "Long Live the Victory of People's War!" *PR*, 1965, no. 36, pp. 26–27.

[15] Chinese evaluation of the power of nuclear weapons, of course, involves not only Peking's interest in the strategy and tactics of foreign revolutionary wars, but also China's own defensive strategy. In the "debate" within the CCP leadership of 1965–1966, prompted by the American military build-up in South Vietnam and fears of war with the US, some Chinese leaders, especially the more professionally oriented military men like Lo Jui-ch'ing, apparently argued for a defensive posture based on a more modernized and mechanized army ultimately protected by the Soviet "nuclear umbrella." The Mao-Lin group apparently disparaged this emphasis on weapons and called for continued struggle against the Soviet revisionists and a defensive strategy based on people's war. See the contributions of Uri Ra'anan and Donald Zagoria in Tang Tsou, ed., *China in Crisis* (Chicago: University of Chicago Press, 1968), vol. 2. And for a study of Chinese attitudes toward nuclear weapons from the Hiroshima blast in 1945 to the present, see Morton H. Halperin's paper in the same volume.

the Chinese of the militant pursuit of their global ambitions (even at the risk of involving the entire world in a catastrophic nuclear war), or an attempt to focus attention on those areas of military strategy and tactics (armed insurrection and small-scale land warfare) in which the Chinese have a proven capability, while at the same time attempting to minimize other aspects of a possible military confrontation in which the Chinese military capability is notably lacking. In fact, however, although the above observations are probably at least partially true, Chinese strategic thinking and especially Mao's writings on revolution have consistently been characterized by a basic commitment to, and confidence in, political power as derived from the politicization and mobilization of the masses. The fundamental concept of strategically despising the enemy while tactically taking him seriously is clearly a consciously conceived ideological formulation constructed in an effort to overcome the psychological barriers to making revolution and to help instill the kind of fighting spirit required to successfully oppose an objectively stronger enemy. It is in this sense that the Chinese speak of being "armed with the thought of Mao Tse-tung"—armed with a view of future victory, a strategic formula that sees the revolution as ultimately more powerful than its opponents, and the confidence to dare to struggle for victory. A *Jen-min jih-pao* editorial in December 1962 put it this way:

The most important question for the Chinese revolution and the fate of the Chinese people was whether we would dare to struggle, dare to make a revolution, and dare to seize victory. It was at this crucial moment that Comrade Mao Tse-tung armed the Chinese Communists and the Chinese people ideologically with the Marxist-Leninist proposition that "imperialism and all reactionaries are paper tigers." . . .

We hold that the question of whether one treats imperialism and all reactionaries strategically as the paper tigers they really are is of great importance for the question of how the forces of revolution and the forces of reaction are to be appraised, is of great importance for the question of whether the revolutionary people will dare to wage struggle, dare to make revolution, dare to seize victory, and is of great importance for the question of the future outcome of the worldwide struggles of the people and the future course of history. . . . *Every oppressed people should above all have the revolutionary confidence, the revolutionary courage and the revolutionary spirit to defeat imperialism and the reactionaries, otherwise there will be no hope for any revolution.*[16]

A major objective of the Chinese ideology of the national liberation struggle, then, is to create a kind of revolutionary mass psychology: a framework of political attitudes which places the blame for economic and political ills on foreign and domestic exploiters, which sees the population as under attack by aggressive reactionary forces, and which demands that the masses join together to make revolution and overthrow the established government, confident of the justice and future success of their struggle.

[16] "The Differences between Comrade Togliatti and Us," *PR*, 1963, no. 1, pp. 13–14 (emphasis added).

3

CHINA'S PROGRAM
FOR REVOLUTION

Having understood the Chinese analysis of the current world situation and grasped Mao's psychology of revolution, what does the potential revolutionary do next? What kind of practical ideology does Peking suggest for the organization of revolutionary activity? What kind of revolutionary model do the Chinese propose for armed struggles in contemporary Asia, Africa, and Latin America?

WARS OF NATIONAL LIBERATION

Any regular television watcher or newspaper reader today knows what kind of revolution Peking proposes for the underdeveloped world: wars of national liberation. The term has become a commonplace, and the brutal battle in Vietnam daily confronts us with an inescapable case in point.

From a classical Marxist-Leninist point of view, the revolution that the Chinese are currently seeking to promote in the underdeveloped world is technically a "national democratic" revolution.[1] Peking rarely speaks of communist-led "socialist"

1 The precise interpretation and application of the concept of national democratic revolution has been at issue in the Sino-Soviet dispute and has

revolution in Asia, Africa, and Latin America—at least, not at this stage. For example, the secret Chinese Army journal *Kung-tso t'ung-hsun* (Bulletin of activities) of April 25, 1961, speaks of the conditions in some areas of contemporary Africa as resembling the situation that existed in China sixty years earlier—twenty years before the Chinese Communist Party was even founded. The journal concludes, "Africa at present is mostly occupied with fighting imperialism and colonialism. Its fight against feudalism is not so important, and, moreover, its role in the Socialist revolution is in a dormant phase. The important part of its activities lies in its national revolution."[2]

In terms of classical Marxism-Leninism, a national democratic revolution is directed primarily against two enemies, foreign imperialism and domestic feudalism, and is characteristically led by the bourgeoisie. Although it is not a socialist revolution, according to Mao Tse-tung it can be turned into a socialist revolution if the proletariat (by which he means the communist party) takes control of the revolution away from the bourgeoisie. In terms of Maoist theory, therefore, there are two possibilities for revolution in the underdeveloped world, both of which are labeled wars of national liberation by Peking. The first is national democratic revolution led by bourgeois nationalists and aimed at the establishment of true independence from foreign control and the abolition of so-called feudal patterns of landholding; the second is national democratic revolution led by communists and comprising the first stage of a two-stage (national then socialist) revolution

---

varied in Chinese and Soviet usage. See, for example, the discussion in Ernst Halperin, "Peking and the Latin American Communists," *CQ*, January–March, 1967, pp. 111–154; and Uri Ra'anan, "Moscow and the 'Third World,' " *Problems of Communism*, January–February, 1965, pp. 22–31.

2 See J. Chester Cheng, ed., *The Politics of the Chinese Red Army: A Translation of the Bulletin of Activities of the People's Liberation Army* (Stanford: The Hoover Institution, 1966), p. 484. This does not mean, however, that the Chinese are not interested in, or see little future for, socialist revolution in Africa. The same paragraph continues, "According to the analysis of Marxism it is to be confirmed that the embryo of national revolution in these countries will become a genuine people's revolution, give rise to Marxists, form political parties of proletariats and go towards the Socialist revolution."

leading eventually to communism. The Algerian Revolution (1954–1962) is a good example of the first possibility; the Chinese Revolution is vigorously promoted by Peking as a model for the second.

What often makes the distinction between the two alternatives unclear is an apparently purposeful Chinese attempt to blur the differences in leadership and ultimate goals of the two revolutions by combining them under the single heading of wars of national liberation. In the Chinese view, both the Algerian and the Chinese revolutions were wars of national liberation; but being led by different economic classes (bourgeoisie and proletariat, respectively), they necessarily resulted in different kinds of political systems.

THE PROBLEM OF ESTABLISHING NATIONALIST CREDENTIALS

Leaving aside for a moment the problem of who leads the revolution, there remains another important distinction to be made with regard to wars of national liberation—one which, again, is somewhat blurred in the Chinese interpretation. This distinction involves the status of the country in which the revolution breaks out: is it a colony, or a supposedly independent country? Is the country an overseas possession of an imperial power and the target of the revolution, therefore, obvious foreign domination? Or, does the revolution occur in a nominally independent country, which appears to run its own affairs, but which revolutionaries claim is actually ruled by indirect foreign influence administered by local "lackeys"? From the Chinese point of view, the policy and political organization of the revolution in both cases is generally the same: both seek to form a broad national united front against an alleged imperialist domination. But the ideological justification for a national liberation revolution in an apparently independent country is considerably more complicated than that for a revolution in an obviously foreign-controlled territory.

When national liberation revolutions occur in obviously foreign-controlled areas (such as the Portuguese possessions of Angola and Mozambique), the nationalist character of the revolution—whether or not it is led by communists—is quite widely accepted. The nationalist credentials of the revolutionaries and the goals they proclaim (the expulsion of the colonial authority and the establishment of indigenous rule) are generally considered to be legitimate and to require little ideological defense.

When a national liberation revolution occurs in a nominally independent country (such as South Vietnam, the Congo, or Peru), the question of establishing the nationalist credentials of the revolution poses a considerably more difficult problem; the country appears to be already independent, and there seems, therefore, to be no legitimate reason for national liberation. In terms of Chinese ideology, however, the enemy in this case is seen to be a new kind of foreign control, "neo-colonialism," which allegedly dominates the affairs of supposedly independent countries by means of indigenous "lackeys" or "puppets," who perform their functions as the government of an apparently independent country but who are in reality only the agents and tools of the foreigners.[3] The case of Peru, where armed struggle against the government broke out in the summer of 1965, provides a good example.

[3] Liu Ta-nien, in "How to Appraise the History of Asia?" (PR, 1965, no. 45, p. 26), described the methods of "neo-colonialism" as follows: "They [the neo-colonialists] foster puppet regimes and practise various subtler methods of colonial control; organize military blocs and build up military bases, and plunder the wealth of countries by means of economic 'aid' and various other forms of economic 'exploitation.' They engage in 'spiritual' infiltration and cultural aggression; organize subversion and engineer military coups d'etat; they engage in direct armed intervention and launch large-scale armed aggression. US armed aggression against Korea and the current US armed aggression against Viet Nam and Laos are only two of these examples." The country most often accused of having neo-colonialist ambitions is the United States, and the targets of this alleged US imperialist domination ("new-type colonies") are of several sorts: (1) former colonies of the "neo-colonial" power itself (e.g., the Philippines); (2) former colonies of other imperial powers (e.g., South Vietnam); and (3) countries which had not formerly been colonies at all (e.g., Thailand).

In the winter of 1966, the Chinese published excerpts from
a report by the pro-Chinese Peruvian Communist Party and
the conclusions and resolutions adopted at the party's Fifth
National Conference, held on November 15–16, 1965. The
documents include a full analysis of the political situation
in Peru and prescriptions for action to be taken by the pro-
Peking splinter party in its struggle for national liberation.
The article begins with an assault on Soviet revisionism and
an endorsement of the recent Chinese formulation concerning
the "principal contradiction" in the contemporary world—a
formulation which, it will be recalled, argues that the national
liberation struggles against imperialism in the underdeveloped world comprise the single most important aspect of the
contemporary world revolution (see pp. 28–29, above). The
report then goes on to analyze the domestic political situation in Peru and to state the party's policy. Peru, it says, is a
"semi-feudal and semi-colonial country," an "appendage of
US imperialism"; therefore, "the strategic objective of the
revolution is anti-imperialist and anti-feudal." The main
tasks of the Peruvian CP, aside from struggling against revisionism, it continues, are to educate and organize the masses
to "wage struggle" against their imperialist and feudal enemies. As a means to defeating these enemies, the Peruvian
CP proposes the organization of a party-led army to wage a
revolutionary war—"a peasant revolution spreading from vil-
lages to cities" with "the peasants as the main force and the
working class (through its party [the Peruvian CP]) as the
leading force." The organizational foundation of the movement should be a patriotic liberation front founded on the
broadest possible popular base: a worker-peasant alliance of
all "who are willing to carry out the anti-imperialist, anti-
feudal, democratic tasks of the first stage of the Peruvian revolution."[4]

4 See *PR*, 1966, no. 12, pp. 20–24. From the Chinese point of view, probably
the main reason for reprinting the Peruvian CP documents was not to illustrate acceptable national liberation ideological positions, but rather to use the

The Peruvian CP program, which is based almost point-for-point on Mao Tse-tung's interpretation of the Chinese Revolution, argues in effect that Peru is not an independent country but a US colony. It claims that, although Peru is recognized in the United Nations and throughout the world as an independent state, it is in reality a semicolonial country (in this case, a "new-type colony") under the influence of US imperialism, which dominates the country by controlling Peru's economy and by secretly manipulating government puppets.

This argument is typical of the general Chinese position with regard to national liberation wars mounted against independent governments. Peking argues that, whereas formerly the imperialist powers of Europe were dominant in the underdeveloped world, now their influence is being replaced by US "neo-colonialism." The Chinese, and many revolutionaries in other parts of Asia, Africa, and Latin America who adopt the Peking line, seem to have learned through hard experience that to be successful a revolution in the contemporary underdeveloped world must be founded on a nationalistic rather than class base in order to tap the prevailing nationalistic feeling. It must, as has often been argued, "capture the nationalist movement." Thus, today's Maoist revolutionaries attempt to disparage the nationalist credentials of existing governments by charging that they are actually nothing more than lackeys of imperialism and puppets of foreigners, meanwhile proclaiming themselves to be the only true nationalist leaders. Characteristically, the Peruvian Communist Party

documents as ammunition in their dispute with the Soviets. The excerpts contain several attacks on revisionism and also criticize Fidel Castro and the Cuban party. The following quotations illustrate the Peruvian CP position in the Sino-Soviet dispute: "Under the cover of revolutionary phraseology and pseudo-unity with those revisionist-led Communist Parties, the present revisionist leaders of the CPSU are taking big strides along the path of compromising with imperialism and restoring capitalism in the Soviet Union." "The glorious center propelling the development of Marxism-Leninism has shifted from Europe to Asia, from the Soviet Union to China. The proof of this is that this life and death struggle against imperialism and world reaction is led by the Communist Party of China."

attempts to wrap itself in the national flag, in the manner frankly advocated by Lin Piao in his article on people's war:

History shows that when confronted by ruthless imperialist aggression, a Communist Party must hold aloft the national banner and, using the weapons of united action, rally around itself the masses and the patriotic and anti-imperialist people who form more than 90 per cent of a country's population. . . . If we abandon the national banner, adopt a line of "closed-doorism" and thus isolate ourselves, it is out of the question to exercise leadership and develop the people's revolutionary cause, and this in reality amounts to helping the enemy and bringing defeat on ourselves.[5]

CHINESE FOREIGN POLICY AND THE UNITED FRONT

For the Chinese, however, support for wars of national liberation comprises but a single part of their overall foreign policy, a policy which is sharply differentiated relative to Peking's evaluation of the foreign country involved, be it socialist, revisionist, imperialist, colonial or whatever.[6] The main thrust of Chinese foreign policy is forcefully radical—anti-revisionist in communist party affairs, and anti-imperialist throughout the world.

During the period 1958–1965, Chinese foreign policy with regard to the underdeveloped areas can perhaps best be seen as an attempt to foster united fronts on two, somewhat analogous, levels: first, a national united front within each of the individual countries of Asia, Africa, and Latin America, based on a patriotic appeal and attempting to unite as many diverse groups in the society as possible to oppose a real or imagined foreign, imperialist enemy; and second, an international anti-imperialist united front comprised, in turn, of the countries and peoples of all the underdeveloped world plus the socialist camp[7] and all others willing to join. The major target of both

5 *PR*, 1965, no. 36, p. 14.

6 For example, see the principles of Chinese foreign policy outlined in *Peaceful Coexistence—Two Diametrically Opposed Policies* (Peking: Foreign Languages Press, 1963), pp. 15–16.

7 As the Sino-Soviet dispute deepened during this period, the Chinese view of the role communist countries should play in the international united front changed. At the outset, the socialist camp was clearly intended to be the

united fronts was imperialism, and specifically US imperialism.

At the national level among the countries of the developing world, the Chinese view of what the patriotic united front should be took different forms. In some cases, it should be directed against the local government; in others, it might be led by the government. If, as in the case of Peru, Peking declared a society to be "semi-colonial" and its government to be "puppets of imperialism," the Chinese would encourage the formation of a united front against both the foreign enemy and the local government and in some cases would support antigovernment wars of national liberation. If, however, the local government was considered by Peking to be truly nationalistic and independent of foreign control, as for example in Tanzania and Cambodia, the local government itself might be seen to be leading the anti-imperialist, patriotic united front.[8]

---

leader of the proposed international united front, but later, some member-states (the revisionists) increasingly were seen by the Chinese not only to be taking an insufficiently active part in the anti-imperialist alliance but, worse, to be actually allying with the enemy, the United States. By the summer of 1965, the term "socialist camp" was only rarely used in Chinese public statements and, then, usually by those Chinese leaders who favored a closer relationship with the Soviet Union and who subsequently became targets of the cultural revolution. See, for example, Uri Ra'anan's analysis in Tang Tsou, ed., *China in Crisis* (Chicago: University of Chicago Press, 1968), vol. 2.

[8] For example, in the China-Tanzania Joint Communique published after the visit of Chinese Premier Chou En-lai to Tanzania in June 1965, the following appraisal of President Nyerere's leadership was made by the Chinese: "The Chinese party expressed great admiration for the indomitable will and revolutionary spirit of the Tanzanian people united as one under the leadership of President Nyerere in opposing imperialist intervention and subversion and safeguarding their national independence and state sovereignty." *PR*, 1965, no. 24, p. 7. Chinese Foreign Minister Ch'en Yi, speaking of Cambodian Prince Sihanouk's leadership, put his remarks in a broader framework: "At present, revolutionary struggles of the people of the world against US imperialism and its lackeys are developing in depth, and all kinds of political forces on the international scene are now going through a drastic process of differentiation and re-grouping. The leader of every country can contribute his share to the cause of world peace and human progress as long as he reflects the will of his people and acts in accordance with the trend of historical development. In the present international situation, His Royal Highness Prince Sihanouk, holding high the militant banner of opposing US imperialism, has given full expression to the national dignity and tremendous courage of the Cambodian people and greatly encouraged all the countries and peoples

On the international level, Chinese thinking regarding united front tactics was based on Lin Piao's image of "the rural areas of the world" (Asia, Africa, and Latin America) surrounding "the cities of the world" (North America and Western Europe); but at times the united front was expanded to include even some of the "cities"—the Western European countries. Probably the most extensive construction Peking has ever given the international united front was a proposal for a "broadest possible united front" (*tsui kuang-fan te t'ung-yi chan-hsien*) to oppose US imperialism, put forward by Mao himself on January 12, 1964, and expounded in detail by a subsequent *Jen-min jih-pao* editorial. Mao declared:

The people of the countries of the socialist camp should unite, the people of the countries of Asia, Africa, and Latin America should unite, the people of the continents of the world should unite, all peace-loving countries and all countries that are subject to US aggression, control, interference and bullying should unite and should form the broadest possible united front to oppose the US imperialist policies of aggression and war and to safeguard world peace.[9]

This was not the first time that Mao had proposed a broad international united front against the United States,[10] but it was perhaps the first time that the united front had been extended to include the non-communist *states* as well as *people* of the countries of Western Europe.[11]

---

fighting against US imperialism. We have great admiration for the firm stand taken by the Cambodian Government and people and their outstanding role in the international struggle against US imperialism." *PR*, 1965, no. 46, p. 4.

9 For Mao's statement, see *JMJP*, January 13, 1964, p. 1. The editorial appears in *JMJP*, January 21, 1964. For an interpretation of the role that this conception subsequently played in the internal CCP leadership dispute of 1965–1966, see Uri Ra'anan in Tang Tsou, ed., *China in Crisis*, vol. 2.

10 Mao made a similar proposal as early as 1946 in his famous interview with Anna Louise Strong. See Mao, *Selected Works*, 4:99–100.

11 The pressures of the deepening Sino-Soviet dispute, plus the opportunity of splitting the Western camp presented by the loosening of the Atlantic alliance, probably led China to seek closer Western European contacts at this time. It is particularly interesting to note that at the time of Mao Tse-tung's statement, Peking was in the process of negotiating the establishment of diplomatic relations with France, finally announced two weeks later on January 27. Peking was also actively seeking to improve its relations with West Germany.

In its attempt to win support for this broadest possible united front against the US, Peking argued that the "US imperialists are the most ferocious and most arrogant aggressors in the history of mankind," and that the US sought not only to make war on the communist world, but also to seize the vast "intermediate zone" lying between the United States and the communist countries—that is, the area of the world composed of both the independent and colonial areas of Asia, Africa, and Latin America ("the first intermediate zone"), and the countries of Western Europe, Oceania, Canada, and other capitalist countries ("the second intermediate zone").[12]

"Despite the different political beliefs among the peoples and the different social systems in various countries," *Jen-min jih-pao* claimed, "there is not a single country or people in the world today which is not subjected to the aggression and threats of US imperialism."[13] To combat this menace, the Chinese proposed that all people throughout the world and all countries "subjected to US aggression, control, interference and bullying" (in other words, everyone in the world except "US imperialism and its lackeys") should join together, form a united front, and struggle against the common enemy.[14]

See, for example, Jean Edward Smith, "Two Germanys and Two Chinas," *The Reporter*, May 19, 1966, pp. 36–38.

12 *JMJP*, January 21, 1964, translated in *PR*, 1964, no. 4, pp. 6–8.

13 *Ibid.*, p. 8.

14 In a particularly candid statement published in late 1965, Peking evaluated the anti-American potential of the non-communist areas of the world as follows: "in the contemporary world opposition to or alliance with US imperialism constitutes the hallmark for deciding whether or not a political force can be included in the united front against the United States.

"In Asia, Africa and Latin America, with the exception of the lackeys of imperialism, personages from the upper strata in many nationalist countries desire in varying degrees to oppose imperialism, colonialism and neo-colonialism headed by the United States. We should co-operate with them in the anti-imperialist struggle.

"In the imperialist countries which are in sharp contradiction with the United States, some monopoly capitalists follow the US imperialists, but there are also others who desire in varying degrees to oppose the United States. In the struggle against the United States, the people of the world can take united action with the latter on some questions and to a certain degree." "Refutation of the New Leaders of the CPSU on 'United Action,'" *PR*, 1965, no. 46, pp. 14–15.

In its appeal to Western European countries, Peking played on what the Chinese saw to be major contradictions among the "monopoly capitalist" countries, contradictions based on a competition for markets and scarce resources, manifesting themselves, for example, in competition between "neo-colonialism" (US) and "old colonialism" (European) in the underdeveloped world, and in stresses and strains within the Atlantic Alliance.

In appealing to the areas of Asia, Africa, and Latin America, the Chinese focused essentially on local nationalistic aspirations and fears of renewed foreign domination. The basic cement of Peking's desired alliance with the underdeveloped world was a common colonial experience and a continuing opposition to any form of foreign intervention or interference. Economically, Peking stressed a common poverty and backwardness in comparison with the prosperous, capitalist countries of the West, and pointed to the danger of new colonial control by "economic imperialism."[15] Culturally, the Chinese argued that each country of Asia, Africa, and Latin America should develop in its own unique way, maintaining its own national heritage and identity, free from the stifling influence of American "cultural aggression."[16] They said in effect: borrow from the West if you will, but beware of becoming westernized or coming under Western control. And, finally, Mao Tse-tung has demonstrated that he was not above at least indirectly suggesting race as an issue if it might be useful. In his statement on American racial discrimination made before a large group of visiting Africans, he linked slavery and racial discrimination to US imperialism, arguing that racial discrimination is a class phenomenon; and he called on people "of all colors in the world, white, black, yellow, brown,

[15] See especially Kuo Wen, "Imperialist Plunder—Biggest Obstacle to the Economic Growth of the 'Underdeveloped' Countries" in *PR*, 1965, nos. 25 and 26; and Nan Han-chen's speech before the Afro-Asian Economic Seminar published in *PR*, 1965, no. 10, pp. 16–26.

[16] See Wen Yuan, "The Cultural Aggression of US Imperialism in Afro-Asian Countries," *SCCS*, 1965, no. 20, pp. 11–14.

etc., to unite to oppose the racial discrimination practiced by US imperialism."[17]

The sum of the various dimensions of China's appeal to the countries of the Third World was an attempt to pit colonials against colonialists, have-nots against haves, colored against white, and East against West in an effort to unify the Third World against the industrialized West, and especially against the United States.

The Chinese appeal to the underdeveloped world, then, is directed at the governments as well as the peoples of Asia, Africa, and Latin America—both governments and people in countries which are "truly independent," but people, and often revolutionary movements, as against their governments in countries which Peking claims to be reactionary, colonial, or semicolonial. Thus, Peking will support a war of national liberation in one country, while seeking friendly relations with the government of its neighbor, both in the name of opposing imperialism and supporting the best interests of the local population. Governments, revolutionary movements, and people alike, all have a place in Peking's anti-imperialist international united front—from Prince Sihanouk of Cambodia to revolutionary leader Pierre Mulele in the Congo, from Tanzania's President Nyerere to the Vietnamese National Front for Liberation. To the extent to which they are willing to oppose the American-supported international status quo, they all have a part to play.

THE UNITED FRONT POLICY

The purpose of the united front policy—whether a national or an international united front—is to bring together as many different groups and individuals as possible to oppose a common enemy. The Chinese Communist Party under Mao's leadership has almost always pursued some kind of a united front policy. Even after the CCP disaster of 1927, caused by

[17] *PR*, 1963, no. 33, pp. 6–7.

the failure of the Comintern-dictated "bloc within," the party returned to a united front policy. The crucial lesson of 1927 was not that the CCP should not participate in united fronts, but that the party should never again enter into a united front which it could not control or within which it could not at least maintain a militarily defensible independence. The Comintern policy of 1924–1927 which required CCP members to operate as vulnerable individuals within the Kuomintang was profoundly discredited by the slaughter of 1927, but the united front under CCP leadership remained and is still today a fundamental element in Peking's approach to both domestic and foreign affairs.[18]

Let us look, then, at the concept of the united front as it may be applied in either the national or the international arena, with regard to either economic classes or nation-states. Essentially, the united front is designed to win over all possible adherents; to neutralize those who will not come over and who might provide support for the enemy; and, insofar as possible, to isolate the enemy. In a discussion of tactics in *The Historical Experience of the Dictatorship of the Proletariat*, a party spokesman writes:

Our experience teaches us that the main blow of the revolution should be directed at the chief enemy to isolate him, while as for the middle forces, a policy of both uniting with them and struggling against them should be adopted, so that they are at least neutralized; and, as circumstances permit, efforts should be made to shift them from their position of neutrality to one of alliance with us, for the purpose of facilitating the development of the revolution.[19]

The united front policy characteristically involves a negative approach; that is, it is most often used in attempts to

[18] For a comprehensive analysis of the united front in CCP history, see Lyman P. Van Slyke, *Enemies and Friends: The United Front in Chinese Communist History* (Stanford: Stanford University Press, 1967). Van Slyke sees Mao's use of the united front as developing from a tactic to a strategy and finally to a significant part of Maoist ideology involving Mao's own self-image and the legitimacy of the CCP regime. See especially pp. 255–259.

[19] *The Historical Experience of the Dictatorship of the Proletariat* (Peking: Foreign Languages Press, 1959), p. 15.

unify diverse political forces on the basis of their common enmity or common fear, rather than because of a consensus on positive goals. Essentially, the basic principle of the united front policy is to seek out all those who are in dispute with your enemy and try to convince them to join you in opposing that enemy. Common opposition to the enemy is the raison d'être of the united front.

The united front is a very practical political tool. Having singled out the major enemy—that country (on the international level) or class (on the national level) which most threatens one's security or most obstructs the attainment of one's objectives—he who uses the united front attempts to isolate that enemy from any possible support or alliance by exploiting disputes or "contradictions" which may exist between the enemy and his allies or potential allies. Mao Tse-tung's view of the imperialist enemy is a good example. His concept of splitting the ranks of the imperialist camp by playing the various imperial powers against one another dates back to his essay, "Why Is It that Red Political Power Can Exist in China?" of 1928,[20] and has its modern counterpart in the "broadest possible united front," in terms of which China has attempted to play the countries of Western Europe against the United States.[21] If a group is allied with the enemy, the Chinese attempt to neutralize it, to bring it into the category of the "middle forces" or "intermediate zone." If it is already sufficiently neutral to be included in the "intermediate zone," Peking then seeks to bend its policy to align it more closely with China's. In fact, Peking's tactical outlook in 1964 was not so different from the policy laid down by Mao Tse-tung in 1940 when the CCP was fighting the Japanese.

20 Mao, *Selected Works*, 1:63–69. Mao's view of the contradictions among imperial powers operating in China was central to his analysis of Chinese politics and to his view of China as a "semicolony."

21 For an indication of the kind of incentives Peking has offered in attempts to woo Western European countries away from close alliance with the US, see the *NYT*, June 1, 1966, account of Chinese negotiations to permit France to fly commercial airlines flights to China—the first such agreement with any Western country.

At that time, Mao wrote that the CCP considered all imperialists as enemies, but, he declared, "Our tactical principle
remains one of exploiting the contradictions among them in
order to win over the majority, oppose the minority, and
crush the enemies separately."[22]

The CCP characteristically speaks differently to each member of the proposed united front—to each in terms of an issue
or issues that are seen to be particularly important to that
group and which may tend to separate that group from the
CCP's enemy. For example, to the underdeveloped world,
Peking speaks of United States "imperialism" and "neocolo-
nialism"; and to Western Europe, China talks of "US control,
interference, and bullying." But the primary Chinese concern is not necessarily the issue they have raised in their effort
to win support, but whether the group being appealed to is
willing to oppose, or at least will not ally with, China's enemy.
For example, clear evidence that classical imperialism and
colonialism, per se, are not China's main targets is the fact
that the greatest remaining colonial power, Portugal, ruler of
some thirteen million colonial people, was barely mentioned
in Peking's strident propaganda blasts. On the contrary, imperial Portugal might even have qualified for membership
in the so-called second intermediate zone, thus technically
making it a part of the Chinese united front against "US imperialism."

The Sino-Soviet dispute provides another good case in
point. In terms of their common Marxist-Leninist philosophy,
China and Russia should be firm friends and allies, but they
are not. The principal issue dividing the two powers through
the early 1960s was Russia's conciliatory attitude toward
China's great enemy, the United States, and Soviet willingness often to cooperate with the US in efforts to maintain the
status quo against China's radical assaults on it. In an article
in 1965, authored jointly by the editorial departments of the
Jen-min jih-pao and *Hung-ch'i*, the problem was explained

[22] Mao, *Selected Works* (New York: International Publishers, 1954), 3:218.

in the following manner: "The sharpest difference of theory and line between Marxism-Leninism [the Chinese position] and Khrushchev revisionism [the Soviet position] concerns precisely the question of handling our relations with enemies and friends, in other words, the question of whether to oppose or unite with imperialism, and above all the question of whether to oppose or unite with US imperialism."[23] The article continued: "The crux of the matter is that, so far from opposing US imperialism, the new leaders of the CPSU are allying themselves and collaborating with it to dominate the world. They have thus set themselves in opposition to the united front against US imperialism."[24]

Thus, a potential united front member's policy with regard to the primary target of the united front, the principal enemy, determines whether in the CCP's view the group can be included in the united front and stand among "the people" and the good "peace-loving countries" and "fraternal socialist allies," or whether it must be excluded and condemned to carry the stigma of "enemy of the people," "reactionary," "imperialist lackey," or "modern revisionist." To Peking, a completely neutral stand (allying with neither the enemy nor China) is grudgingly tolerated, but collaboration with the enemy is inexcusable.[25]

Properly handled the united front is the tool of the leadership. It can be expanded and contracted in accordance with changes in the political scene, and can be used to try to bring lesser enemies together to battle against a greater enemy (and later to defeat the lesser enemies, one by one). Enemies

23 "Refutation of the New Leaders of the CPSU on 'United Action,'" PR, 1965, no. 46, p. 13.
24 Ibid., p. 15.
25 Peking made this point quite clear, for example, in its dispute with the Russians: "We must tell them the truth: So long as their line of Soviet-US collaboration against world revolution remains unchanged, and so long as they do not abandon their alliance with US imperialism and reaction, we absolutely refuse to take any 'united action' with them. We absolutely refuse to serve as a pawn in their secret diplomacy with US imperialism or help them to cover up their assistance to US imperialism in suppressing the people's revolution in various countries." Ibid.

change, but the tactic remains essentially the same. Those who join the united front are China's friends—at least for the moment; those who do not are beyond the pale. In 1964, for example, in terms of Peking's proposed broad international united front against the United States, those governments in Asia, Africa, and Latin America that remained allied with the US had, in Peking's view, to be America's "lackeys" or "puppets"; and their countries, by definition, were not independent as the local governments claimed, but were American "semicolonies." From the Chinese point of view, the task of winning true "national liberation" in such countries could not be performed by the officals in power (compromised as Peking saw them to be by their ties to the US), but had to depend on popular struggles against the government and perhaps on armed struggle by national liberation military forces.

THE CHINESE REVOLUTIONARY MODEL

When Peking does advocate a war of national liberation for a country in Asia, Africa, or Latin America, what kind of war are they talking about? What sort of guidelines or model have the Chinese proposed?

The so-called Chinese model has been much defined and discussed by scholars,[26] and it is not my intention here to attempt to evaluate or even compare the various interpretations that have been offered. Rather my objective is to isolate those elements of the Chinese revolutionary experience that the CCP leadership has explicitly pointed to as being definitive of a universally applicable mode of operation for making successful revolution in colonial and semicolonial societies. Clearly, the Chinese do not suggest that all aspects of the Chi-

26 For a variety of conceptions of the Chinese model, see the contributions by Robert A. Scalapino and Chalmers Johnson in Scalapino, ed., *The Communist Revolution in Asia* (Englewood Cliffs: Prentice-Hall, 1965); Werner Klatt, ed., *The Chinese Model* (Hong Kong: Hong Kong University Press, 1965); A. M. Halpern, "The Foreign Policy Uses of the Chinese Revolutionary Model," *CQ*, July–September, 1961, pp. 1–16; and John K. Fairbank, "How to Deal with the Chinese Revolution," *New York Review of Books*, February 17, 1966, pp. 10–14.

nese Revolution will or should be replicated abroad. A constant theme in Mao's writings is the emphasis placed on adapting Marxism-Leninism to fit the particular circumstances of each individual country; and Mao's own contribution to Marxist theory, for example, is said to have resulted from his application of universal Marxism-Leninism to the unique conditions of China. Hence, the interpretation of the Chinese revolutionary model presented here is not based on an independent analysis of the revolution Mao led in China. Rather, it is a description of the CCP's view of its own experience in terms of those aspects of the Chinese Revolution which they feel are presently applicable, and which they actively and explicitly advocate, for revolutions in the countries of the Third World. Thus, this definition of the Chinese revolutionary model does not depend so much on how scholars have previously interpreted the Chinese Revolution, as on how the CCP *itself* interprets the Chinese Revolution for the purpose of promoting it as a revolutionary prototype for contemporary revolutions in the countries of the developing world.

The most comprehensive and specific definition of the Chinese revolutionary model to be made by the Chinese in recent years appears in Lin Piao's article on people's war published on September 3, 1965.[27] The underlying significance of Lin's essay has been widely debated;[28] but at least one important

27 Lin Piao's essay was published concurrently in all of the national newspapers of Communist China and in the party journal *HC* (1965, no. 10). It is available in translation in *PR* (1965, no. 36), and the following quotations are taken from that text. The earliest definition of the Chinese revolutionary model to be published after the establishment of the People's Republic on October 1, 1949, was that put forward by Liu Shao-ch'i in his address to the Asian and Australian Trade Union Conference convened in Peking in November of the same year. See *Hsin-hua yueh-pao*, December 15, 1949, pp. 440–441.

28 Lin's essay has been variously interpreted as Mao's equivalent of Hitler's *Mein Kampf*; primarily as a contribution to the internal leadership "debate" over China's defense strategy; as a message to Hanoi and the NFL that the Vietnamese ought to take a more defensive posture in response to the American build-up in the South, and that China was extremely reluctant to become directly involved in the conflict; etc. For a thoughtful discussion of the various interpretations of the essay, see Donald Zagoria, "The Strategic Debate in Peking," in Tang Tsou, ed., *China in Crisis*, vol. 2.

element in it is a clear statement of the Maoist position with regard to wars of national liberation and the strategy of people's war, most of which had been explicit or implicit in Chinese policy for several years.

Defense Minister Lin Piao, since the cultural revolution Mao Tse-tung's successor-designate, begins his article with a statement of purpose. The essay, "Long Live the Victory of People's War!" has been written to commemorate the twentieth anniversary of the victory of the war against Japan, to analyze the strategy ("people's war") that enabled the Chinese to defeat the Japanese, and to comment on its contemporary relevance:

Today, the US imperialists are repeating on a world-wide scale the past actions of the Japanese imperialists in China and other parts of Asia. It has become an urgent necessity for the people in many countries to master and use people's war as a weapon against US imperialism and its lackeys. In every conceivable way US imperialism and its lackeys are trying to extinguish the revolutionary flames of people's war. The Khrushchev revisionists, fearing people's war like the plague, are heaping abuse on it. The two are colluding to prevent and sabotage people's war. In these circumstances, it is of vital practical importance to review the historical experience of the great victory of the people's war in China and to recapitulate Comrade Mao Tse-tung's theory of people's war.[29]

Discussing the international significance of Mao's theory of revolution, Lin Piao begins by describing the Chinese and Russian revolutions and noting their similarities and differences:

The Chinese revolution is a continuation of the Great October Revolution. The road of the October Revolution is the common road for all people's revolutions. The Chinese revolution and the October Revolution have in common the following basic characteristics: (1) Both were led by the working class with a Marxist-Leninist party as its nucleus. (2) Both were based on the worker-peasant alliance. (3) In both cases state power was seized through violent revolution and the dictatorship of the proletariat was established. (4) In both cases the socialist system was built after vic-

29 PR, 1965, no. 36, p. 10.

tory in the revolution. (5) Both were component parts of the proletarian world revolution.

Naturally, the Chinese revolution had its own peculiar characteristics. The October Revolution took place in imperialist Russia,
but the Chinese revolution broke out in a semi-colonial and semi-
feudal country. The former was a proletarian socialist revolution,
while the latter developed into a socialist revolution after the complete victory of the new-democratic revolution. The October Revolution began with armed uprisings in the cities and then spread
to the countryside, while the Chinese revolution won nation-wide
victory through the encirclement of the cities from the rural areas
and the final capture of the cities.

Comrade Mao Tse-tung's great merit lies in the fact that he has
succeeded in integrating the universal truth of Marxism-Leninism
with the concrete practice of the Chinese revolution and has en-
riched and developed Marxism-Leninism.

Comrade Mao Tse-tung's theory of people's war . . . has not
only been valid for China, it is a great contribution to the revolutionary struggles of the oppressed nations and people throughout
the world.[30]

Thus, the two revolutions, Russian and Chinese, stand as
models for their respective kinds of countries: the Russian
model for revolutions in imperialist countries such as those
of North America and Western Europe, and the Chinese model for revolutions in colonial and semicolonial countries like
many of those in Asia, Africa, and Latin Amercia.[31]

Lin Piao goes on to specify in greater detail the particular

30 *Ibid.*, pp. 22–23.

31 Liu Ta-nien in his essay "How to Appraise the History of Asia?" (*PR*,
1965, no. 45, pp. 23–28) makes this claim quite clear: "the victory of the Chinese
democratic revolution and the advent of socialism in Chinese history have
set a brilliant example for the colonial and semi-colonial countries of the
world. The victory of the Chinese people over imperialism and its lackeys and
the founding of the People's Republic of China have greatly inspired the
people of many colonial and semi-colonial countries in their struggle for
national independence and the complete victory of their people's democratic
revolution. The Russian October Socialist Revolution served as an example
for revolution in the oppressor nations, that is, for revolution in the imperialist countries; while the Chinese revolution set an example for revolution in the oppressed nations, that is, the colonial or semi-colonial countries.
In studying the changes in Asian history since World War II, we need to make
an adequate appraisal of the path as well as the influence of the Chinese
revolution. For it is of significance for the whole world, far beyond the East
or Asia."

contribution of Mao Tse-tung to the revolutionary struggles of the underdeveloped world in terms of an exposition of Mao's theory of the "new-democratic revolution":

The October Revolution opened up a new era in the revolution of the oppressed nations. The victory of the October Revolution built a bridge between the socialist revolution of the proletariat of the West and the national-democratic revolution of the colonial and semi-colonial countries of the East. The Chinese revolution has successfully solved the problem of how to link up the national-democratic with the socialist revolution in the colonial and semi-colonial countries.

Comrade Mao Tse-tung has pointed out that, in the epoch since the October Revolution, anti-imperialist revolution in any colonial or semi-colonial country is no longer part of the old bourgeois, or capitalist world revolution, but is part of the new world revolution, the proletarian-socialist world revolution.

Comrade Mao Tse-tung has formulated a complete theory of the new-democratic revolution. He indicated that this revolution, which is different from all others, can only be, nay must be, a revolution against imperialism, feudalism and bureaucrat-capitalism waged by the broad masses of the people under the leadership of the proletariat.

This means that the revolution can only be, nay must be, led by the proletariat and the genuinely revolutionary party armed with Marxism-Leninism, and by no other class or party.

This means that the revolution embraces in its ranks not only the workers, peasants and the urban petty bourgeoisie, but also the national bourgeoisie and other patriotic and anti-imperialist democrats.

This means, finally, that the revolution is directed against imperialism, feudalism and bureaucrat-capitalism.

The new-democratic revolution leads to socialism, not to capitalism.[32]

Finally, Lin Piao, in the same article, provides us with a definition of Mao's strategy of waging revolutionary warfare, the strategy of people's war, which comprises the following six major elements:

(1) *Leadership by a revolutionary communist party* which will properly apply Marxism-Leninism in analyzing the class

[32] *PR*, 1965, No. 36, p. 24.

character of a colonial or semicolonial country, and which can formulate correct policy to wage a protracted war against imperialism, feudalism, and bureaucratic capitalism.[33]

(2) *Correct utilization of the united front policy* to build "the broadest possible" national united front to "ensure the fullest mobilization of the basic masses as well as the unity of all the forces than can be united," in an effort to take over the leadership of the national revolution and establish the revolution on an alliance of, first, the workers and peasants and, second, an alliance of the working peoples with the bourgeoisie and other "non-working people."[34]

(3) *Reliance on the peasantry and the establishment of rural bases,* because in agrarian and "semifeudal" societies the peasants are the great majority of the population; "subjected to threefold oppression and exploitation by imperialism, feudalism, and bureaucrat-capitalism," they will provide most of the human and material resources for the revolution. In essence, the revolution is a peasant revolution led by the communist party: "to rely on the peasants, build rural base areas and use the countryside to encircle and finally capture the cities—such was the way to victory in the Chinese revolution."[35]

(4) *Creation of a communist party-led army of a new type,* for a "universal truth of Marxism-Leninism" is that "without a people's army the people have nothing." A new type of communist party-led army in which "politics is the commander" must be formed, one which focuses on instilling in the minds of the population a "proletarian revolutionary consciousness and courage" and which actively seeks the "support and backing of the masses."[36]

(5) *Use of the strategy and tactics of people's war* as interpreted by Mao Tse-tung, in a protracted armed struggle to annihilate the enemy and take over state power, based on the

33 *Ibid.*, pp. 10–12.
34 *Ibid.*, pp. 12–14.
35 *Ibid.*, pp. 14–16.
36 *Ibid.*, pp. 16–17.

support of a mobilized mass population and the use of guerrilla warfare, and ultimately mobile and even positional warfare as the revolution progresses.[37]

(6) *Adherence to a policy of self-reliance*, because "revolution or people's war in any country is the business of the masses in that country and should be carried out primarily by their
own efforts; there is no other way."[38]

Here, then, was an explicit Chinese revolutionary model
for communist-led wars of national liberation in the colonial
and semicolonial countries of Asia, Africa, and Latin America. Fundamental to Lin Piao's entire exposition of the Chinese
model and Mao's theory of new-democratic revolution is the
requirement of communist party leadership—the idea that
the local CP should gain control of the nationalist movement
and use it as a vehicle to attain state power, after which it can
transform the national revolution into a socialist one. This
idea is at the heart of Mao Tse-tung's whole theory of new
democracy.[39]

It is therefore somewhat surprising to read further on in

[37] *Ibid.*, pp. 17–19.

[38] *Ibid.*, pp. 19–22. Lin Piao's six-point formulation of the Chinese revolutionary model expanded upon the original Liu Shao-ch'i conception of November 1949 which included only four points. In Lin's version, points number
three (reliance on the peasantry and the establishment of rural bases) and
number six (adherence to a policy of self-reliance) were added.

[39] In a book review in the *Journal of Asian Studies* (May, 1966, pp. 507–508),
Stuart Schram, prominent analyst of the political thought of Mao Tse-tung,
inexplicably states, "Mao's original essay [*On New Democracy*] in 1940 explicitly stated that hegemony during the new-democratic phase would belong
to the bourgeoisie." The original 1940 edition of Mao's essay *On New Democracy* was somewhat ambiguous about the leadership role of the proletariat, but it left no doubt that the bourgeoisie could *not* lead in the new-
democratic stage. If it did, there would be no *new* democracy, only *old*
democracy. Mao writes, "The first step or stage in our revolution [the new-
democratic revolution] is definitely not, and cannot be, the establishment of
a capitalist society under the dictatorship of the Chinese bourgeoisie, but
will result in the establishment of a new democratic society under the joint
dictatorship of all the revolutionary classes of China" (Mao, *Hsin min-chu chu-
yi lun* [Liberation Association, 1940], p. 11.) Alterations in the texts of subsequent versions of the essay (see, for example, Mao, *Hsuan-chi* [Peking, 1964],
2:661, 665, 671) clearly indicate that, according to the contemporary interpretation of Mao's theory of new democracy, the leadership role of the proletariat
or communist party should definitely be paramount. Lin Piao's 1965 conception follows this pattern.

Lin Piao's article—when he gets down to specific cases—that people's wars need not necessarily be communist-led.[40] In contrast to his earlier demand for CP leadership, Lin Piao now cites Algeria and Indonesia, among other countries, as victorious examples of people's war and declares, in complete contradiction with what he has said before, that "the classes leading these people's wars may vary."[41]

What soon becomes clear, although not explicitly so stated, was that Peking pragmatically (or opportunistically, if you like) conceived of both a maximum and a minimum program in its support for wars of national liberation during this period. What Lin Piao had defined in terms of his long exposition of a Chinese revolutionary model was an ideal type—the kind of revolution Peking would probably most like to see in contemporary Asia, Africa, and Latin America. But after having defined this maximum program in detail, he implicitly acknowledged a minimum program as well, a kind of revolution at least minimally acceptable to Peking. Whereas the former, the ideal type, required communist leadership and was based on Mao's theory of new democracy, the latter was apparently construed broadly enough to include almost all vigorously pursued, anti-imperialist revolutions, regardless of leadership.

[40] *PR*, 1965, no. 36, p. 26.
[41] *Ibid.*, p. 26.

PART II
REVOLUTION IN PRACTICE: CHINESE SUPPORT FOR WARS OF NATIONAL LIBERATION, 1965

Part I of this study dealt with the Maoist theory of the national liberation struggle; this section, Part Two, attempts to describe and analyze the actual practice of Communist China's support for wars of national liberation in the period before the cultural revolution. To simplify the analysis and to put the subject matter in sharper focus, the time dimension in this part is narrowed to a single year, 1965. Chinese policy for the period is drawn from a systematic content analysis of the official newspaper *Jen-min jih-pao* (People's daily) and the two mainland magazines that are most concerned with foreign affairs, *Shih-chieh chih-shih* (World knowledge) and the English language weekly, *Peking Review*. Concentrating on China's relations with the countries of the Third World during a single year, the analysis seeks to reveal underlying patterns of Chinese foreign policy behavior which will provide the basis for a better understanding of the function and importance of support for wars of national liberation in China's general approach to international politics.

The year 1965 began as a good year for Chinese foreign policy, but ended as one of the most disastrous. Peking greeted New Year's Day 1965 with the happy recollection of autumn 1964 still very much in mind. The Chinese arch-enemy,

Khrushchev, had been overthrown by his own subordinates in the Soviet Union; and China had exploded an atomic device, the first non-Western nation to do so. The war of national liberation being waged by the National Front for Liberation in Vietnam was going well for the rebel side, and US and Belgian intervention in the Congolese civil war in November had provoked Africans into their greatest concerted outburst against imperialism yet.

The Chinese had high hopes for 1965. The second Afro-Asian summit conference was scheduled to be held in Algiers in June, and Peking's long preparation for the conference seemed destined to bear the fruit of increased Afro-Asian militancy against the West and perhaps even the exclusion of the "revisionist" Soviet Union from the meeting. Two events of spring 1965 served to heighten Chinese confidence: a second Chinese atomic device was exploded, and the hasty US intervention in the uprising against military dictatorship in the Dominican Republic provided the Chinese anti-American campaign with a fresh propaganda issue and prompted new outbursts of Latin American hostility against the "Yankees" from the north. By early June, it appeared at least possible that the Chinese delegation at the Algiers Conference, armed with the support of several of the more radical Asian and African states, might be able to prevent the Soviet Union from being seated at the meeting and to succeed in convincing a majority of the Asian and African countries represented to adopt a more radical and forceful policy against "US imperialism" in Asia, Africa, and Latin America.

However, the beginning months of 1965 were marred for the Chinese, first by Burundi's suspension of diplomatic relations with Peking in January, and second by the beginning of continuous American bombing of North Vietnam in February—harbingers of events to come. The new American commitment to the Vietnam War (both the bombing in the North and the build-up of American military forces in the South begun later in the year) prompted a reappraisal in Peking of how to respond to the American escalation and a debate within the CCP leadership as to how best to prepare

China for the possibility of war with the United States.[1] This debate helped to exacerbate earlier differences within the CCP primarily relating to domestic policy, all of which led subsequently to Chairman Mao's portentous decision to mount the Great Proletarian Cultural Revolution against his opponents within the party.

The month of June brought more difficulties for Peking. Just ten days before the scheduled opening of the Afro-Asian summit meeting, and while the Chinese delegation was en route to Algiers, Algerian Defense Minister Houari Boumedienne moved with quiet military dispatch to unseat his president, Ahmed Ben Bella, and to topple the government of Algeria. By the time Chinese Foreign Minister Ch'en Yi arrived on the scene, there was already grave doubt that the conference would be convened. Many governments were voicing their opposition to holding the meeting, and earlier opponents of the conference were now attempting to use the coup d'etat as a pretext to either postpone or even cancel the conference. Trying desperately to keep the conference together despite the change of government, Ch'en Yi suffered the first major defeat for Chinese foreign policy in 1965 when the conference was finally postponed, the first of a string of setbacks to come during the next four months.

Events of the summer and early fall did little to help the Chinese cause. The anticipated NFL summer offensive never materialized, and there were increasing reports that the burgeoning American military build-up in Vietnam had begun to turn the war against the rebels. When hostilities broke out between Pakistan and India over Kashmir, Peking leaped to Pakistan's defense, denouncing "Indian aggression," only to have Pakistan ultimately turn to the United Nations and the Soviet Union for a solution rather than yield to Chinese incitements to take the offensive against India.

On October 1, the sixteenth anniversary of the establishment of the People's Republic of China, a leftist coup attempt aimed primarily at conservative leaders of the Indonesian

---

[1] See the essays by Uri Ra'anan and Donald Zagoria in Tang Tsou, ed., *China in Crisis* (Chicago: University of Chicago Press, 1968), vol. 2.

Army was launched in Djakarta. Interpretations of the motivation behind the coup and the parties involved in it vary, but it was soon suppressed by the Indonesian Army which blamed the coup on its major competitor for power in Indonesia, Partai Komunis Indonesia, the actively pro-Peking communist party. In the slaughter which followed, at least 100,000 people were killed, and the PKI, previously the third largest communist party in the world, was almost entirely wiped out.[2]

As a result of the coup attempt, the Peking-Djakarta axis was strained to the breaking point, and on the basis of allegations of Chinese involvement in the coup, a new army-dominated Indonesian government moved swiftly to curtail Peking's influence in the country. Subsequent Chinese evaluations of the events in Indonesia no doubt mourned the loss of China's immensely promising alliance with the Sukarno government as much as casualties among the membership of the PKI.

The remainder of 1965 went no better for Chinese foreign policy. Peking's dispute with the Soviets appeared to deepen in the aftermath of the March meeting of communist parties and Russia's mediation of the India-Pakistan conflict at Tashkent. And as 1965 closed and 1966 began, Peking was once again locked in battle with Moscow, this time at the Tri-Continental People's Solidarity Conference in Havana, where Cuban Premier Fidel Castro made an unprecedented attack on the Chinese for allegedly reneging on trade agreements and several weeks later broadened his attack to include allegations of Chinese interference in Cuban internal affairs.

Such in brief was the stormy sixteenth year of the People's Republic of China, the setting for this analysis of Chinese support for wars of national liberation.

2 Official Indonesian estimates of people killed in the several months following the abortive October first coup have placed the number of dead at less than 100,000, but other sources argue that several times that figure would be a more accurate estimate. For example, Stanley Karnow, a veteran American correspondent in East Asia, traveled through Indonesia in early 1966 exploring the dimensions of the violence and the nature of the struggle, and is quoted (*Far Eastern Economic Review*, May 12, 1966, pp. 282–283) as concluding that at least 500,000 people were killed in the post-coup violence.

4

ENDORSEMENT OF REVOLUTIONS

"Export of revolution" is a term commonly used in the American press to describe Communist China's foreign policy, and reports from Peking would seem to confirm that Peking was vigorously mounting a worldwide revolutionary assault on established authority. During 1965, mass rallies in the Chinese capital and public statements by Chairman Mao militantly proclaimed support for revolutionary struggles in Vietnam, the Congo, the Dominican Republic, and elsewhere; and Defense Minister Lin Piao outlined a model of revolutionary strategy in metaphoric detail—a plan to turn the US "vicious wolf" into a "mad bull" dashing in futile circles, destined ultimately to be consumed by the "blazing fires of people's war." But beneath the fine rhetoric and militant phraseology, what actually was official Chinese policy with regard to revolutions in Asia, Africa, and Latin America? Aside from making broad generalizations about "an exceedingly favourable situation for revolution" prevailing in Asia, Africa, and Latin America,[1] which specific revolutions and revolutionary movements did the Chinese leadership in Peking actually endorse and support?

[1] For example, see the report of comments made by Chou En-lai during his visit to Tanzania in June 1965 in *PR*, 1965, no. 24, p. 6.

In theory, Peking has committed itself to support for all revolutions against imperialism and other kinds of oppression throughout the underdeveloped world, but practice is something else again. The official Chinese analysis of imperialism and the problem of attaining state power (discussed in chapter 1) leads to the conclusion that wherever "progressives" confront "reactionaries" in a contest for state power—and especially wherever the "oppressed peoples" of colonial and semicolonial areas confront "imperialism and its lackeys"—there must almost inevitably be armed struggle and revolution. Moreover, the Chinese have continually insisted that it is the "internationalist duty" of all communist party states to support such efforts, and they have chastised the Soviets for failing to do so. When faced with making such a commitment themselves, however, the Chinese have been surprisingly selective in their official endorsements of specific revolutions and revolutionary movements. As we will see, during 1965, Peking endorsed revolutionary armed struggles in only 23 of a possible total of some 120 independent and nonindependent countries of Asia, Africa, and Latin America—those areas which the Chinese had proclaimed to be so ripe for revolution.

Earlier in this study, Chinese support for foreign revolutions was defined minimally as public endorsement in the official Chinese press of the armed struggle of any group or organization that is publicly committed to and actively pursuing the overthrow by force of the established government of any foreign country or territory. Now, let us look at what endorsement in practice actually means.

ENDORSEMENT: EXPLICIT AND IMPLIED

As often as not, Chinese support for a specific war of national liberation is not indicated by mass rallies in Peking or statements from Chairman Mao, but by implication. Moreover, Peking rarely explicitly endorses foreign revolutionary organizations. Quite common are articles in *Jen-min jih-pao* and other mainland periodicals that describe in general terms armed struggles in the various parts of Asia, Africa, and Latin America; and maps indicating areas in which revolutions are being carried out are occasionally published. Often, the Chinese press reprints the programs and proclamations of revolutionary organizations, and reports on visits to China by foreign revolutionaries. But relatively rare are explicit public endorsements by official Chinese spokesmen that exclusively identify either the Chinese government or people with a specific group of revolutionaries. When support is announced, usually it is termed support for "the people" of a certain area, without naming any particular organization, even when representatives of that organization may happen to be present when the statement is being made. Sometimes, the Chinese press will report on the activities and reprint the programs of competing revolutionary movements within a single country, making no attempt to discriminate among them. The exceptions to this general pattern are pro-Peking communist parties which usually do receive specific Chinese endorsements.

In general China implicitly endorses virtually all organizations in a particular country that are attacking Chinese-approved targets; but supports none to the exclusion of the others, and none explicitly unless it is the local communist party or until it has gained sufficient predominance to merit an explicit commitment.

Peking gains both influence and flexibility by maintaining a militant worldwide propaganda line that appears to give full endorsement to all actively operating anti-imperialist political organizations, while at the same time generally withholding specific endorsement for organizations that have not yet proved a capacity to win local mass support, and that may eventually be defeated or discredited and superseded by other revolutionary organizations. Implied Chinese endorsement or endorsement of "the people" of a country provides the public impression of Chinese support without identifying Peking with any particular organization. Minimizing local involvement while appearing to support vigorously the goals of the local revolution, Peking is less likely to become publicly involved in costly local political disputes, while at the same time the Chinese can claim to be making a full public commitment to the local popular struggle.

Another possible reason for Chinese reluctance to endorse local revolutionary movements explicitly is that a public endorsement by Peking may be more detrimental than helpful to the revolutionary organization. A Chinese Communist endorsement might provide cause for the local government to move more forcefully against the organization; it might also detract from the organization's nationalist appeal by implying foreign (Chinese) control; and it may even serve as grounds for foreign (Western) intervention to suppress the local revolutionary movement.

TYPES OF ENDORSEMENT

Peking's endorsement of revolutions in Asia, Africa, and Latin America generally falls into several fairly clear-cut categories. What I have called implicit endorsement is usually indicated in one of three ways: by reprinting the policy statements of foreign revolutionary movements in *Jen-min jih-pao* or other mainland periodicals; by publishing articles in the Chinese press in news report style, which describe the recent activities of revolutionaries operating in a particular country, but which do not state Chinese policy toward them; or finally, by designating certain countries, on maps published in official periodicals, as sites of ongoing revolutionary armed struggles against imperialism.

A good example of the first type of implicit endorsement, the reprinting of policy statements, is the article cited earlier (pp. 54–56) in which the revolutionary program of the Peruvian Communist Party was quoted at some length. Another example is an article in the May 10, 1965, issue of *Shih-chieh chih-shih* in which the political programs of two Thai revolutionary organizations, the Thailand Independence Movement and the Thailand Patriotic Front, are quoted and discussed, side by side.

The second kind of implicit endorsement, the publication of news reports concerning areas in which revolutionary wars are going on, is typified by four articles appearing together in the November 23, 1965, *Jen-min jih-pao*, characteristically accompanied by a picture of revolutionaries in the field.[2] The four short articles appear in a marked-off section in the top third of page five under a general headline which reads, "A Single Spark Can Start a Prairie Fire"—an allusion to Mao Tse-tung's essay of the same name of January 1930 in which he analyzed the revolutionary potentialities of China at that time. Each of three of the articles deals with a separate armed struggle under way in the three major areas of Portuguese Africa (Angola, Guinea, and Mozambique) and discusses recent "victories" and the spread of armed struggle. The fourth article is an "editor's comment" headlined "People's War— Once Grasped, It Is Effective," which generalizes on the three cases and discusses the strategy of armed struggle. These are not Chinese policy statements as such—China is not mentioned—but rather supposedly objective news reports and commentary on the revolutionary situation in Portuguese Africa.

A final type of implicit Chinese endorsement of revolutions is the publication of maps on which certain areas are marked as sites of armed struggle. One of the most comprehensive of these maps to appear in recent years is a world map published by *Shih-chieh chih-shih*.[3] This map purports to show, among other things, all "countries and areas in which armed struggle against imperialism and its lackeys is being carried out" for the year 1965. Accompanying textual material discusses the world revolutionary situation in 1965 by continent and mentions each of the sites of armed struggle by name. Those in Asia are Aden, Laos, Malaysia, Oman, the Philippines, Thailand, and Vietnam; those in Africa comprise the Congo (for-

[2] *JMJP*, November 23, 1965, p. 5. This kind of article, which is rarely if ever translated by the US Consulate's *Survey of the China Mainland Press*, almost invariably appears on either page 3, 4, or 5 of the *JMJP* together with other reports of international news events.

[3] This map appeared as an unattached enclosure to *SCCS*, 1966, nos. 2–3.

merly Leopoldville, now Kinshasa) and the Portuguese territories of Angola, Guinea, and Mozambique; and those in
Latin America include Colombia, the Dominican Republic,
Guatemala, Honduras, Nicaragua, Paraguay, Peru, and Venezuela.

But how can these three types of "news reports" be said to
constitute implicit endorsement? One might say, for example,
that the three types of press reports discussed above are simply
objective accounts of world events carrying no indication one
way or the other of official Chinese sanction. They are endorsements in the following sense. In the first place, these "objective" reports actually present a very selective view of reality. In 1965, there were, for example, similar armed struggles
going on—many of which were considerably more intense
than the ones noted—in Kashmir, Kenya, and Burma, but
these areas were not included in Chinese news reports or, if
included, were placed in a distinctly different category than
those of the endorsed revolutionary armed struggles against
imperialism. Secondly, Peking has stated as a matter of principle that it supports all so-called struggles against imperialism
and its lackeys, armed or otherwise. Therefore, when in official
publications certain areas are designated as areas in which
armed struggles against imperialism are being carried on,
there is, at the very least, a strong implication of official Chinese endorsement.

Explicit, as opposed to implicit, endorsements can best be
categorized with regard to who made them or in whose name
they were made. Explicit Chinese endorsements of foreign
revolutions generally take the form of either highly publicized statements of support by Chairman Mao, specific endorsements by Chinese officials other than Mao, or Chinese
Communist Party endorsements of revolutions being fought
by other communist parties. Moreover, explicit endorsements
usually are made in the name of either the Chinese people or
the Chinese Communist Party. The Chinese government, as
such, does not customarily endorse revolutions, since its formal activities with regard to foreign affairs are generally lim-

ited to relations with other governments, rather than with mass organizations or political parties.[4]

Among the various kinds of explicit endorsement, a statement by Mao Tse-tung is clearly the most important. From the summer of 1963 through 1965, Chairman Mao made six highly publicized statements on foreign policy, one each in support of the American Negroes and the peoples of South Vietnam, Panama, Japan, the Congo, and the Dominican Republic.[5] The theme of each statement was the same: a call for unity of the people to oppose "US imperialism." Three of the statements were made in support of continuing or newly initiated armed struggles; three others were made in support of militant demonstrations against US government policy.

Mao's statements were all fairly short, averaging about 800 characters, and pointedly aimed at the United States. The following excerpts from Mao's statement in support of the insurrection in the Dominican Republic of April–May 1965 provide some of the characteristic flavor of his proclamations:

> Recently, a coup d'etat overthrowing the Cabral dictatorship of traitors took place in the Dominican Republic. The Johnson Administration of the United States has dispatched more than 30,000 troops there to carry out sanguinary suppression. This is a grave provocation by US imperialism to the Dominican people, to the people of Latin America and to the people of the whole world.

4 Occasionally, however, the Chinese government will endorse the struggle of another government or make a statement at the official governmental level that relates to a particular revolutionary armed struggle. For example, various Chinese officials and official organizations, acting in their governmental capacities, have several times stated their support for the North Vietnamese government and in passing have included the Vietnamese people as well, both North and South. Also, during the hostilities in the Dominican Republic of April and May 1965, and prior to Mao Tse-tung's own statement on the subject, a Chinese government statement was published—but one which was technically made in denunciation of the American government rather than in support of the Dominican people.

5 All except the statement on the Dominican Republic of May 1965 are published together in the pamphlet *Ch'uan shih-chieh jen-min t'uan-chieh-ch'i-lai ta-pai mei-kuo ch'in-lueh-che chi ch'i yi-ch'ieh tsou-kou* (Peking: People's Press, 1965). The statement on the Dominican Republic, like the others, was reprinted widely in Chinese and in translation, and is available in *JMJP*, May 13, 1965, p. 1. More recently, following the assassination of Dr. Martin Luther King, Mao published a second statement of support for the American Negroes. See *PR*, 1968, no. 16, pp. 5–6.

The patriotic Dominican people are now waging a heroic fight against the US aggressor and his lackeys.

The Chinese people firmly support the Dominican people in their patriotic armed struggle against US imperialism. . . .

US imperialism has never ceased to subject Latin American countries to its interference, control, subversion and aggression. . . .

US aggression against the Dominican Republic has forcibly brought home to the Dominican people and all the other people of Latin America that in order to safeguard national independence and state sovereignty, it is imperative to wage a tit-for-tat struggle against aggressive US imperialism. . . .

The people in the socialist camp should unite, the people of every continent should unite, all peace-loving countries and all countries subjected to US bullying, interference, control and aggression should unite, and form the broadest united front to oppose the US imperialist policies of aggression and war and to safeguard world peace.

The struggle of the people of the world against US imperialism is bound to triumph!

US imperialism, the common enemy of the people of the world, is bound to fail![6]

A statement by Mao Tse-tung is the strongest kind of verbal public support Peking can provide. Each statement is inevitably accompanied by mass rallies, statements by other Chinese officials, and propaganda campaigns throughout the country and abroad. Public support does not stop there; usually a statement of support by Chairman Mao implies a continuing Chinese interest in and commitment to the particular area chosen for endorsement (for example, the anniversaries of Mao's statements are often celebrated, and with a good deal of publicity).[7] Thus, considering the apparent significance of Mao's statements and also the fact that pubic statements and published articles signed by Mao were extremely rare in the 1963–1965 period, his endorsement of the armed struggles in Vietnam, the Congo, and the Dominican Republic should be seen to have a special importance.

[6] This quotation is excerpted from the translation in *PR*, 1965, no. 20, p. 6.

[7] See, for example, the report of the celebration of the third anniversary of Mao's first statement in support of the American Negroes in *JMJP*, August 9, 1966, p. 6.

Explicit endorsements of particular revolutions by lesser Chinese officials occur more frequently; however, they clearly carry less weight than those by Chairman Mao. These statements are often part of a general endorsement in which the struggles (armed or otherwise) of as many as twenty different peoples may be endorsed. For example, Nan Han-chen, the head of the Chinese delegation to the Afro-Asian Economic Seminar held in Algeria in February 1965, voiced Chinese support for the peoples of eighteen individual areas, plus "the people of the Arab countries," in his major speech before that particular gathering.[8] Moreover, endorsements by Chinese officials other than Mao receive only a small fraction of the publicity which Mao's statements receive, even when an endorsement happens to coincide with such occasions as the so-called Day Against Colonialism (April 24), a time when mass demonstrations throughout the country in support of foreign revolutions are common.

The final category of explicit endorsement is endorsement by the Chinese Communist Party, as a party. Such endorsement characteristically takes the form of publicly stated support by a CCP representative for the program of a foreign communist party that is engaged in waging revolutionary armed struggle. For instance, in a letter dated April 15, 1965 and published in *Peking Review*, the Central Committee of the CCP congratulated the Malayan Communist Party on the thirty-fifth anniversary of its founding; discussed the party's leadership of "the armed struggle against British imperialism and its hireling, the Rahman clique" and the MCP's opposition to "modern revisionism"; and concluded by affirming continuing support for the "just struggle of the Communist Party of Malaya and the Malayan people."[9]

The CCP's relations with foreign communist parties and the whole question of Peking's relations with overseas revolutionary movements will be discussed in more detail in chapter 5.

[8] *PR*, 1965, no. 10, p. 26.
[9] *PR*, 1965, no. 19, p. 6.

PEKING'S ENDORSEMENT OF REVOLUTIONS IN 1965

Table 1 is a compilation of the various revolutionary armed struggles endorsed by Peking, either explicitly or implicitly,

TABLE 1

CHINESE ENDORSEMENT OF REVOLUTIONS, 1965

Country	Mao Tse-tung Statement[a]	Other Explicit Endorsement[b]	Implicit Endorsement[c]
Asia			
Aden		x	x
Laos		x	x
Malaysia:			
Malaya and Singapore[d]		x	x
North Borneo		x	x
Oman			x
Philippines			x
Thailand		x	x
South Vietnam	x	x	x
Africa			
Congo (Leopoldville)	x	x	x
Portuguese Africa:			
Angola		x	x
Guinea		x	x
Mozambique		x	x
Latin America			
Argentina			x
Bolivia		x	x
Brazil			x
Colombia			x
Dominican Republic	x	x	x
Guatemala			x
Haiti			x
Honduras			x
Nicaragua			x
Paraguay			x
Peru			x
Venezuela		x	x

[a] Vietnam and the Congo: *Ch'uan shih-chieh jen-min t'uan-chieh-ch'i-lai ta-pai mei-kuo ch'in-lueh-che chi ch'i yi-ch'ieh tsou-kou* (Peking: People's Press, 1964). Dominican Republic: *JMJP*, May 13, 1965, p. 1.

[b] Once having been explicitly endorsed, the various revolutions are usually repeatedly endorsed by Chinese officials; the following citations

in 1965. The data included in the table refer only to endorsements made during 1965 or to endorsements that, though published later, refer explicitly to that year. The exceptions to this rule are the statements by Mao Tse-tung, which because of their obvious significance are included in spite of the fact that two of them (those with regard to the Congo and Vietnam) were actually made earlier than 1965. In order to simplify the analysis, while maintaining the distinctions between types of endorsement as rough measures of the strength of the endorsement, the table has been arranged so as to distinguish only three categories of endorsement: statements by Mao Tse-tung, all other explicit endorsements, and implicit endorsements.

Asia

During 1965, Peking's major preoccupation was with Asia, and with Vietnam in particular. Reports of events in Vietnam took up more space by far in the Chinese press than those of any other area, and the struggle in both North and South Vietnam was endorsed in almost every conceivable manner by the Chinese.[10] Appropriately, the symbol indicating armed struggle in Vietnam appears larger on the *Shih-chieh chih-shih* world map mentioned earlier than similar symbols indicating armed struggles in all other areas throughout the world.

---

note a single case, not necessarily the first instance, in which explicit endorsement was made: Laos, North Borneo, Vietnam, the Congo, Angola, Portuguese Guinea, and Mozambique—Nan Han-chen's speech at the Afro-Asian Economic Seminar in Algiers, trans. in *PR*, 1965, no. 10, pp. 16–26. Aden—NCNA (English), October 9, 1965. Malaya and Singapore—*PR*, 1965, no. 19, p. 6. Thailand—*PR*, 1965, no. 17, p. 5. Bolivia—NCNA (English), May 20, 1965. Dominican Republic—*JMJP*, May 14, 1965, p. 1. Venezuela—*JMJP*, July 22, 1965, p. 4.

c World map in *SCCS*, 1966, nos. 2–3, and map of Latin America in *JMJP*, May 27, 1965, p. 4.

d On August 9, 1965, Singapore broke away from the Federation of Malaysia and became an independent state (*NYT*, August 10, 1965, p. 1).

10 See the series of pamphlets published by Foreign Languages Press entitled *Support the People of Viet Nam, Defeat US Aggressors*, which begins with a Chinese government statement of February 9, 1965, and continues for four volumes which include a variety of Chinese editorials, official statements, speeches, and commentaries in support of the Vietnamese war.

Also in Asia, the special case of Laos, where Peking supports both the government (or, more accurately, the Chinese conception of what that government should be) and a revolutionary alternative to it, also received wide press coverage and endorsement, as did to a lesser extent the incipient armed struggle across the border in Thailand.

According to the official Chinese view, the battle to overthrow the government of Malaysia proceeded in the form of two separate national liberation struggles, one for the liberation of "Malaya and Singapore" and another to liberate "North Kalimantan" or northern Borneo. Peking does not recognize the legitimate existence of Malaysia as it was constituted in 1963—a federation of the former Federation of Malaya and Singapore on the Malay peninsula, in combination with two former British colonies in northern Borneo, Sarawak and North Borneo (now Sabah). On the contrary, Chinese maps in 1965, showed Malaya as an independent country, indicated as having attained its freedom in 1957 (the date of the founding of the former Federation of Malaya), but Sarawak and Sabah are shown to be still under colonial rule.[11]

The three remaining armed struggles in Asia endorsed by Peking during 1965, those in the Philippines, Aden (South Yemen), and Oman, all received only minimal news coverage and commentary in the Chinese press during the year.

A final Asian country which is *not* included in the table is Israel. The Palestine Liberation Organization, a revolutionary organization which had sought most actively to overthrow the Jewish government of Israel and reestablish Arab rule, had publicly called for armed struggle against Israel,[12] and Peking had explicitly endorsed the Arabs' struggle against Israel (although the Chinese had not specifically endorsed *armed* struggle).[13] However, the lack of revolutionary activity precluded listing Israel in the table as a site of ongoing armed

11 *SCCS*, 1965, no. 7, p. 5.

12 United States Consulate, Hong Kong, *SCMP*, no. 3425, p. 37; and in 1966, more specifically, *JMJP*, May 17, 1966, p. 6.

13 See, for example, Liao Ch'eng-chih's statement of support translated in *PR*, 1965, no. 21, p. 16.

struggle, and apparently it was also the reason for Israel's being excluded from Peking's listing on the *Shih-chieh chih-shih* world map.

Africa

The lack of revolutionary activity also precluded placing the names of some African countries, such as Rhodesia (Zimbabwe), South Africa, and Basutoland among others, in the table. China had explicitly endorsed the independence movements of all of these areas;[14] but during 1965 armed struggle did not occur in any of these countries. A map of Africa published by the Chinese in early 1965 tallies with the *Shih-chieh chih-shih* world map; each shows only four areas in Africa specifically designated as areas of revolutionary armed struggle—the Congo (Leopoldville) and the Portuguese territories of Angola, Guinea, and Mozambique.[15]

Latin America

Aside from the war in Vietnam, American intervention in the Dominican Republic provided Peking with its biggest anti-US issue of the year. In their enthusiasm over the hostile Latin American reaction to the intervention, the Chinese published a "Simplified Map of Conditions in Latin America" in May[16] which designated twelve areas as "countries having anti-US and anti-dictatorship armed struggles and guerrilla activities." They included the eight countries later designated as sites of armed struggle by the *Shih-chieh chih-shih* world map, plus four additional countries: Argentina, Bolivia, Brazil, and Haiti.

The reasons for the discrepancy between the two maps, one supposedly depicting the situation in Latin America in May 1965 and the other indicating the world situation for all of

14 *PR*, 1965, no. 10, p. 26.

15 *SCCS*, 1965, no. 3, p. 7. This particular map also indicated a separate category of "countries and areas having some armed activities" (Rhodesia, South Africa, and Spanish Guinea); but the accompanying text made it clear that only the Congo, Angola, Mozambique, and Portuguese Guinea were considered as sites of armed revolutionary activity.

16 *JMJP*, May 27, 1965, p. 4.

1965, were at least partially explained by later Chinese analyses. According to subsequent Chinese press reports, by the end of 1965 the armed activities of striking workers in Bolivia had subsided, and the "bold initiative" of an armed insurrection against the government of Brazil had failed.[17] Apparently for these reasons, the world map, published after the end of 1965, failed to indicate Bolivia and Brazil as sites of armed struggle. Argentina and Haiti present more of a mystery. A general survey article on Argentina, appearing in *Shih-chieh chih-shih* in February 1965,[18] almost in passing confirmed Chinese interest in the "people's guerrilla forces" reputed to be operating in several parts of Argentina, but there was no further mention in the Chinese press of armed struggle in Argentina during the rest of the year.[19] A search for Chinese reports of armed activities in Haiti also reveals little. Apparently, by the end of 1965, the Chinese felt that the armed activities in these two countries were not currently significant enough to merit being included in the 1965 year-end world survey. However, since all four countries were at one point indicated as areas of revolutionary armed struggle by the Chinese, and therefore given at least implicit endorsement, they are all included in Table 1, above.

In sum, then, armed struggle against the governments of twenty-three countries or colonies received at least implicit endorsement by Peking in the year 1965. Twelve of these (East and West Malaysia counting as one) received explicit Chinese endorsements, and three qualified for special statements of support by Chairman Mao.

REVOLUTIONS NOT ENDORSED BY PEKING IN 1965

Contrary to popular belief, however, Peking does not publicly endorse and support all antigovernment armed struggles in

---

[17] See *PR*, 1966, no. 5, pp. 15–17.

[18] *SCCS*, 1965, no. 4, pp. 19–20.

[19] For a discussion of the background of the guerrilla effort in Argentina by an attorney who defended guerrilla prisoners, see Ricardo Rojo, *My Friend Che* (New York: Dial Press, 1968), chapter 7.

the Afro-Asian world. In some cases, even communist-led revolutionary movements and violent struggles against Western colonial governments fail to gain Chinese support. In other cases, certain revolutionary efforts are viewed from Peking as special kinds of armed struggles, not wars of national liberation. During 1965, armed struggles against the governments of five countries (French Somaliland, Kenya, Kashmir, Burma, and Indonesia) occurred, but none of them was endorsed by Peking as a war of national liberation or a struggle against imperialism. Chinese policy toward each of these countries provides a particularly interesting example of Peking's unwillingness, under certain circumstances, to support revolutions in the Afro-Asian world.

The first country, French Somaliland, is one of the last remaining outposts of French colonialism. It borders on the countries of Ethiopia and Somalia on the east coast of Africa, standing at the strategic gateway to the Red Sea and the Suez Canal, and has the dubious distinction of constituting the last foothold of Western colonialism in the vast area of northeastern continental Africa. Although Peking explicitly endorsed anticolonial revolutionary struggles in other parts of Africa during 1965, the Chinese Communists neither explicitly nor implicitly endorsed the intermittent armed struggle against the colonial government of French Somaliland. Armed activities in the area were not on the scale of those in the Congo or Angola, but they clearly equaled the magnitude of the antigovernment violence of other countries in the underdeveloped world which were endorsed by Peking as legitimate targets of anti-imperialist revolutionary warfare. Moreover, since French Somaliland was obviously a colonial territory ruled by a foreign power, it would have been expected that the anti-imperialist emphasis of Chinese foreign policy would have produced an unequivocal endorsement of the rebels by Peking. A characteristic example of the Chinese position with regard to French Somaliland during 1965 is an important speech delivered at the Afro-Asian Economic Seminar in Algiers in February 1965 by the chief Chinese delegate, Nan

Han-chen, entitled "Let Us Resolutely Struggle Against Imperialism and Neo-Colonialism and for the Economic Emancipation of the Afro-Asian Peoples."[20] At the end of his long oration, Nan Han-chen endorsed by name the struggles (armed and otherwise) of the peoples of nineteen Afro-Asian countries, but failed to include the anticolonial effort in French Somaliland.[21] In striking contrast, the Afro-Asian Economic Seminar as a whole published a general declaration at the end of the meeting, which specifically endorsed the nationalist struggle in French Somaliland, proclaiming support for it in two separate paragraphs in the document.[22]

The second case, also in East Africa and not far to the south of French Somaliland, was the continuing battle being waged against the government of the independent African state of Kenya. The rebels there, members of a Somali minority which the Kenyan government calls *shiftas* or bandits, were fighting to separate the northeastern part of Kenya—their homeland— from Nairobi's control and to annex it to neighboring Somalia, the nation-state of the Somali people. As a result of the conflict which had been going on since Kenya became independent in 1963, relations between Kenya and Somalia had so deteriorated that by June 1966 Nairobi had severed all trade relations with Somalia and had even revoked the landing privileges in Kenya of the Somali Airlines.[23] At times, Kenyan President Jomo Kenyatta had seemed to imply that he felt that Peking was aiding the *shiftas*,[24] but the Chinese themselves, once again, made no explicit or implicit statement of support for the rebels during the year.

A somewhat similar situation, but one about which the Chinese have made much public comment, prevailed in disputed Kashmir, scene of domestic insurrection and repeated border conflict between India and Pakistan during the latter half of 1965. Unlike the insurrections in Kenya and French

20 An English translation was published in *PR*, 1965, no. 10, pp. 16–26.
21 *Ibid.*, p. 26.
22 *PR*, 1965, no. 11, pp. 17–19.
23 *NYT*, June 22, 1966, p. 3.
24 *NYT*, June 2, 1965, p. 3.

Somaliland about which Peking had little if anything to say, the Chinese fully endorsed the struggle of the Kashmir people and the government of Pakistan against Indian "aggression," and placed full blame for the hostilities on India.[25] The Chinese press spoke of a "Revolutionary Committee of India-Occupied Kashmir" and declared support for the Kashmir people's struggle, but Peking stopped short of proclaiming the hostilities a war of national liberation. Rather, Peking endorsed the "Kashmir people's struggle for national self-determination"[26] and thus, in effect, adopted the Pakistani position which calls for the Kashmiris, who like the Pakistanis are overwhelmingly Moslem, to decide for themselves whether they want to become part of Pakistan or India, which is predominantly Hindu. To have endorsed a war of national liberation for Kashmir would have implied that the Kashmiris should have their own nation-state; but to call for self-determination neatly coincided with Pakistan's hopes to make Kashmir a part of that country.

Several hundred miles to the east, in Burma, Communist China's relations with that republic provided an even more peculiar exception to Peking's repeatedly declared support for revolution. The Burmese government, which maintained an embassy in Peking and was signatory to several treaties with the Chinese, continued during 1965 as it had for several years to try to put down an insurrection in the hinterland being carried on by several different revolutionary organizations, one of which was a pro-Peking communist organization called the White Flags. Fatalities resulting from the hostilities during the year were estimated at some fifty people a month,[27] and the violence was at least on a par with that of the Chinese-endorsed revolutions in Malaya, the Philippines, and Thailand. Moreover, the Burmese government was understandably concerned about the antigovernment activities, as was

---

[25] See, for example, the *JMJP* editorial of September 11, 1965, translated in *PR*, 1965, no. 38, pp. 12–14.

[26] *Ibid.*, p. 14. See also *JMJP*, September 22, 1965, p. 4.

[27] *CSM*, December 10, 1965, pp. 1, 12.

indicated in *New York Times* correspondent Harrison Salisbury's interviews with the Burmese head of state, General Ne Win.[28] But Chinese policy toward Burma was ostensibly one of seeking to develop the closest of friendly government-to-government relations, and there was no mention nor endorsement in the Chinese press during the year of the communist rebels operating in the Burmese jungles who were attempting to overthrow the government. On the contrary, the Chinese press was full of reports of friendly visits between Chinese and Burmese officials, including trips to Burma by Chinese Premier Chou En-lai and Foreign Minister Ch'en Yi, and a visit to Peking by General Ne Win himself in July.[29] In fact, Peking's relations with Rangoon were often pointed to by the Chinese as a model of China's policy of friendly "peaceful co-existence" with non-communist countries.[30]

Looking back at these four cases (French Somaliland, Kenya, Kashmir, and Burma), as well as that of Indonesia which requires a more detailed analysis and will be discussed separately below, one can see at least one striking similarity: in every case Peking had established and was maintaining diplomatic relations with the government under attack by the revolutionaries. One obvious inference to be drawn is that Peking did not publicly endorse wars of national liberation against the governments of these countries for fear of jeopardizing its own state relations with those governments.

With regard to the French government, which maintains control over colonial French Somaliland, Peking had, after extensive negotiations, finally won diplomatic recognition by President De Gaulle in January 1964 and had since that time actively encouraged French independence from the United States, especially with regard to NATO and SEATO military

28 *NYT*, June 22, 1966, p. 6.

29 The colorful welcome given to Ne Win by "hundreds of thousands" of Chinese congregated in Tien An Men Square and on the route from the airport when he visited China in July 1965 was said by the Chinese press to properly express the close *paukphaw*, or kinfolk, spirit between the two peoples and the good neighbor relationship between the two countries. *PR*, 1965, no. 31, p. 6.

30 See, for example, *ibid.*, pp. 6–7.

commitments and American policy in Vietnam. It will be recalled that fundamental to Communist China's view of the world and its contemporary world strategy was the idea of forming the broadest possible worldwide united front against the United States, a concept based in part on the hope of dividing the West against itself by exploiting the "contradictions" among the Western powers, particularly those between the United States and its European allies. In this connection, De Gaulle's independence from, and often opposition to, US policy had provided the Chinese with a most hopeful opportunity of encouraging dissension within the Western alliance.[31] Moreover, potential French influence on the new governments of former French colonies in Africa was probably also an important consideration in determining Chinese policy toward France. In any case, Peking apparently felt that developments in French foreign policy had proved sufficiently beneficial from Peking's point of view to cause the Chinese to refrain from endorsing a national liberation war in French Somaliland at this time, one which might have reversed the trend of Sino-French relations and caused President De Gaulle to once again seek closer ties with his US ally.[32]

In Kenya, in spite of deteriorating government-to-government relations due to alleged Chinese interference in that

[31] With regard to the anti-US orientation of China's policy toward France during this period, see André Malraux's report of his interview with China's leaders when he traveled to China in the capacity of French minister of culture in the summer of 1965. *Atlantic*, October 1968, pp. 95–120, especially pp. 100, 102–105.

[32] By the middle of 1966, French Somaliland had finally been added to the list of African anti-imperialist struggles endorsed by the Chinese, though nothing was said about *armed* struggle (see Foreign Minister Ch'en Yi's speech reported in *PR*, 1966, no. 27, p. 33). The reasons for this change in Chinese policy seem to have been, first, that the independence movement in French Somaliland was gaining increasing international publicity (this was particularly true later in the year when a visit by General De Gaulle to Djibouti prompted widespread rioting and violence) and the Chinese were probably under increasing pressure to support the anti-French effort; and, second, that the Sino-French detente seemed to have become somewhat strained by 1966, as Paris sought to develop closer ties with the Soviet Union and made efforts to find a basis for negotiations to end the Vietnam War, neither of which initiatives were popular in Peking. In this connection, see *PR*, 1966, no. 30, p. 28, and no. 52, p. 31.

country's domestic affairs and the subsequent expulsion from Kenya of Chinese officials, Peking apparently still hoped to benefit from its official ties there. Although Peking protested the official Kenyan rebuffs, the Chinese demonstrated no eagerness to endanger their diplomatic relationship with Nairobi by endorsing an armed struggle against the Kenyan government.[33]

The situation in Kashmir was somewhat different. There, Peking vocally endorsed the struggle against India, but tailored its policy to suit the interests of Pakistan, a country which Peking had actively and somewhat successfully courted over the previous few years. The Sino-Indian border war of 1962 and Peking's continued demands for a realignment of the Sino-Indian frontier, accompanied by the possibility of renewed hostilities, indicated little concern for improved relations with New Delhi; but throughout the several years of constant propaganda agitation and intermittent military action against the Indian government, Peking had refrained from endorsing a national liberation war against that government and had stopped short of recalling its diplomatic mission from New Delhi. In fact, Peking has never unilaterally broken diplomatic relations with any country, even when Chinese missions have been forcibly entered and destroyed and Chinese diplomats physically assaulted.

Finally, the case of Burma is the most striking example of Peking's giving precedence to state relations over support for revolution—particularly striking since, in this case, the revolution was being led by pro-Peking communists. Although Peking no doubt maintained some contact with the pro-Peking rebels, facilitated by the common Sino-Burmese border, it appeared clear, at least in the short run, that the Chinese had chosen to maintain friendly relations with the neutralist Ne Win government (to which Peking had given substantial

[33] In October 1967, the governments of Kenya and Somalia finally agreed to work together to end the insurrection by Somalis against Kenya, and in January 1968, the two countries resumed formal diplomatic relations. *NYT*, February 1, 1968, p. 40.

amounts of economic aid), rather than to support its over-throw by cooperating with the revolutionary White Flag Communists. In fact, by 1965 Peking and Rangoon had maintained friendly government-to-government relations for over a decade, during which time Peking had consistently respected Burma's national security interests.[34]

In confirmation of this particular line of argument with regard to Chinese policy in Asia and Africa, it is interesting in conclusion to note that during 1965 there were no antigovernment armed struggles of any consequence in Latin America that did not receive at least implicit Chinese endorsement. Having been entirely unsuccessful in establishing diplomatic relations with any Latin American country except Cuba, Peking stood to lose nothing in terms of hard-won diplomatic ties by publicly endorsing revolutions in the American hemisphere.

INDONESIA AND THE ATTEMPTED COUP OF OCTOBER 1[35]

China's relationship with Indonesia, the so-called September 30 Movement, and the coup attempt of October 1, 1965, require a more extensive treatment, first, because the organization and motivation behind the coup have been subject to differing interpretations and, second, because of the immensely complicated relationships among three of the major figures in the incident—the Chinese government, Indonesian President Sukarno, and the Indonesian Communist Party (PKI).

The events in Indonesia of the first days of October 1965

[34] John H. Badgley, "Burma and China: Policy of a Small Neighbor," in A. M. Halpern, ed., *Policies Toward China: Views from Six Continents* (New York: McGraw-Hill, 1965), especially pp. 307–308, 326.

[35] This interpretation of events in Indonesia owes much to a long conversation with Roger K. Paget and to his article "The Military in Indonesian Politics: The Burden of Power," *Pacific Affairs*, fall and winter, 1968, pp. 296–314. Mr. Paget was one of the few foreign social scientists resident in Indonesia at the time of the September 30 Movement, and he has done extensive field research on the subject. I do not want to imply, however, that he would necessarily endorse or agree completely with the interpretation presented here.

are well known. Lieutenant Colonel Untung, Tjakrabirawa
Battalion commander assigned to guard the Presidential Palace in Djakarta, announced early on the morning of October 1 that he had taken action against several Indonesian
Army generals, who, he alleged, were conspiring against the
Sukarno government in cooperation with the US Central Intelligence Agency. Later the same day, the Untung-held radio
station further announced the establishment of a forty-five-
member Revolutionary Council to be headed by Indonesia's
pro-leftist Foreign Minister Subandrio, and it was learned
that during the night of September 30, soldiers of the palace
guard and members of the Pemuda Rakjat, a communist
youth organization, had entered the homes of several of the
most important Indonesian Army generals, including Army
Chief of Staff General Yani, had taken the officers prisoner,
and had later tortured and killed them with the assistance of
members of another communist organization, Gerwani. However, the rebels were not as careful as they might have been,
for two of the highest ranking generals, Defense Minister
Nasution and Major General Suharto, eluded the assassins and
rallied loyal elements of the army against Untung's coup attempt. By the afternoon of October 1, less than twenty-four
hours after the rebellion had begun, General Suharto re-
gained control of Djakarta and soon thereafter put down the
insurrection. Ultimately, the army singled out its long-time
enemy, the PKI, as the prime instigator of the coup attempt;
in the following weeks, in cooperation with newly confident
anticommunist mass organizations, it carried out one of the
bloodiest reprisals in modern history. By May 1966, a journalist who had traveled extensively throughout Indonesia estimated that at least 500,000 people had lost their lives in the
violence which followed the events of October 1.[36] Only a
year before, on May 23, 1965, the forty-fifth anniversary of
the founding of the PKI, party Central Committee Chairman
D. N. Aidit, at elaborate ceremonies attended and warmly

---

[36] *Far Eastern Economic Review*, May 12, 1966, p. 282.

endorsed by President Sukarno, had bragged that the PKI was the third largest communist party in the entire world (after the Chinese and the Russian) and had spoken glowingly of the party's successes.[37] A year later, Aidit himself was dead[38] and the party shattered, its members either dead, defected, or in hiding. The membership of the PKI had suffered the most extensive suppression of any communist party in the history of the Marxist-Leninist movement.

Interpretations of the role and motivation of the parties involved in the coup attempt vary. The Indonesian Army and some foreign commentators unequivocally assert that the PKI was the originating force behind the coup, whereas other writers have claimed that the coup was primarily an internal affair of the army and deny that the PKI instigated the action. Although a truly definitive interpretation of the events in Indonesia of October 1965 has yet to be published, it is, I think, useful for the purposes of this study to try briefly to reconstruct the role and motivation of three major actors in the piece—the PKI, Peking, and President Sukarno—in an attempt to better understand Chinese policy and Peking's involvement in the September 30 Movement. In this connection, it is important to note carefully the objectives of the coup and to specify the degree to which it was indeed an assault on the Indonesian government. The September 30 Movement, as it was implemented, did represent a coup attempt in the sense that if it had been successful, it would have replaced the existing Dwikora cabinet with the proposed Revolutionary Council. However, the September 30 Movement clearly did *not* represent a revolutionary attempt to overthrow the Indonesian state or to oust the chief-of-state, President Sukarno. On the contrary, as we shall see, there is a good deal of evidence that the president himself was deeply involved in the movement.

Few analysts now deny that the PKI, Partai Komunis Indo-

---

37 *PR*, 1965, no. 23, pp. 8–12.
38 Aidit's death is confirmed by several sources. See, for example, Seymour Topping's account in the *NYT*, August 23, 1966, pp. 1, 2.

nesia, played some significant role in the events of October 1, 1965.[39] The PKI had for several years adopted a paradoxical position with regard to the international communist movement. In terms of the Sino-Soviet dispute, the party since 1963 had been quite consistently more pro-Peking than pro-Moscow; but in terms of its own domestic strategy, it had followed more of a Soviet line, pursuing a policy that might well have been cited by Moscow as a successful example of the Soviet philosophy of "peaceful transition." Having tried armed insurrection and failed disastrously at Madiun in 1948, the PKI had subsequently adopted a peaceful strategy, involving close cooperation with the nationalist Sukarno government and enabling the party to expand its size and influence greatly over the years.

The PKI's main competitor for power in Indonesia was the army, and as the party increased its influence throughout the country (in the government, in various social organizations, and even within the army itself), a violent confrontation between the army and the PKI appeared increasingly imminent. For years, political analysts had spoken of President Sukarno as maintaining himself in power in large part by playing the army against the PKI and vice versa. However, by 1965, Sukarno seemed increasingly to be favoring the PKI over the army in domestic policies, while at the same time allying Indonesia ever more closely with China in foreign affairs.

It seems clear that whatever the motivation behind the events of October 1, 1965, the PKI and the Indonesian Army had been at swords' points for some time, each fearing a swift stroke by the other that would irrevocably establish the victor as predominant. An attempted coup by the army must have appeared very likely to the PKI, whether or not the army was actually planning one (this question is still in dispute), because it was the PKI which was most benefiting from the recent trend of events and which appeared to stand to benefit even more in the future. For instance, there is little evidence to

[39] Paget, "The Military in Indonesian Politics," p. 298.

support the contention that the PKI felt its peaceful strategy had not been successful. On the contrary, the evidence would seem to indicate that the PKI had benefited substantially from its cooperation with the Sukarno government and looked forward to improving its position in the future.

Hence, perhaps fearful of an army coup d'etat which would drastically change the existing situation or hopeful of sharply improving its own political position with a minimum of risk, the PKI apparently became deeply involved in organizing the September 30 Movement and may in fact have been its principal instigator, as Guy Pauker and others have argued.[40] Promoting what appeared to be an attempt within the Army to exterminate some of its most conservative leaders, PKI Chairman Aidit may have opportunistically felt that, even if the attempt failed, the party would not be implicated or suffer army retaliation; whereas, if the coup were successful, the PKI would diminish significantly the potential threat from the army and would take an important step toward attaining predominant power in Indonesia.

Although the precise role and motivation of the PKI in the events of October 1 remain a matter of contention, it is President Sukarno himself who presents the real mystery. Early accounts of the coup generally described Sukarno as a passive figure waiting out the succession of events, but later versions speak of Sukarno's alleged involvement in the coup and desire to clear away army obstruction to his gradual move to the left. The testimony that has provided some of the most substantial evidence of President Sukarno's involvement has been that offered by Omar Dhani, former commander of Indonesia's air force.[41]

It seems clear that after the coup had failed, Sukarno sought to protect some individuals involved in the affair, like Omar

40 See, for example, Guy J. Pauker, "The Rise and Fall of the Communist Party of Indonesia," RAND Corporation Memorandum RM-5753-PR, February 1969.
41 See *NYT*, December 6, 1966, p. 9; December 7, 1966, p. 8; December 22, 1966, p. 7; and December 25, 1966, p. 5.

Dhani, and attempted to prevent the army's suppression of the PKI. Charges that the president was even more deeply implicated (that he had advance knowledge of the coup and approved the murder of the generals) led to demands that he be dismissed from office and tried for treason.[42] Those charges were finally used to force Sukarno to relinquish his authority and to give up even his official position, which he did in March 1967 when General Suharto became acting president.

Generally speaking, China has been absolved of any major part in the coup, even by some of those analysts who place greatest emphasis on implicating the PKI.[43] There is evidence that Peking agreed to supply 100,000 light weapons to arm an Indonesian "people's militia," which would doubtlessly have been controlled by the PKI;[44] but these weapons had not been delivered by October 1, and the army itself admitted finding only very few Chinese weapons in the aftermath of the coup—these among weapons from a wide variety of arms-producing countries.[45]

The allegation that Peking ordered the PKI to make a revolutionary assault on the Indonesian government is extremely doubtful for at least two very good reasons. First, communist parties of the size and influence of the PKI no longer respond with unquestioning obedience to orders from either Moscow or Peking. Not only have communist-governed states increasingly moved away from subservience to either the Russians or the Chinese, but nongoverning CP's have also come to think of themselves first and Peking and Moscow much later, and have begun to pursue policies designed to serve their own interests rather than those of the Chinese or Russian Communists. In the second place, Peking before the coup attempt appeared to be extremely happy with the status quo in Dja-

---

[42] For example, both the Indonesian Supreme Court and the Indonesian Parliament demanded that Sukarno be brought to trial. *NYT*, February 4, 1967, p. 1.

[43] See, for example, John Hughes, *Indonesian Upheaval* (New York: David McKay, 1967), especially p. 110.

[44] *NYT*, December 25, 1966, p. 5.

[45] John Hughes, *Indonesian Upheaval*, p. 110.

karta and was probably fearful of drastic action that might endanger the existing political situation. Sukarno had moved ever more leftward in his domestic and foreign policies and had willingly cooperated with Peking on many issues of special importance to the Chinese—for instance, the Afro-Asian conference, opposition to the United Nations, and mutual interests in Southeast Asia particularly involving Vietnam and Malaysia. There were even rumors that Sukarno might convert to communism on the Castro model or prepare the way for a PKI succession after he was gone.[46] Also, the Chinese knew from their own experience in 1927 the vulnerability of an unarmed CP opposed in battle by a fully armed modern army; they would, it seems, have been reluctant to see the PKI risk the gains so painstakingly won since the debacle of 1948 by becoming involved in violent action when it appeared that the PKI's peaceful strategy might ultimately be successful.

One qualification to this line of argument relates to Sukarno's health and assessments by the Chinese and the PKI of contingencies in the event the Indonesian president became gravely ill or died. There had been rumors before October 1 that Sukarno was ill; on the basis of their assessment of the effect of these rumors on the existing situation, the Chinese may have concurred in the PKI's decision to become involved in a preemptive attack against the army. Yet, here again, the evidence of Sukarno's own role in the coup would tend to cast doubt on the importance of the health question in actually motivating the various parties to take action.

In any case, the Chinese public position regarding the coup was cautious in the extreme. Not until nineteen days after the fact did Chinese newspapers report the events of September 30 and October 1, 1965. On October 5, however, *Jen-min jih-pao* did report that Chairman Liu Shao-ch'i and Premier Chou En-lai had sent President Sukarno a cable on October 3; and the newspaper prefaced its text of their message with the

---

[46] Donald Hindley, "Political Power and the October 1965 Coup in Indonesia," *Journal of Asian Studies*, February 1967, pp. 237–249.

following brief comment: "Owing to a sudden incident which occurred in Indonesia, President Sukarno has left Djakarta. According to a broadcast on October 3rd from Djakarta radio, President Sukarno announced in a taped broadcast that he is in good health."[47] The message Liu and Chou sent to Sukarno read: "We have learnt from the radio broadcasts from Djakarta that Your Excellency the President is in good health. We hereby extend to you our cordial regards and heartfelt wishes. May the great Indonesian people, under the leadership of Your Excellency the President, develop still further the spirit of opposing imperialism and old and new colonialism, and of opposing 'Malaysia.' "[48]

But not until two weeks later did the Chinese people begin to learn of the events taking place in Indonesia, when the Chinese press published the first government protests against anti-Chinese attacks by Indonesian anti-communist youth organizations and the Indonesian Army and when, on October 20, *Jen-min jih-pao* published a long interpretative article on the events of the preceding weeks and four full pages of documents relating to the September 30 Movement.

After their initial silence, the Chinese reacted to events in Indonesia primarily by protesting to the Indonesian government for specific actions taken against Chinese missions and officials in the country and by reprinting the allegations made by the September 30 Movement (that a "Council of Generals" had been formed within the Indonesian Army in cooperation with the American CIA which planned to mount a coup d'etat against the Indonesian government) and the interpretation of the movement made by Aidit and the PKI (that the September 30 Movement was an internal affair within the Indonesian Army, but that PKI stood for safeguarding President Sukarno and opposed the "Council of Generals"). Chinese accounts blamed "Indonesian rightists" for the anti-Chinese and anti-PKI attacks, accusing them of pursuing "an anti-China, anti-

47 *JMJP*, October 5, 1965, p. 1.
48 Translation from *PR*, 1965, no. 41, p. 5.

communist and anti-popular policy . . . to cater for the needs of US imperialism and its lackeys."[49]

Later, as it became clear that the Indonesian Army was determined to emasculate the PKI and perhaps hoped to precipitate a break in diplomatic relations with Peking, Chinese protests became stronger and Peking's denunciation of the new army-dominated government more violent. Articles in the Chinese press accused the Indonesian army of usurping power by coup d'etat, and of seeking to suppress the Indonesian people and to destroy Sino-Indonesian friendship. And finally, an editorial in *Jen-min jih-pao* on April 16, 1966, entitled "A Full-Scale Fascist Outrage," went to the extreme of comparing anti-Chinese activities in Djakarta with Hitler's fascist violence and declared that the new Indonesian government was run by agents of imperialism: "Only Hitlerite hordes were capable of such behaviour. What the Indonesian Right-wing reactionary forces have done proves that they are nothing but a gang of fascists. . . . This small handful of Indonesian Right-wing army-men and reactionary politicians have all along been agents of imperialism. Their counter-revolutionary military coup d'etat was engineered by US imperialism and Japanese reaction."[50]

At no point, however, did Peking explicitly support the September 30 Movement or publicly endorse any revolutionary activities against the Indonesian government, although the Chinese did remain loyal to Aidit.[51] Rather, once Peking began to comment publicly on the Indonesian situation, Chinese policy seemed tailored to protesting specific acts taken against the Chinese mission in Indonesia and to ameliorating the adverse effects of the Indonesian Army's reaction to the September 30 Movement. Implicitly, Peking endorsed the allegations made by the movement's leaders and the interpre-

---

49 *PR*, 1965, no. 43, p. 6.
50 Translation from *PR*, 1966, no. 17, pp. 11–12; see also "Most Urgent and Strongest Protest to Indonesian Government," in the same issue, pp. 8–9.
51 See, for example, "Aidit—Outstanding Helmsman of Indonesian CP," *PR*, 1965, no. 50, p. 8.

tation of the entire episode made by the PKI; but the focus of Chinese policy, at least in the initial stage, appeared centered on salvaging as best as possible what remained of Sukarno's and the PKI's influence and attempting to reconstitute the pre-September 30 status quo. In spite of repeated attacks on Peking's official representation in Indonesia and even though the PKI (the foremost pro-Peking communist party in the world) was fighting for its life against army suppression, the Chinese refrained from either unilaterally severing relations with the Indonesian government or endorsing a popular armed uprising to overthrow it. Peking chose to hold on to its diplomatic ties with Djakarta, once again giving priority to state relations over revolution.

In the entire Indonesian affair what is most significant from the point of view of this study is that, even if some day an irrefutable case can be made that the PKI was unquestionably the leader and organizer of the September 30 Movement, and even if Peking can be shown to have been an important party to the affair as well (which has not as yet been shown), the movement nevertheless was not involved in making revolution against the Indonesian government; rather, it apparently was an attempt to facilitate the advancement of Sukarno's move to the left. Ultimately, both the PKI and Peking took their stand, as they had for several years previously, on cooperating with—not trying to overthrow—the Sukarno government of Indonesia.

5
RELATIONS WITH
REVOLUTIONARY MOVEMENTS

Theoretically, the Chinese have adopted what seems to be a contradictory position on the question of supporting wars of national liberation. On the one hand, they argue that it is not actually necessary for China to help fight or even give material aid to foreign revolutions, because revolution in each country is made by the people of that country, not by Chinese or any other foreigners. When Lin Piao specified the main elements of the Chinese revolutionary model, he particularly included a commitment to self-reliance as a major factor: "revolution or people's war in any country is the business of the masses in that country and should be carried out primarily by their own efforts; there is no other way."[1]

On the other hand, however, Mao has consistently placed great emphasis on the importance of international moral support for the success of any revolutionary effort. When leading the CCP to power in China, he clearly felt the need for foreign encouragement; and since taking power in 1949, Mao has continually pointed to the obligation of "progressive" peoples everywhere—and especially communists—to make a pub-

[1] *PR*, 1965, no. 36, p. 19.

lic commitment to foreign revolutionaries in their battles against the imperialist enemy. As we have seen, a constant theme in Chinese denunciations of the Soviets has been that Moscow is backing down on its "internationalist duty" to support wars of national liberation.

Hence, in Mao's own terms, a public, verbal commitment of support for wars of national liberation would seem to be an inescapable minimum obligation (and it is in this sense, of course, that Chinese failure to support certain revolutionary efforts as indicated in chapter 4 is so significant); but at the same time, the doctrine of self-reliance permits China to limit its actual commitment of military or material aid to that which Peking deems appropriate.

MILITARY AND MATERIAL ASSISTANCE

The Chinese have been accused of spending millions of dollars to support revolutionary efforts throughout Asia, Africa, and Latin America, and of often employing the most despicable methods in attempting to overthrow governments in these areas. Paradoxically, they have also been accused of making a great deal of propaganda noise, but actually being either unwilling or unable to do much else in support of overseas revolutions. Both accusations are to some extent true.

Generally speaking, it has not been Peking's policy to commit Chinese troops to support foreign wars of national liberation. As of 1965, the only Chinese troops known to be stationed outside China's borders for any purpose were Chinese service troops engaged in rebuilding bombed out roads and railroads in North Vietnam.[2] Subsequently, in 1966 and 1967, as the American military build-up in the South approached a half million men, the Chinese supplied more men to North Vietnam to help build airfields, man antiaircraft weapons, and take over national defense duties from North Vietnamese troops being sent to fight in the South.[3] However, no Chinese

[2] *NYT*, December 1, 1965, p. 1.
[3] *CSM*, March 8, 1967, p. 4; and April 18, 1968, p. 1.

combat troops have yet been known to have fought in the revolution in the South. The situation that would be most likely to prompt a Chinese decision to commit troops to the battle in the South would be one in which Peking felt that the national security and integrity of China were drastically threatened (analogous to the Korean situation in the autumn of 1950), but this would be very different from committing Chinese troops for the purpose of advancing a war of national liberation per se. Actually, Peking's reluctance to commit combatants to foreign wars of national liberation is in striking contrast to the policy of at least one other communist state. Cuba, both in its official statements[4] and its recent behavior (with respect to Bolivia, Argentina, and Venezuela), has demonstrated quite clearly that it views sending Cuban cadres abroad to participate in and even to lead foreign revolutions as an important part of its policy of support. The Chinese have never done this sort of thing as far as is known.

The Chinese have, however, provided substantial material support to foreign revolutionary movements, often in the form of arms and ammunition. During 1965, tons of Chinese-made weapons were intercepted by US and South Vietnamese troops in South Vietnam,[5] and by early 1967 Peking was reported to have supplied an estimated $600 million worth of aid to Hanoi.[6] Substantial shipments of Chinese arms have been sent to other Asian countries, and also to Africa. In May 1965, for instance, authorities of the government of Kenya halted a shipment of seventy-five tons of Chinese weapons, including antitank guns, mortars, rocket launchers, land mines, and heavy machine guns—all part of a truck convoy escorted by Ugandan troops and apparently destined for rebels in the Congo.[7]

Military training is another aspect of Chinese support for wars of national liberation. Some prospective revolutionaries

[4] For example, see the statement by Osmany Cienfuegos, secretary of the tricontinental solidarity organization, reported in *MR*, April 1966, pp. 4–5.
[5] For example, see *NYT*, June 21, 1966, p. 1.
[6] *NYT*, May 28, 1967, p. 1E.
[7] Associated Press, May 21, 1965.

are brought to China for training, but probably more often
they are given instruction at less distant training centers which
are financially supported and often partially staffed by the
Chinese. In Africa, camps established to provide guerrilla
training for revolutionaries have been reported in several
countries and especially in Congo (Brazzaville) and Tanzania,
both bordering on Congo (Kinshasa), site of the continent's
most active antigovernment struggle in early 1965. Also, in-
vestigations in Ghana, undertaken since the overthrow of
Kwame Nkrumah in February 1966, have revealed Chinese-
staffed guerrilla training facilities in that country, allegedly
established in connection with a continent-wide underground
network to train exiles from both independent and colonial
African countries.[8]

Yet, not all Chinese financial support for revolutionary
movements is invested in weapons and military training. Some
funds are spent in more prosaic fields, for example, for cover-
ing the organizational and maintenance costs of revolutionary
movements or for supporting potential revolutionaries such
as Watusi refugees in Kenya and Uganda, dispossessed from
their native country of Rwanda in central Africa.[9] Other
funds are allegedly earmarked for more sinister activities,
such as providing support for organized political terror or
bribing government officials. Prime Minister Hastings Banda
of Malawi has several times claimed that Peking was trying to
buy diplomatic recognition in return for a promised $18 mil-
lion in aid[10] and, having failed at that, was supplying financial support to dissident government officials in an effort to
overthrow the Malawi government.[11] And at a news conference in January 1965, President Felix Houphouet-Boigny of
the Ivory Coast is reported to have said that in Nanking,
China, "Africans are being taught to assassinate those whose
eyes are open to the Chinese danger, in order to replace them

8 CSM, June 30, 1966, p. 4; NYT, June 10, 1966, p. 20.

9 CSM, September 29, 1965, p. 1; John K. Cooley, East Wind over Africa:
Red China's African Offensive (New York: Walker, 1965), pp. 70–71.

10 NYT, August 16, 1965, p. 8.

11 CSM, October 13, 1965, p. 2.

with servile men who will open the gates of Africa to China."[12]

However, no one but the Chinese really knows the full dimensions of Peking's financial support for revolutionary movements. Largely because of Vietnam, the annual budget is clearly over $100 million; but any attempt to estimate it more precisely on the basis of the incomplete and unreliable information available would probably be more misleading than instructive. The Chinese press almost never mentions the size of Peking's aid even when it is provided to governments rather than revolutionary movements, and the Western anti-communist press no doubt often overestimates it. Nonetheless, both documentary evidence and personal interviews confirm that the Chinese have widely provided financial support to individuals and revolutionary organizations of which they approve, and often in quite generous amounts.

CHINESE PROPAGANDA

Considerably less tangible a form of support than military or financial assistance, but one of immense importance for the worldwide national liberation movement, is Chinese propaganda.

Daily, Peking reaches out to virtually the entire world with its extensive propaganda apparatus: radio broadcasts, cinema, touring performers, "cultural delegations," and a great variety of printed material. Chinese news magazines and beautifully illustrated picture magazines, for example, are widely available throughout the underdeveloped world, and subscriptions to them are solicited at nominal cost. Probably the most widely circulated is *China Pictorial*, a monthly published in nineteen different languages.[13] More explicitly political in content is the *Peking Review*, also published in several languages and available to subscribers in an inexpensive airmail

---

[12] Cooley, *East Wind over Africa*, p. 181; Agence France Presse, January 24, 1965.

[13] Chinese, Mongolian, Tibetan, Uighur, Korean, Chuang, Russian, English, German, French, Japanese, Vietnamese, Indonesian, Hindi, Spanish, Arabic, Swedish, Swahili, and Italian.

edition. Announcing itself as a "weekly magazine of Chinese news and views," it, too, is almost universally available.

Chinese radio broadcasts apparently receive highest priority among Peking's various overseas propaganda media and probably reach the widest audience in Asia, Africa, and Latin America. Almost every year since the communists took power on the mainland in 1949, the number of weekly broadcast hours of programs beamed abroad from China has substantially increased: in 1953 China broadcast only 100 hours per week to countries outside its borders, but by 1965 weekly broadcast hours had increased tenfold to 1,027 hours per week.[14] Over half the broadcasting time during 1965—582 hours per week—was devoted to programs for listeners in the Far East, which were heard in five Chinese dialects and thirteen other languages.[15] To South Asia and the Near East, as well as to Africa, Peking broadcast only 70 hours per week, and in six languages to each area.[16] Latin America, lowest in priority, received only 39 hours of programs from China a week, and only in Spanish and Portuguese.[17]

The fine arts and performing artists also play an important role in China's overseas propaganda. In early 1966, for instance, the *China Pictorial* published pictures of a 114-figure series of realistic sculptures done by the Sculpture Department of the Szechuan Fine Arts Institute on the general theme of the *shou tzu yuan* or rent collection court. The display reputed to portray the brutality of the feudal tenant agricultural system as it operated in preliberation China—complete with whippings, forced sale of children to pay overdue rent, and the horrors of the "water-prison." The theater is also a

14 Research and Reference Service, United States Information Agency, *Communist China's Propaganda Activities: 1965* (May 1966), p. 6.

15 Chinese dialects: Amoy, Cantonese, Chaochow, Hakka, and Mandarin. Other languages: Burmese, Cambodian, English, Esperanto, Indonesian, Japanese, Korean, Laotian, Malay, Mongolian, Tagalog, Thai, and Vietnamese.

16 To South Asia and the Near East: Arabic, English, Hindi, Persian, Tamil, and Turkish. To Africa: English, French, Hausa, Italian, Portuguese, and Swahili.

17 Research and Reference Service, USIA, *China's Propaganda Activities*, pp. 6–7.

popular vehicle for propaganda. The subject matter and social content of the ever popular Peking Opera have been changed in order to convey modern political themes without—I am told by people who have seen the new reformed theater—losing the excitement and audience appeal of the traditional form. Probably the best known single play is the extravaganza *The East Is Red*.[18] Of course, fine arts exhibits and Chinese theatrical productions staged in China have only a limited effect on the international scene; but these productions are reported on the Chinese radio and in Chinese publications sent abroad, and traveling Chinese art troupes help to establish the link between the Chinese Revolution and present-day wars of national liberation.

Plays dealing with foreign revolutions have also been particularly popular in recent years and are apparently written and produced both to involve the Chinese people at home more closely in the revolutionary activities of people abroad and to demonstrate to foreigners Chinese concern and support for their struggles. In 1965, for example, *Battle-Drums on the Equator: A Play Dedicated to the Anti-US Patriotic Struggle of the Congolese (L) People* was produced,[19] as well as a continuing series of dramas in support of the war in Vietnam, one of which was entitled *Letters from the South*, the story of an attack on a US-controlled Vietnamese strategic hamlet.[20] The official description of a similar drama which appeared in 1966 (but this time with a Vietnamese cast) provides a good example of the anti-US theme which pervades much of this kind of modern politicized theater. The play, *Under the Banner of the Liberation Front*, is said to expose "the heinous crimes of US imperialism and its lackeys in South Vietnam and de-

18 Both the reformed Peking Opera and the rent collection court sculptures were subsequently seen to be "pioneer efforts" in the attempt by the Maoists to revolutionize Chinese art and literature, which culminated in the Great Proletarian Cultural Revolution. See, for example, "Summary of the Forum on the Work in Literature and Art in the Armed Forces with Which Comrade Lin Piao Entrusted Comrade Chiang Ching," *PR*, 1967, no. 23, pp. 10–16.
19 See *China Pictorial*, 1965, No. 12, pp. 28–29. An English translation of the full script of the play appears in *Evergreen*, Special Number, August 1965.
20 *China Pictorial*, 1965, no. 4, pp. 18–19.

scribes how the South Vietnamese people full of class and national hatred, wage resolute struggles against the aggressors."[21] Also in 1966, a play about revolution in Latin America called *Storm over the Andes* was produced, which told the story of an American imperialist agent named Murphy, his attempt to suppress the revolutionary struggle, and how the people of the Andes organized themselves into revolutionary guerrilla bands to defeat him.[22]

But how can such propaganda actually serve to support ongoing wars of national liberation, or help to build popular support for revolutions in the future? Systematic measurement of the effectiveness of Chinese propaganda in Asia, Africa, and Latin America is beyond the scope of this study, but let us speculate briefly on how Chinese propaganda tends to influence popular political attitudes.

Clearly, it seems, the most important single effect of Chinese propaganda is to provide the potential revolutionary cadres of the underdeveloped world—the alienated and disaffected young intellectuals profoundly dissatisfied with the status quo and searching for a way to change it—with a "practical ideology," a theoretical plan for making revolution and upsetting established authority. Translations of Mao's works, especially his *Selected Military Writings*, and other theoretical material widely published by Peking, such as Lin Piao's essay "Long Live the Victory of People's War!" can provide potential revolutionary leaders with the theoretical tools not only to develop their own commitment to revolution as a means of social change, but also to help enable them to guide popular discontent into revolutionary channels by providing the ideological foundation and organizational principles for the formation of revolutionary movements.

On the mass level, the problem is somewhat different. The most important problem facing the Chinese propagandist who wants to help foreign revolutionary movements is how to help mobilize the mass support that is so vital to the success of vir-

21 *Ibid.*, 1966, no. 4, p. 34.
22 *Ibid.*, no. 6, pp. 30–31.

tually any revolutionary effort. Let us hypothesize that mass thought processes in the underdeveloped world, especially among rural people, can be characterized somewhat as follows: large sectors of the population of many countries, independent as well as colonial, are still primarily bound by traditional ties; and although not necessarily content with their lot (which objectively seen is often very bitter indeed), the people of these areas are still resigned to their "fate," to the continuing existence of things as they are. But people throughout the underdeveloped world, even in the most traditional areas, are beginning to change and beginning to develop what Daniel Lerner has called "empathy," or the capacity to identify with others and imagine oneself living in a different situation.[23] It is this empathy or psychic mobility, Lerner argues, which is the predominant personal style of modern society and which is an important prerequisite to social change, be it peaceful or revolutionary.

Propaganda alone usually cannot initiate the empathy process, nor can continued harsh social conditions of themselves create the psychological prerequisites for social change. After all, men have endured the most difficult living conditions for entire lifetimes and even generations without giving a thought to revolution or rebellion. But once people have begun to empathize—often prompted by personal experiences with the more modernized aspects of their society—and have learned to imagine something better for themselves and their families, the propagandist can then plant the seeds of discontent and the hope for change. By daily elaborating the same themes, he can begin to "demonstrate" to poverty-ridden peoples that what they had considered to be their unalterable fate is actually exploitation, unjustly carried out by an aggressive ruling class in cooperation with malevolent foreigners. When conditions begin to be perceived as unjust, then, and perhaps only then, can they begin to be seen as intolerable. Analyzing

[23] For a definition and discussion of the concept of empathy, see Daniel Lerner, *The Passing of Traditional Society: Modernizing the Middle East* (Glencoe: The Free Press, 1958), pp. 47–52.

local conditions from the perspective of a different view of reality, the propagandist not only can demonstrate the evil of the existing system, but can also project a tempting vision of an alternative system and describe the means of attaining it.

An article appearing in *Foreign Affairs* in 1966 noted an interesting example of the activation of discontent in a previously apathetic Panamanian school teacher—in this case produced with the aid of radio propaganda:

Time is not with us [the US] in Latin America. The pressures of population and revolution are increasing. I recall a year ago visiting a remote village in the Panamanian highlands, a sleepy place, nestled deep in its own poverty and ignorance, unconscious of the outside world or of the changes taking place there. The wife of the local storekeeper, also the school teacher of the village, was at that time a listless woman, resigned to the unchanging life around her, to the drought then threatening the village's meager food supply, to the lack of even the most rudimentary medical treatment for her children, to the dull drudgery of her daily work. This year I returned to the village to find this woman a completely different person. She had been listening to a transistor radio and was filled with anger. Her eyes flashed as she pointed to the misery around her, as she spoke of the landlord who owned the land on which the village was located, as she demanded answers to the thousand questions of why everything was not better.[24]

After men have become actively discontented and have begun to think in terms of a revolutionary solution to their problems, propaganda can perform the function of reinforcing these new ideological inclinations by continually reassuring both leaders and rank and file that their cause is just and that China and the world supports them in their struggle. To cite an example of the reinforcement effect of radio propaganda as applied to the other side of the barricades in a revolutionary situation, Frantz Fanon in *Studies in a Dying Colonialism* describes how French radio programs helped support and maintain French colonial views and values among listening French settlers, living in the midst of an increasingly hostile social

[24] *Foreign Affairs*, January 1966, p. 197.

environment during the Algerian war for national independence.[25]

But, of course, helping to formulate revolutionary ideas is not the same thing as making revolution. Thinking revolutionary thoughts is one thing; taking revolutionary action is something quite different. Marx's call to the barricades, "You have nothing to lose but your chains," is simply not true. Anyone who dares to make revolution risks not only his own life, liberty, and possessions, but also those of his family and friends. Yet, if activating and reinforcing revolutionary political opinions is not making revolution, it is a beginning—and a beginning without which there can be no popular-based revolution.

Thus, given China's limited economic resources, a sustained propaganda program is probably the single most fruitful kind of support that Peking can currently provide to the revolutionary movements of Asia, Africa, and Latin America.

CONTEMPORARY REVOLUTIONARY ORGANIZATIONS

Chinese theoretical statements on the subject of the national liberation struggle would seem to require that, in practice, Peking support only those revolutionary movements led by revolutionary communist parties. Both Lin Piao's definition of the maximum Chinese revolutionary model and persistent Chinese attacks on Soviet Russia in the name of preserving Marxist-Leninist orthodoxy would seem to assure that Peking would support only those insurrectionary movements in Asia, Africa, and Latin America led by communist parties of unquestionable Marxist-Leninist credentials.

In fact, however, this is not always the case; as we have seen, the Chinese conceive of both a maximum and a minimum revolutionary model. The characteristic type of revolutionary organization that Peking actually supported in 1965 was not a pro-Peking communist party (although they were

25 Frantz Fanon, *Studies in a Dying Colonialism* (New York: Monthly Review Press, 1965), pp. 96–97.

supported as well), but a nationalist united front organization in which the local communist party (if there was one) may or may not have played a dominant role. These nationalist or "patriotic front" revolutionary organizations characteristically make a broad nationalist appeal, declaring as their objectives the attainment of true national independence, democracy, peace, and the economic improvement of the people.[26] They vary in composition and organization, from those similar to the Algerian FLN (essentially a nationalist alliance of dissimilar social groups organized for the specific purpose of winning independence and led by no single group), to those more closely approximating the South Vietnam National Front for Liberation (a CP-led united front organization ostensibly established for the purpose of gaining "true" independence but committed to continuing social revolution under CP direction).

Since the advent of the Sino-Soviet dispute and the loosening of Soviet control and authority over communist parties throughout the world, the international communist movement has undergone a profound crisis. Communist parties on every continent, especially in Asia, Africa, and Latin America, have become faction ridden and in some cases have split into two separate communist parties, one pro-Peking and the other pro-Soviet. In other countries, entirely new Marxist-Leninist parties have emerged which usually do not even carry the name of communist (among these are the Castroite parties in Latin America and so-called Trotskyite parties). In many countries the political left is in a serious state of chaos. A recent listing of world communist parties, for example, cited six separate organizations for both Ceylon and Mexico and four for the Dominican Republic.[27] Particularly in Western Europe and Latin America, some traditional communist parties pursuing a policy of "peaceful transition," have adopted

[26] See, for example, the policy statement of the Thailand Patriotic Front, published in *PR*, 1965, no. 7, p. 25.

[27] *Survey*, January 1965, pp. 190–196.

the posture of political parties of the moderate left and appear, at least temporarily, to have given up the idea of attempting to overthrow the government by force. At the same time, however, as traditional communist parties in some countries have moved to the right, radical new Marxist-Leninist organizations have arisen to the left of the communist party, holding high the banner of armed struggle.

The confused and divided state of the international communist movement has certainly not contributed to the capacity of traditional communist parties to lead effective revolutionary movements. Where communist parties are not divided and bickering among themselves, they are often flatly committed to a peaceful pro-Soviet line and unwilling to wage armed struggle. Elsewhere, communist parties have been effectively suppressed or discredited, or there is virtually no communist party in existence at all.

Yet, the splintering of the international communist movement and the diminishing of its central authority (either from Moscow or Peking) have not been without advantages for local Marxist-Leninist leaders. Although local communist parties continue to reflect the Sino-Soviet competition and conflicting loyalties and disputes over policy tend to wrench communist parties apart, local communists appear to be gaining the substantial benefit of being able to operate more credibly as truly nationalistic leaders rather than as agents of Moscow or Peking. The strict discipline of the international communist movement, operating as it has in the past from Moscow, has often worked to the detriment of local communists—forcing them into untenable political positions, providing cause for suppression by local authorities as being agents of a foreign power, and perhaps most important of all detracting from their credibility as true nationalists. Thus, the new state of affairs in the international communist movement, though weakening the movement as a worldwide, centrally-directed political force, provides local communists with a new flexibility and a better opportunity to win the popular support without which no revolution today can be successful.[28]

Moreover, as the viability of traditional communist parties in many areas has declined, paradoxically the likelihood of communist leadership of wars of national liberation has increased. Today, not only are independent Marxist-Leninists capable of making a more effective nationalist appeal as revolutionary leaders, but the revolutions they are seeking to lead are different from those that have characterized the political development of Asia and Africa since the end of World War II. Except for southern Africa, by and large the struggles for national independence which have shaped Asian and African politics for the last two decades have been won; and the so-called wars of national liberation being waged today are not aimed at the overthrow of colonialist domination, but the toppling of already established, independent governments.

Although it is extremely dangerous to generalize about the politics of a single continent, let alone that of the three vastly dissimilar continents of Asia, Africa, and Latin America, it does seem that at least three factors can be said to be increasing the chances of communist leadership of the armed struggles in the underdeveloped world. The first is the Cold War, defined more in terms of a US confrontation with China than a struggle between the US and Russia. Throughout the underdeveloped world, now that independence has been won in almost all areas, the United States appears committed to defending the status quo against any further revolutionary efforts, justified or not, apparently fearful that new revolutions would result in communist takeovers. China, on the other hand, appears to be actively supporting the overthrow of the status quo and has come to be seen by many revolutionaries as the only major power willing to support their struggles. The result of the confrontation of US-supported counterinsurgency efforts to suppress contemporary revolutionary movements on the one hand, and Chinese support for them on the

28 See the discussion by the Latin American journalist Adolfo Gilly, in "A Guerrilla Wind," MR, November 1965, pp. 41–45.

other, seems very likely to have a profound influence in defining these revolutions as communist *versus* anti-communist struggles.[29]

Secondly, mass-based revolutions against independent national governments seem certain to become more deeply involved in social and economic issues—that is, to become more social revolutionary—than earlier wars against the foreigner. In independent nations, the struggle is no longer one of virtually the whole country against a foreign ruler, but of the less privileged against the more privileged within the nation. Although the struggle is usually defined by the revolutionaries as a national one—against a new kind of foreign domination, neo-colonialism—in fact, domestic issues are often uppermost. Even if the initial source of armed struggle is a dispute between middle class leaders, it would seem inevitable that challengers of the established government ultimately would have to raise class issues in order to build a mass following. Insofar as the revolution becomes an effort to reshape the entire social system of a country, the applicability of Marxist-Leninist ideology and organizational techniques would seem to enhance the chances of communists taking over its leadership. An example of a Marxist view of class participation in contemporary revolutions in Latin America is provided by the following analysis written by the editors of the American Marxist magazine *Monthly Review*:

No considerable section of the bourgeoisie, especially after the experience of the Cuban Revolution, is going to support, still less fight for, the establishment of such a [peasants and workers] state. With the (very important) exception of those—mostly students and intellectuals—who are ready to throw in their lot with the workers and peasants, the Latin American bourgeoisies are not interested in any kind of a revolution: they prefer to throw in *their* lot with the imperialist defenders of the status quo. Under these circum-

29 Even in southern Africa where the United States has taken more of a neutral stand with regard to revolutionary movements than it has in other areas of the world, the Cold War still seems destined to play an important part. See George M. Houser, "African Liberation Movements: Report on a Trip to Africa, Spring 1967," *Africa Today*, August 1967, pp. 11–13.

stances, Latin American revolutionaries are finding that it is vastly preferable to rouse the morale and enthusiasm of workers and peasants by boldly proclaiming a full-fledged socialist program than to seek vainly to enlist the backing of a largely non-existent anti-imperialist bourgeoisie. What this means is not that carrying through the national democratic revolution as a preliminary to the construction of socialism has lost any of its importance, but rather that in Latin American conditions the national democratic and socialist revolutions are apparently going to be carried out under a single unified program and in this sense are being telescoped into one.[30]

Finally, the third factor that seems to favor communist leadership of contemporary wars of national liberation is that Marxism-Leninism seems to many revolutionaries to provide the most suitable theoretical framework and military strategy for conditions in their particular countries. Marxism-Leninism offers a systematic world view and practical prescriptions for revolutionary action. Moreover, Marxists can point to an impressive tradition and important revolutionary successes, at least two of which, the Chinese and Cuban experiences, appear to have direct relevance to the kinds of problems revolutionaries are facing in the countries of the underdeveloped world. For example, the Chinese concept of neo-colonialism offers revolutionaries a nationalist issue around which to rally popular support even after national independence has been won; and Mao's guerrilla strategy, calling for an alliance of workers and peasants to wage war from rural areas in order to capture the cities, appears to suit the revolutionary potentialities of many of the primarily agrarian countries of Asia, Africa, and Latin America. That is not to say, however, that objectively seen, the examples of the Chinese or Cuban revolutions have in the past or will in the future provide the key to instant revolutionary success. On the contrary, many revolutionaries have met disaster (for example, the Guevara movement in Bolivia in 1967) trying to replicate revolutionary models; and particularly in Latin America, in the face of many recent revolutionary defeats, much discussion

[30] *MR*, November 1965, p. 11.

has been carried on with regard to what aspects of earlier revolutionary experiences actually can be applied with success today.[31] Nevertheless, Chinese and other Marxists speak with relevance to the problems of the Third World, and they can provide foreign revolutionaries with intellectual sustenance as well as moral and material support.

Generally speaking, the revolutionary situation in the underdeveloped world in 1965 seemed to be in a period of transition. Revolutionary patriotic fronts led by traditional communist parties characterized the situation in Southeast Asia, and revolutionary movements there seemed increasingly to be modeled on the South Vietnamese NFL. In Latin America, a new, independent or pro-Cuban Marxist-Leninist leadership was arising to vie for the leadership of revolutions. But Africa perhaps best reflected the sense of transition. Would the battles for national independence and self-determination being fought in the Portuguese territories and white supremacist southern Africa develop on the non-communist Algerian model? Or was the Algerian Revolution the last major revolutionary armed struggle that could avoid the Cold War and a communist *versus* anti-communist confrontation?[32]

PEKING'S RELATIONS WITH REVOLUTIONARY ORGANIZATIONS

As was stated earlier in this study, Chinese diplomacy, or the implementation of Chinese foreign policy, operates on three levels: the official governmental level; the semiofficial level, comprising relations carried out by nominally nongovernmental or "people's" organizations; and the communist party level, which involves relations between the Chinese Commu-

---

31 See, for example, Régis Debray, "Revolution in the Revolution?" in *MR*, July–August 1967, and the criticism of Debray published the following year by the same magazine, "Regis Debray and the Latin American Revolution," *MR*, July–August 1968.

32 The assassination in February 1969 of Eduardo Mondlane, president of FRELIMO and one of the few remaining African revolutionaries with close contacts in the West, left the chances for non-communist revolution in southern Africa considerably poorer than before.

nist Party and the other parties comprising the international communist movement.

During 1965, Peking's relations with revolutionary organizations were handled through the second and third levels, by means of semiofficial or communist party contacts, depending on the character of the revolutionary organization. The full extent of China's contacts with foreign communist parties during the year is not fully known, but mention in the Chinese press of foreign communist parties with specific regard to wars of national liberation was relatively rare. China's main public interest in foreign communist parties seemed to focus on winning a pro-Peking commitment from them for the purpose of building China's influence within the international communist movement. Peking often reprinted the policy statements and programs of foreign communist parties, which frequently dealt with strategic questions relative to waging wars of national liberation; but generally these statements seemed primarily intended to provide ammunition for China's battle against the Soviet Union. At the same time, Chinese press reports of overseas revolutionary activities and of Chinese relations with foreign revolutionary movements usually spoke of semiofficial Chinese contacts with national front organizations. As a result, during 1965 there was something of a division of labor implied by the Chinese press treatment of communist parties as opposed to national front revolutionary organizations. Foreign communist parties were most often mentioned with regard to their position in the Sino-Soviet dispute, whereas national front organizations were generally referred to as leading wars of national liberation, and Chinese relations with these movements were publicly said to be handled through semiofficial rather than communist party channels.[33]

[33] With regard to China's relations with some areas of the world, this division of labor appears to go deeper than just public image-making. For example, Ernst Halperin argues that the Chinese effort among Latin American communists has been focused almost exclusively on countering Soviet influence on that continent, rather than organizing to defeat the American imperialist enemy. See "Peking and the Latin American Communists," CQ, January–March 1967, pp. 111–154.

In part, the reason for this press treatment of foreign revolutionary movements was no doubt an attempt to portray communist-led national front organizations as being more broadly representative of the countries they claimed to represent than in fact they actually were. However, the use of semi-official channels for contacts with foreign revolutionary movements also reflected the fact that in some countries there was no formal communist party, or that, even where there was a communist party, the actual leadership of the revolution had been taken over by other, often more radical, elements in the society. In Guatemala, for example, the traditional communist party (Partido Guatemalteco del Trabajo) had given lip service to the strategy of armed struggle;[34] but the revolution had actually been mounted by a disparate group which later split, one branch being led by independent Marxists some of whose policies were even more radical than those proposed by Lin Piao in his definition of the Chinese revolutionary model. (The Guatemalan Movimiento Revolucionario 13 de Noviembre [MR-13], for example, has rejected the Chinese-endorsed concept of a broad national united front that includes the national bourgeoisie; instead it argues that there is no anti-imperialist bourgeoisie in Guatemala and calls for "socialist revolution" and a "workers' and peasants' government.")[35]

During the year, the Chinese practice of publicly supporting revolutionary movements was generally broadly inclusive, rather than exclusive. Lin Piao's injunction that a revolution on the Chinese model must be led by a Marxist-Leninist revolutionary party did not, in practice, preclude Peking from supporting movements not having such leadership. Moreover, if two or more separate organizations were seen to be leading armed struggle within a single country, Chinese practice was generally to *imply* support for all of them by mentioning them

34 See, for example, José Manuel Fortuny, "Has the Revolution Become More Difficult in Latin America?" *World Marxist Review*, August 1965, pp. 38–45.

35 For a discussion of MR-13, its program, background, and operations, see Adolfo Gilly, "The Guerilla Movement in Guatemala," *MR*, May and June 1965.

in press reports and reprinting their programs, while *explicitly* supporting none to the exclusion of the others,[36] except perhaps for pro-Peking communist parties.

However, some revolutionary organizations, other than communist parties, did receive explicit Chinese endorsement and even formal diplomatic status in Peking. For example, the 1965 edition of *Jen-min shou-ts'e* (People's handbook), at the end of a long list of countries with which China maintains formal government-to-government diplomatic relations, includes both the South Vietnamese NFL Mission in China and the Office of the Palestine Liberation Organization in Peking.[37] Since the publication of the 1965 *Jen-min shou-ts'e,* three more revolutionary organizations have established permanent missions in China: the Malayan National Liberation League, the Thailand Independence Movement, and the Thailand Patriotic Front.[38] Chinese hosts to both the permanent missions and visiting delegations from revolutionary movements in 1965 were customarily either the Chinese People's Institute of Foreign Affairs, which welcomed Gaston Soumialot and his six-member Congolese delegation in August 1965, or the Chinese Committee for Afro-Asian Solidarity.

Parenthetically, it should be noted that Afro-Asian organizations of many types proved increasingly important in Chinese relations with the underdeveloped world during 1965. Much to Peking's regret, the Afro-Asian summit conference at the governmental level failed to be convened, but China's failure to gather Afro-Asian governments together did not diminish Chinese persistence in organizing international Afro-Asian conferences at the nongovernmental or mass organization level. The principal problem Peking faced in sponsoring

[36] *SCCS,* of May 10, 1965, for example, carries the programs of two Thai revolutionary organizations side by side.

[37] *Jen-min shou-ts'e 1965* (Peking: Ta Kung Pao, 1965), p. 226. When in June 1969 the Provisional Revolutionary Government of the Republic of South Vietnam was proclaimed, the Chinese government raised the diplomatic level of the NFL Mission in China, declaring it to be the official embassy of the new South Vietnamese rebel government. *PR,* 1969, no. 25, pp. 5–6.

[38] *JMJP,* May 7, 1966, p. 6; *PR,* 1965, no. 45, p. 31; *PR,* 1966, no. 2, p. 12.

the Afro-Asian mass organization meetings was Soviet competition for control of the meetings. The customary result was a public battle between the Chinese and Soviet delegations, such as that which occurred in Havana in January 1966 at the long-planned Tricontinental Conference of people's solidarity organizations. More recently, Peking has apparently decided that the convening of rump meetings which include only those delegations that favor the Chinese position would be more profitable. These gatherings, such as the Afro-Asian Writers Emergency Meeting held in Peking in July 1966, are often so radical in complexion that their resolutions adopt positions even to the left of the official Chinese position.[39] By organizing the extreme radicals of Asia, Africa, and Latin America, Peking apparently hoped to build international organizations that were both anti-US and anti-Soviet, and which would, therefore, help buttress China's own anti-imperialist and antirevisionist foreign policies.

Although Asia, Africa, and Latin America are often lumped together in Chinese political analyses and policy statements, at least two important factors tend to make for differences in Peking's approach to the three continents. From the Chinese point of view, geographical proximity is probably the most important distinction among the three continents. Asian nations pressing close on China's borders obviously make them of more immediate concern to Peking than the far away countries of Africa and Latin America. Also, receptivity to Chinese policy overtures—such as an offer from Peking to establish diplomatic relations—is another significant determinant of Chinese attitudes toward the three continents. For example, by the end of 1965 Peking had established formal diplomatic relations with fifteen of the thirty-one Asian nations, with seventeen of the thirty-seven sovereign states of Africa, but with only one (Cuba) of the twenty-four independent states in the American hemisphere.

[39] Compare Foreign Minister Ch'en Yi's address to the meeting, translated in PR, 1966, no. 27, pp. 32–36, with the 37 resolutions later passed by the meeting, PR, 1966, no. 29.

In the following pages, China's relations with the major revolutionary organizations of Asia, Africa, and Latin America during 1965 are discussed continent by continent. Accompanying the discussion of each continent is a table that attempts both to summarize Peking's relations with the principal revolutionary organizations of that area and to measure in a rudimentary fashion the intensity of China's relationship with each organization. Three criteria are used to measure this relationship: whether the organization had established a permanent mission in China; whether a delegation from the particular organization visited China in 1965; and whether the organization was mentioned in the Chinese press in connection with the armed struggle going on in its home country. Generally, no subordinate organizations are included; for example, if a revolutionary movement has both a political and a military organization, only the dominant one will be listed. Also, those relationships between Peking and foreign revolutionary organizations that do not appear in the Chinese press, such as secret trips to China by organization members, are not listed. If a country was mentioned in the Chinese press as the site of revolutionary activity but no particular revolutionary organizations were named, I have simply listed the name of the country followed by a dash (—).

Asia

During 1965, Communist China endorsed revolutions in a total of twenty-three countries and territories throughout the world; seven of these were in Asia (see Table 2), and Vietnam was clearly the most important of all to Peking. The armed struggle in Vietnam was continually the subject of official Chinese pronouncements and news reports, and the South Vietnam NFL, the organization leading the revolution, received the most firm, explicit, and repeated Chinese public support.[40]

[40] See *Support the People of Viet Nam, Defeat US Aggressors,* 4 vols. (Peking: Foreign Languages Press, 1965).

US and Belgian intervention in the Congo temporarily placed Africa in the spotlight of world attention in the fall of 1964, and the Dominican Republic revolt and subsequent US intervention there brought much attention to Latin America in the spring of 1965; but, although Peking made the most of both events (Mao made highly publicized statements concerning each), the Chinese leadership remained preoccupied with Vietnam and Southeast Asia throughout 1965.

Early in the year the chances of the rebels winning the struggle in South Vietnam looked extremely promising; and although it is unclear to what extent the Chinese may have subscribed to the so-called domino theory, Lin Piao described Vietnam as a "testing ground" and suggested the possibility of a "chain reaction" of US international defeats to follow American defeat in Vietnam. He described the Vietnam war and Chinese support for the rebels there as follows:

The struggle of the Vietnamese people against US aggression and for national salvation is now the focus of the struggle of the people of the world against US aggression. The determination of the Chinese people to support and aid the Vietnamese people . . . is unshakable. No matter what US imperialism may do to expand its war adventure, the Chinese people will do everything in their power to support the Vietnamese people until every single one of the US aggressors is driven out of Viet Nam.[41]

However, at the same time, Lin placed great emphasis on the need for the Vietnamese ultimately to rely on their own efforts, and he indicated quite clearly that China was not eager to become directly involved in the war.

Continuous American bombing of North Vietnam (begun in February 1965) and the build-up of American armed forces in the South had apparently prompted a major debate within the Chinese leadership with regard to how China should deal with the new situation in Vietnam and what implications followed from the different policy alternatives for China's own

41 *PR*, 1965, no. 36, p. 29.

TABLE 2

CHINA'S RELATIONS WITH MAJOR ASIAN REVOLUTIONARY ORGANIZATIONS, 1965

Endorsed Revolution	Revolutionary Organization	Permanent Mission in China[a]	Delegation Visited China in 1965[b]	Mentioned in Chinese Press[c]
Aden	Front for the Liberation of Occupied South Yemen (FLOSY)			x
	National Liberation Front			x
Laos	Neo Lao Haksat		x	x
Malaysia:				
Malaya and Singapore	Malayan Communist Party			x
	Malayan National Liberation League[d]			x
Northern Borneo	North Kalimantan Unitary State Revolutionary Government		x	x
Oman	—			
Philippines	—			
Thailand	Thailand Patriotic Front[e]	x	x	x
	Thailand Independence Movement	x	x	x
South Vietnam	South Vietnam National Front for Liberation (NFL)	x	x	x

a Thailand Patriotic Front: *PR*, 1966, no. 2, p. 12. Thailand Independence Movement: *PR*, 1965, no. 45, p. 31. South Vietnam NFL: *Jen-min shou-ts'e*, 1965, p. 226.

b Neo Lao Haksat: *SCMP*, no. 3442, p. 34. North Kalimantan Unitary State Revolutionary Government: *SCMP*, no. 3551, p. 39. Thailand Patriotic Front: *SCMP*, no. 3442, p. 38. Thailand Independence Movement: *JMJP*, March 27, 1965, p. 6. South Vietnam NFL: *SCMP*, no. 3583, p. 37.

c (Sources cited only for those organizations not referred to in notes a or b.) Front for the Liberation of Occupied South Yemen (FLOSY): *JMJP*, October 7, 1965, p. 4. National Liberation Front:

PR, 1965, no. 46, pp. 35–36. Malayan Communist Party: *PR*, 1965, no. 19, p. 6. Malayan National Liberation League: *PR*, 1965, no. 27, pp. 18–20.

d A mission from the Malayan National Liberation League arrived in China just after the close of 1965, in January, 1966, and established a permanent office. See *PR*, 1966, no. 4, pp. 3–4; and *JMJP*, May 7, 1966, p. 6.

e *JMJP*, December 15, 1965, p. 3, announced that the Thailand Independence Movement had decided to become a part of the Thailand Patriotic Front, so by the end of 1965 there remained only the one organization, the Thailand Patriotic Front.

defense and its relations with the Soviet Union.[42] The debate was finally resolved, it seems, with a decision to limit Chinese support for Vietnam to giving material aid to both the North and the South and providing Chinese construction battalions and later even Chinese military forces to aid in the defense of the North.[43] Peking made it clear that the Chinese were not eager to risk American retaliation against the mainland by intervening directly in the Vietnamese war, but this did not mean that Peking would not intervene at some future point if China's national security were to become compromised in the process of subsequent escalations of the war.

Elsewhere in Southeast Asia, Chinese actions implied that Peking had sharply divided the countries of Southeast Asia into friends and enemies. Of the nine countries of the area, four (all of which maintained diplomatic relations with Peking) were treated as close friends: North Vietnam, Cambodia, Burma, and Indonesia (before the October 1 coup attempt). Four others were endorsed as legitimate targets for revolution: South Vietnam, Thailand, Malaysia, and the Philippines. Laos fell in between; Peking both maintained a diplomatic mission in Vientiane accredited to the official government and, at the same time, publicly supported a revolutionary alternative to it.

The dilemma in Laos stemmed from the breaking apart of the neutralist coalition government which had been set up in 1962 as a result of the Geneva Conference on Laos, and which was based on the sharing of political power between three factions (right, left, and neutralist), with neutralist Prince Souvanna Phouma as premier. Less than a year after the agreements had been concluded in Geneva, the various factions had once again become engaged in violent competition, and an intermittent state of war had resumed in Laos. During

42 See the essays by Uri Ra'anan and Donald Zagoria in Tang Tsou, ed., *China in Crisis* (Chicago: University of Chicago Press, 1968).

43 See *NYT*, December 1, 1965, p. 1; *San Francisco Chronicle*, July 2, 1966, p. 6, and August 12, 1966, p. 1; and *CSM*, March 8, 1967, p. 4, and April 18, 1968, p. 1.

1965 Chinese policy constantly reiterated support for the government as originally constituted under the Geneva agreements, as a neutral coalition government; but, in the meantime, Peking supported the revolutionary efforts of the left faction under the leadership of Prince Souphanouvong and the Neo Lao Haksat.[44] For example, at the same time he was publicly supporting Souphanouvong's revolutionary activities, Liu Shao-ch'i, chairman of the People's Republic of China, in May 1965 sent the following polite message to the king of Laos: "On the occasion of the National Day of the Kingdom of Laos, I extend my warm greetings to Your Majesty and the Laotian people. I wish prosperity to your country and happiness to your people. May the friendship between the Chinese and Laotian peoples develop daily."[45] Symbolic of this paradoxical policy, Peking maintained two separate diplomatic missions in Laos: an embassy accredited to the royal government in Vientiane and a "Chinese Economic and Cultural Mission" in the Neo Lao Haksat "liberated areas."

Chinese policy with regard to the other countries of Southeast Asia where Peking had endorsed revolution was considerably less ambiguous. Since its inception, Malaysia had been under attack by China and Indonesia and had been described by Peking as "a dagger thrust in the heart of Southeast Asia by the US and British imperialists" and "an implement of old and new colonialism."[46] Cooperating closely with Djakarta, the Chinese considered the peoples of northern Borneo (or so-called North Kalimantan) and those of the Malay Peninsula (the people living in Malaya and Singapore) to be different peoples deserving separate states. Appropriately, it supported

[44] See, for example, the article by "Commentator" in *JMJP*, June 23, 1965, and translated in *PR*, 1965, no. 26, p. 11; and the report of the Chinese Foreign Ministry statement of January 20, 1965, in *PR*, 1965, no. 4, p. 4. For a description of the war in Laos, see Zalin Grant, "Report from Laos: The Hidden War," *New Republic*, April 20, 1968, pp. 17–19; and for a Neo Lao Haksat view of the recent history of Laos, see *20 Years of Lao People's Revolutionary Struggle* (Neo Lao Haksat Publications, 1966).
[45] NCNA (English), May 10, 1965, in *SCMP*, no. 3457, p. 37.
[46] *PR*, 1965, no. 3, p. 14.

separate national liberation organizations for the two areas: the North Kalimantan Unitary State Revolutionary Government for North Kalimantan, and the Malayan National Liberation League and the Malayan Communist Party for Malaya and Singapore. All three organizations received public Chinese support,[47] and the Malayan National Liberation League was invited to establish a permanent diplomatic mission in Peking. Working in concert with Indonesia (until October 1965 when events in Indonesia brought about a drastic change in that country's foreign policy), Peking apparently hoped to split the Malaysian Federation in two and eventually see revolutionary governments established in both sections.

In Thailand there had been some sporadic terrorist activity in earlier years, but in 1965 full-scale guerrilla warfare was begun against the Bangkok government. Reports from Thailand's vulnerable northeastern region drew parallels between the situation there in 1965 and that which had existed early in the Vietnamese conflict.[48] The Chinese press described Thailand as a "bridgehead of US aggression against Indo-China,"[49] and Thai revolutionaries called it a "new-type colony."[50] The *Jen-min jih-pao* increasingly published reports of antigovernment activities in Thailand and quotations from radio broadcasts by "The Voice of the Thai People," a radio station thought to be located in either North Vietnam or China.[51] During the year, two new Thai revolutionary organizations appeared, both of which received rapid recognition by Peking. In December Peking announced that they had been merged into one; the original Thailand Independence Movement was reported to have resolved on the first anniversary of its founding (November 1, 1965) to become a part of the second organi-

[47] Malayan Communist Party, *PR*, 1965, no. 19, p. 6; the North Kalimantan Unitary State Revolutionary Government, *SCMP*, no. 3555, p. 38; and the Malayan National Liberation League, *PR*, 1966, no. 4, p. 3.

[48] See, for example, NYT (international edition), May 17, 1965, p. 2; *CSM*, November 30, 1965, p. 15.

[49] *PR*, 1965, no. 42, pp. 8–9.

[50] *SCMP*, no. 3443, pp. 34–35.

[51] *NYT*, December 16, 1965, p. 5.

zation, the Thailand Patriotic Front.[52] The frequency and tone of Chinese press reports through the year made it obvious that Peking looked upon Thailand as an important new site of revolutionary activity in Southeast Asia.

New guerrilla activity was also reported in the Philippines during 1965. Communist rebels of the original Hukbalahap movement against the Japanese had developed into a formidable revolutionary force in the years after Philippine independence, but had subsequently been almost entirely wiped out by government initiatives taken under the leadership of Ramon Magsaysay during the middle 1950s. Now there was a resurgence of revolutionary activity; and although there was as yet little comment in the Chinese press, it seemed clear that any organization which appeared successful in fielding a guerrilla force against the Manila government would be likely to receive Peking's blessings.[53]

The two remaining Asian countries endorsed by the Chinese as proper targets for revolution in 1965 were both located on the southern tip of the Arabian peninsula: Aden (subsequently to become independent South Yemen) and Oman. Little was said in the Chinese press of the guerrilla war being fought (apparently under the leadership of the Dhofar Liberation Front) for the independence of Oman from the British-"protected" sultanate of Musquat and Oman;[54] but occasional Chinese reports encouragingly made mention of the revolutionary activities of both the Front for the Liberation of Occupied South Yemen (FLOSY) and the National Liberation Front, the major organizations engaged in trying to expel British rule from the colony of Aden and the protectorate of the South Arabian Federation.[55]

---

[52] *JMJP*, December 15, 1965, p. 3.

[53] See *CSM*, July 18, 1966, p. 10; *San Francisco Chronicle*, July 26, 1966, p. 11; and Denis Warner, "President Marcos and the Huk Resurgence," *Reporter*, November 3, 1966, pp. 28–31.

[54] *CSM*, May 5, 1966, p. 7.

[55] Aden ultimately became independent on November 28, 1967 (*NYT*, November 29, 1967, p. 11) and shortly thereafter established diplomatic relations with Peking (*JMJP*, February 3, 1968, p. 1).

Africa

If Asia took first importance in Peking's assessment of the revolutionary potentialities of the underdeveloped world, Africa (see Table 3) came in a close second. An analysis published in the secret People's Liberation Army journal *Kung-tso t'ung-hsun* in April 1961 declared that "The center of the struggle against colonialism is in Africa; the center of the battle between East and West for the intermediate zone is in Africa; hence, Africa has become the focus of contemporary world problems."[56] This assessment, in turn, was confirmed by Premier Chou En-lai's announcement on his visit to Somalia in Febuary 1964 that "Revolutionary prospects are excellent throughout the African continent."[57]

Actually, the Peking government's assessment of the political situation in Africa seemed to be based on its perception of the instability in that continent resulting from extremely rapid and widespread decolonization during the early 1960s, rather than on any firm belief in the immediate likelihood of socialist revolution in Africa. Of the three continents of the underdeveloped world, Africa in 1965 was clearly the most politically unstable, the most potentially explosive, and the most vulnerable to outside influence. The reasons for this are fairly obvious. Africa was undergoing social and political change at a fantastic rate of speed. New states were being established almost daily (twenty-seven in the six years from 1960 through 1965); already independent governments were struggling to form nations out of their heterogeneous populations and build viable political systems; and in the South, their African brothers were still fighting, in the jungles and on the streets, to win their independence from unbending colonial and white supremacist regimes. National boundaries based on colonial divisions made for border disputes and even border wars, and tribal and ideological differences created domestic

[56] *Kung-tso t'ung-hsun*, No. 17, April 25, 1961, p. 22.
[57] *Afro-Asian Solidarity Against Imperialism* (Peking: Foreign Languages Press, 1964), p. 274.

TABLE 3

CHINA'S RELATIONS WITH MAJOR AFRICAN REVOLUTIONARY ORGANIZATIONS, 1965

Endorsed Revolution	Revolutionary Organization	Permanent Mission in China	Delegation Visited China in 1965a	Mentioned in Chinese Pressb
Congo (Leopoldville)	Congo (L) Supreme Council of Revolution		x	x
Portuguese Africa: Angola	Angola People's Liberation Movement (MPLA)		x	x
	Angola National Liberation Army			x
Guinea —	African Independence Party of Guinea and the Cape Verde Islands (PAIGC)			x
Mozambique	Mozambique Liberation Front (FRELIMO)		x	x
	Mozambique National Democratic Union (UDENAMO)			
	Mozambique Revolutionary Committee (COREMO)		x	x

a Congo (L) Supreme Council of Revolution: PR, 1965, no. 35, p. 5. Angola People's Liberation Movement: SCMP, no. 3447, p. 27. Mozambique Liberation Front: SCMP, no. 3436, p. 34. Mozambique Revolutionary Committee: SCMP, no. 3510, p. 32.

note a.) Angola National Liberation Army: JMJP, August 13, 1965, p. 4. African Independence Party of Guinea and the Cape Verde Islands: JMJP, August 13, 1965, p. 4. Mozambique National Democratic Union: JMJP, May 31, 1965, p. 3.

b (Sources cited only for those organizations not referred to in and international conflicts. An indication of the vulnerability of the new governments to internal disruption is the fact that, in the nine months from June 1965 to March 1966, there were violent changes of government in seven, or almost 20 percent, of the thirty-seven independent African states—Algeria, Congo (Leopoldville), Dahomey, Central African Republic, Upper Volta, Nigeria, and Ghana—plus suspension of the constitution and seizure of special powers by President Obote in Uganda and a unilateral declaration of independence from Britain by the white supremacist government of Rhodesia.

Following the CCP victory in 1949, the first official Chinese diplomatic mission was posted to Africa in 1956 when Egypt (now the United Arab Republic) agreed to establish relations with Peking. By the end of 1960, China had established diplomatic relations with seven African countries and, by the end of 1965, with seventeen governments. Peking had long supported the anti-imperialist and anticolonial movements in Africa and frequently pointed to the Algerian example as a model for African political development. Apparently both the protracted and violent nature of the Algerian Revolution and the leadership of Algerian President Ben Bella appealed to the Chinese. It often seemed as though Peking was hopeful that Ahmed Ben Bella, like Fidel Castro, might decide one day to steer his country away from nonalignment and into the communist camp,[58] thus establishing the first communist government on African soil. As late as December 1964, these hopes still appeared strong in Peking when Chou En-lai, reporting to the National People's Congress, spoke of the Algerian Revolution as "a brilliant example for the national-liberation movement in Africa."[59] But several months later, after the fall of Ben Bella, the rise of the more conservative Boumedienne, and the postponement of the Algiers summit conference, Algeria seemed to have lost its appeal for the

[58] Burmese Communist Party documents indicate that some Chinese leaders had at least thought of this kind of possibility with regard to Ne Win. PR, 1967, no. 36, p. 20.

[59] PR, 1965, no. 1, p. 18.

Chinese and to have fallen from its eminence as a "brilliant example" for Africa.[60]

By 1965 the only areas in Africa that had not won their national independence were the Spanish Sahara, small colonial enclaves on the east and west coasts (under French, Spanish, and Portuguese rule), and the extensive territories of southern Africa, including Angola, Mozambique, Southwest Africa, Bechuanaland, Basutoland, and Swaziland.[61] South Africa and Rhodesia were both perhaps technically independent but were also colonies in the sense that their governments were remnants of former colonial regimes and controlled by white supremacist minorities. Characteristic of British colonial policy since World War II, London was preparing to withdraw from its remaining territories in Africa; but Portugal and the governments of Rhodesia and South Africa remained adamant in their refusal to consider African self-determination.

Repressive police measures in South Africa had thus far been successful in preventing the outbreak of armed struggle in both that country and its protectorate, Southwest Africa; and the initial reaction of African nationalist leaders in Rhodesia (which they call Zimbabwe) to the white settlers' Unilateral Declaration of Independence from Britain on November 11, 1965, had been nonviolent opposition rather than armed struggle.

In the Portuguese territories of Guinea, Angola, and Mozambique, however, the situation was quite different. Armed struggle against the colonial government of Guinea erupted in January 1963; and by the end of 1965 it was estimated that the rebels, led by the African Independence Party of Guinea and the Cape Verde Islands (PAIGC), controlled at least 30

[60] See, for example, the almost impolite (when compared with usual Chinese greetings) message sent by Liu Shao-ch'i and Chou En-lai to Houari Boumedienne on October 31, 1965, on the eleventh anniversary of the Algerian Revolution, translated in *PR*, 1965, no. 45, p. 3.

[61] Bechuanaland, Basutoland, and Swaziland subsequently gained independence as the sovereign states of Botswana (September 1966), Lesotho (October 1966), and Swaziland (September 1968).

percent of the country. Estimates of the strength of the rebel forces varied from 5,000 to 15,000, but separate sources agreed that Lisbon had committed some 20,000 troops backed by air and naval support to suppress the revolution.[62] PAIGC, which operated from the sanctuary of the neighboring state of Guinea, was reported to be led by a Cape Verde agronomist, Amilcar Cabral, and to have received support from both African and communist nations, and also from the African Liberation Committee of the Organization of African Unity.[63] The degree of Chinese support for the PAIGC was unclear, but Chinese press reports often mentioned the organization[64] and delegations from the organization had visited China.[65] A competing nationalist organization, Fight for the National Independence of Guinea, was reported to be based in neighboring Senegal to the north; but it was apparently not engaged in armed struggle.[66]

By 1965 rebel forces in Angola had been waging a sporadic guerrilla war against Portuguese colonialism for four years, longest of any of the three armed struggles against Portuguese rule in Africa. Peking had continually endorsed the revolutionary effort to win independence for Angola and neighboring Cabinda; and on February 4, 1965, the fourth anniversary of the uprising, the Chinese celebrated Angola Day throughout the country.[67] The leadership of the Angolan revolution had been divided into factions from the beginning. During the year, the Chinese press mentioned two major revolutionary organizations: the Angola People's Liberation Movement

[62] Cooley, *East Wind over Africa*, pp. 129–132; and *CSM*, December 2, 1965, p. 10.

[63] *CSM*, December 2, 1965, p. 10.

[64] See, for example, *JMJP*, January 31, 1965, p. 4; *JMJP*, February 21, 1965, p. 5.

[65] For example, Aristides Pereira, member of the Political Bureau and Deputy General Secretary of the party, led a delegation to China and attended the National Day celebrations on October 1, 1964. *PR*, 1964, no. 41, p. 7.

[66] *CSM*, December 2, 1965, p. 10. For more recent reports of guerrilla activity in Spanish Guinea, see *CSM*, January 12, 1968, p. 1, and *NYT*, January 15, 1968, p. 12.

[67] *JMJP*, February 4, 1965, p. 3.

(MPLA) and the Angola National Liberation Army which is apparently the military arm of Holden Roberto's Revolutionary Government of Angola in Exile.[68] Recent discoveries of vast amounts of oil in Cabinda would seem to assure that the Portuguese will fight even more tenaciously to maintain their hold on these important territories.[69]

Mozambique, the most populous of Portugal's African territories, was the last to rise in revolt—in the fall of 1964. The major revolutionary organization in Mozambique, the Mozambique Liberation Front (FRELIMO) with headquarters in the Tanzanian capital of Dar es Salaam, had proclaimed a general armed insurrection against Portuguese colonial rule on September 25, 1964;[70] and guerrillas, operating mainly in the northern provinces and from bases across the border in Tanzania, had waged armed struggle with mixed results since then. Peking proclaimed a Day of Solidarity with the Mozambique People on the first anniversary of the revolution and fervently declared Chinese support for the "just struggle" of the Mozambique people.[71] Chinese press reports on the Mozambique hostilities spoke of FRELIMO and two other revolutionary organizations: the Mozambique National Democratic Union (UNDENAMO), the oldest of the three organizations, and the Mozambique Revolutionary Committee (COREMO), reportedly formed in the summer of 1965 by consolidating three smaller liberation organizations.[72] Peking consistently and explicitly endorsed armed struggle in each of the three Portuguese territories and had apparently developed contacts with all the major revolutionary organizations, many of which had sent delegations to Peking. However, the full extent of Chinese material support for the various organizations is not known.

Yet, for Peking the most important armed struggle in Africa

---

[68] See Cooley, *East Wind over Africa*, pp. 124–129.
[69] See *NYT*, September 20, 1967, p. 61, and July 7, 1968, p. 3.
[70] *PR*, 1965, no. 39, p. 31.
[71] NCNA, September 24, 1965, in *SCMP*, no. 3547, p. 35.
[72] *El Moudjahid* (Algiers), June 27, 1965, p. 5.

in 1965 was not in any of the colonial areas but rather in independent Congo (Leopoldville), where civil war had raged intermittently since the initial army mutiny in 1960. The rebels by mid-1964 had gained control of roughly one-fifth of the country[73] and had won broad international support in their vigorous opposition to the widely despised Tshombe government, supported in power by white mercenary troops recruited from South Africa and other colonial areas of Africa. The high point of this stage of the Congolese insurrection for Peking was the US-Belgian intervention in the Congo in November 1964 which provoked a virtual storm of protest throughout Africa. Peking attempted to capitalize on the incident with a worldwide propaganda campaign, featuring a statement on the Congo by Chairman Mao.

By the spring of 1965, however, Leopoldville government forces were having increasing success in bringing the insurrection under control; and as the fortunes of the rebels declined, so, too, did their outside African support. The revolutionary movement began to crumble. Under the pressure of the Leopoldville suppression, the rebel leadership splintered into several factional organizations. In April, Gaston Soumialot, a major figure in the insurrection, organized the Supreme Council of Revolution in an apparently futile attempt to bring other Congolese revolutionary leaders (such as Christophe Gbenye and Pierre Mulele) into a single unified organization; and in August (by which time many Congolese revolutionaries were seeking refuge in exile) Soumialot led a delegation from the Supreme Council to Peking where he was received by Mao Tse-tung and other Chinese leaders.[74] Throughout 1965 and early 1966, Peking continued to publish glowing reports of armed activities in the Congo, but these appeared more hopeful than factual—especially after Tshombe was deposed in October 1965 and the Leopoldville government began to alter

[73] Cooley, *East Wind over Africa*, p. 118.
[74] *SCMP*, no. 3524, pp. 22–24, and no. 3528, p. 22. For the Chinese view of the Supreme Council and its activities at that time, see *JMJP*, November 28, 1965, p. 5.

its domestic and foreign policies in an active effort to win
domestic popular support and the endorsement of neighboring African governments.[75]

Latin America

From Peking's point of view and in terms of Chinese press
coverage, the continent that received lowest priority among
the three continents of the underdeveloped world in 1965
was Latin America (see Table 4). Geography was part of the
reason. Whereas the nearest point in Africa was some two
thousand miles from China's borders, Latin America was virtually on the other side of the globe. Government policy was
another reason. Latin American governments had staunchly
maintained anti-communist and pro-US foreign policies; and
no country in the American hemisphere, except Cuba, had
agreed to establish diplomatic relations with Peking. What is
more, in spite of a history of often oppressive and dictatorial
governments on the one hand and militant leftist activism in
the universities on the other, Latin American societies had
generally remained quite stable; attempts to mold the lowest
strata of society into a revolutionary force had usually met
with little enthusiasm. The various Latin American governments effectively controlled the cities and most of the countryside of their nations in spite of extensive poverty, unem-
ployment, and discontent. In the rural areas, US-supported
counterinsurgency measures and the traditionalism and suspi-
cion of destitute Indian populations combined to place great
obstacles in the path of those who sought to overturn the social
and political order in the American hemisphere. Moreover,
Latin America generally lacked the single condition that
had most contributed to the development of contemporary
revolutions in Asia and Africa—direct, foreign colonial domination. National independence having been won long ago in
Latin America, oligarchic oppression and widespread human

[75] See, for example, the extremely interesting report in the *NYT*, July 1,
1966, p. 2, of General Mobutu's Independence Day speech and the new official
policy of the Congolese government.

misery in the contemporary setting had not yet created the conditions under which revolutionaries could effectively mobilize the populations of Latin American countries to take up arms against their governments.

Nevertheless, this did not mean that the Chinese had overlooked the strategic importance of Latin America nor had they become resigned to the status quo in the area—quite the contrary. Peking spoke of the countries south of the Rio Grande as being the "backyard" (*hou yuan*) of the United States[76] upon which the US was economically and strategically dependent; and the Chinese wrote hopefully of lighting fires of revolution in Washington's Latin American backyard, pointing to the case of Cuba as proof that it could be done. The Chinese apparently felt that they had little to lose and everything to gain by generally pursuing a revolutionary policy in Latin America. Chile, Mexico, and Argentina had developed some degree of semiofficial contact and trade with mainland China, but they had not been willing to break away from the official Latin American line of opposition to Peking; the Chinese were probably skeptical about how durable even semiofficial ties might be, considering their recent experience in Brazil after the overthrow of the Goulart regime.[77] Moreover, Chinese contacts with Latin America were being increasingly restricted by 1965. The United States and Latin American governments, fearful of the example set by the Cuban Revolution and the active efforts being made by Havana to export revolution to the Americas, had moved to

[76] See, for example, *SCCS*, 1965, no. 3, p. 13.

[77] Following the overthrow of the liberal Goulart government in the spring of 1964, nine Chinese citizens, members of the New China News Agency and the China Council for the Promotion of International Trade staffs in Brazil, were arrested by the new military government and charged with espionage. The Chinese government demanded their release and claimed that the arrested Chinese were being framed by the Brazilian government which, Peking said, was plotting with the United States and the Chinese Nationalist government to discredit Peking. The Chinese Communists continuously agitated for the release of the nine Chinese during the following year and made the incident a major propaganda issue. Finally, in April 1965, the nine men were released and returned to China.

TABLE 4

CHINA'S RELATIONS WITH MAJOR LATIN AMERICAN REVOLUTIONARY ORGANIZATIONS, 1965

Endorsed Revolution	Revolutionary Organization	Permanent Mission in China	Delegation Visited China in 1965[a]	Mentioned in Chinese Press[b]
Argentina	—			
Bolivia	—			
Brazil	Communist Party of Brazil			x
Colombia	Communist Party of Colombia			x
	National Liberation Army (ELN)			x
	United Front Movement (Frente Unido del Pueblo)			x
Dominican Republic	June 14 Revolutionary Movement			x
	Dominican People's Movement			x
Guatemala	Alejandro de Leon November 13 Revolutionary Movement (MR-13)			x
Haiti				
Honduras	Revolutionary Liberation Movement			x
Nicaragua	Sandino National Liberation Front			x
Paraguay	Commander Lopez Guerrilla Force			x
Peru	Peruvian Communist Party			x
	Movement of the Revolutionary Left (MIR)			x
	Revolutionary Students Front			x
Venezuela	Communist Party of Venezuela (PCV)		x	x
	National Liberation Armed Forces (FALN)			x
	Movement of the Revolutionary Left (MIR)			x

a Communist Party of Venezuela: SCMP, no. 3531, p. 44.
b Communist Party of Brazil: JMJP, May 23, 1965, p. 5. Communist Party of Colombia: JMJP, August 13, 1965, p. 3. National Liberation Army: JMJP, March 23, 1965, p. 5. United Front Movement: PR, 1966, no. 11, p. 28. June 14 Revolutionary Movement and the Dominican People's Movement: JMJP, December 25, 1965, p. 4. Alejandro de Leon November 13 Revolutionary Movement: SCCS, 1965, no. 21, p. 19. Revolutionary Liberation Movement: SCCS, 1965, no. 18, p. 22. Sandino National Liberation Front. SCCS, 1965, no. 19, p. 29. Commander Lopez Guerrilla Force: SCCS, 1965, no. 17, p. 29. Peruvian Communist Party: JMJP, December 16, 1965, p. 4. Movement of the Revolutionary Left: JMJP, June 22, 1965, p. 5. Revolutionary Students Front: JMJP, August 6, 1965, p. 4. Communist Party of Venezuela, National Liberation Armed Forces, and Movement of the Revolutionary Left: SCCS, 1965, no. 1, ...

tighten security measures and isolate the hemisphere from communist influence to the greatest extent possible. China's relations with Latin America had suffered as a result. Also, Peking's relations with Havana were deteriorating in 1965,[78] making for additional difficulties in Chinese contacts with the Americas.

Inevitably, the Cuban experience had had a profound impact on the development of revolutionary movements in Latin America. If they identified with any foreign country at all, most of the organizations actually leading armed struggles in Latin America during 1965 acknowledged their inspirational or ideological debt to Havana rather than to Moscow or Peking. The possible applicability of Chinese military strategy and guerrilla warfare tactics was recognized; but for a revolutionary model, Latin American revolutionaries seemed to prefer one closer to home, one which symbolized a successful effort to deal with Latin American social and political problems.

Actually, the Cuban precedent has had an ambivalent effect on contemporary revolutions in Latin America. Fidel Castro demonstrated that a revolution in the American hemisphere which opposed the United States could succeed and be defended, and in this sense he has inspired the confidence of revolutionaries throughout the hemisphere. But the Castro revolution—its leadership having converted to communism and adopted a socialist domestic policy and an anti-US foreign policy[79]—has, on the other hand, also provided the US govern-

[78] See Daniel Tretiak, "China and Latin America," *Current Scene*, March 1, 1966.

[79] The Cuban revolutionary experience adds an interesting twist to Mao's theory of new democratic revolution, which conceives of a single CP-dominated multiclass leadership guiding the revolution through both its "national democratic" and "socialist" stages, as opposed to the classical Marxist-Leninist view of revolutionary development, in which the bourgeoisie leads the national democratic stage and the CP the socialist stage. The Cuban Revolution was a combination of both. When Castro led the national democratic stage of the revolution, he was a bourgeois nationalist; but after completing the national democratic stage, he converted to communism to lead the socialist stage. The leadership of both stages, therefore, was the same, Castro; but it was also

ment with a handy "negative example" of what could happen
if contemporary revolutions in Latin America were successful.
The lesson the US government chose to draw from the Cuban
experience is plainly demonstrated by the great emphasis in
military aid to Latin America on counterinsurgency warfare,
and by the military intervention in the Dominican Republic
in April 1965. Moreover, apparently the middle classes in
Latin America have kept close watch on the experience of the
Cuban bourgeoisie under the Castro regime, and it seems
clear that they have generally decided (with the immensely
important exception of certain middle class intellectuals) that
their best interests would not be served by armed revolutions
in their own countries.

As for communist parties, they have existed for many years
in Latin America. Unlike Africa, where there are very few
indigenous communist parties, Latin America has a long tradition of Moscow-dominated communist movements. However, in 1965, Latin American CP's were generally not the
organizations that were leading the revolutions. As in the case
of Cuba, the revolutions had begun independently, and the
traditional communist parties were either disclaiming the
revolutionaries or dashing madly to catch up with them.

The Latin American communist movement at this time was
also suffering from a malady common to almost all the organizations in the international communist movement, that is,
intraparty factional struggles reflecting the Sino-Soviet dispute
and the centrifugal nationalist tendencies within the worldwide movement. Latin American communist parties had generally been firmly pro-Moscow and usually committed to
policies of parliamentary cooperation or peaceful struggle
rather than to strategies involving revolutionary violence. But
by 1965, debates within the various parties over both domestic
strategy and international allegiance had begun to produce
important divisions in several organizations; and of the twelve

different, because in terms of Marxist interpretations at the time, Castro represented different classes during the two different stages.

Latin American countries in which Peking endorsed revolutons in 1965, the communist parties of four (Brazil, Colombia, Paraguay, and Peru) had already split along pro-Peking, pro-Moscow lines.

Peking's approach to the new pro-Peking splinter parties seems to be based on two separate considerations: Chinese support for Latin American revolutions and the Sino-Soviet dispute.[80] Initially, the appearance of new pro-Peking communist parties in Latin America presented the Chinese with the opportunity to gain greater influence within the traditional communist movement in the American hemisphere and to muster additional support for the Chinese position in Peking's dispute with Moscow. However, in most cases the pro-Peking CP's were not in control of the more effective revolutionary efforts in Latin America; if the Chinese wanted to maintain contact with the revolutionary movements in the hemisphere, they also had to develop relations with non-CP revolutionary leaders. As a result, in 1965 Peking appeared to be cultivating pro-Chinese CP elements in Latin America mainly for the purpose of the Sino-Soviet dispute, while giving credit in the official press to almost all of those non-CP revolutionary organizations that were actually leading armed struggles, no doubt hoping eventually to merge the two, CP and non-CP, into unified national front organizations under pro-Peking CP leadership.

In all, Peking endorsed revolutions in a total of twelve Latin American countries during 1965. However, only in five of the twelve were significant armed struggles actually being carried on during the year.

So little was published in the Chinese press about many of the Latin American revolutions that it is sometimes difficult to get a clear picture of Peking's view of them. However, several themes are repeated time and again: that the governments under attack are tools of US "neo-colonialism"; that the coun-

[80] As was mentioned earlier (see p. 128, n. 33), Ernst Halperin argues that Chinese policy in Latin America was actually focused almost exclusively on anti-Soviet efforts within the communist movement.

tries in which revolutions have occurred are "semifeudal" and "semicolonial" societies; and that armed struggle against local authorities and the United States is the only way to solve local problems. Moreover, the political programs of the pro-Peking communist parties, reprinted in the Chinese press, consistently called for the unification of the various national revolutionary movements under the framework of a patriotic liberation front and unwaveringly proclaimed a strategy of armed struggle.[81]

With regard to the five countries—Colombia, the Dominican Republic, Guatemala, Peru, and Venezuela—in which a good deal of revolutionary activity was going on during 1965, Peking usually quite accurately mentioned not one but several revolutionary organizations as active in the struggle. However, Chinese press reports generally implied a much greater degree of unity among the various revolutionary organizations than actually existed and usually overstated CP participation (pro-Peking CP's gave verbal support to armed struggle but were rarely involved in the fighting); but the reports also gave credit to non-CP revolutionary organizations.

By 1965, probably the longest continuous armed struggle in Latin America and the one in which there was the least unity and central authority among the rebels was that being waged in Colombia. Originally begun in 1948 as a dispute between feuding Liberals and Conservatives, Colombia's *la violencia* subsequently involved a variety of organizations, Marxist and otherwise.[82] Chinese press reports in 1965 generally spoke of three major revolutionary organizations: the pro-Peking Communist Party of Colombia and its subsidiary united front organization, the Patriotic Front for Liberation; the National

[81] See the following for statements of the programs of the pro-Peking Communist Party of Brazil, Communist Party of Columbia, and Peruvian Communist Party, respectively: *JMJP*, May 23, 1965, p. 5; *JMJP*, August 13, 1965, p. 3; and *JMJP*, December 16, 1965, p. 4.

[82] See *CSM*, January 14, 1966, p. 9; *NYT*, July 6, 1966, p. 16; and Adolfo Gilly, "Guerrillas and 'Peasant Republics' in Colombia," *MR*, October 1965, pp. 30–40.

Liberation Army, or Ejercito de Liberacion Nacional (ELN); and Father Camilo Torres' United Front Movement, or Frente Unido del Pueblo. All three organizations had been actively seeking to bring the national revolutionary movement under central control but apparently with little success. Camilo Torres, a radical young Catholic priest, was killed during a raid in February 1966, after having spent only a few months working in the hills with the guerrillas.[83]

In April 1965 when a group of young army officers attempted to overthrow the government of the Dominican Republic, Peking was not long in declaring its support. And when US troops were sent to intervene in the Dominican insurrection, China responded with a resounding barrage of propaganda; Mao made a statement, and cities of mainland China reverberated with the sounds of demonstrations of Chinese support for the Dominican people against US aggression. What appeared most significant to the Chinese about the Dominican insurrection was apparently that in the Dominican Republic—as in Vietnam and the Congo—"the people" were directly confronted by US forces, and the issue could be sharply defined as one of direct aggression by US imperialism. The Chinese press discussed Francisco Caamano Deno and other major figures in the conflict, but generally referred to the struggle as one led by the "patriotic army and people of the Dominican Republic." When specific organizations were mentioned, they were usually the June 14 Revolutionary Movement and the Dominican People's Movement, both generally considered to be either independent or pro-Castro communist organizations.[84]

In contrast, the armed struggle in Guatemala received little attention in the Chinese press. During 1965, the guerrilla war in that Central American country seemed to be gaining

[83] For a biographical eulogy of Camilo Torres, see *Ramparts*, April 1966, pp. 23–28.
[84] See "The State of the [Communist] Parties," *Survey*, January 1965, pp. 190–196; Bureau of Intelligence and Research, US Department of State, *World Strength of the Communist Party Organizations*, 18th annual report (January 1966), pp. 152–154.

ground in its battle to overthrow the Guatemalan government, and a series of audacious kidnappings of prominent commercial and political leaders brought the revolutionaries much notoriety. The Chinese press reported that several guerrilla organizations were operating in the Guatemalan countryside, but implied that they were all unified under the general leadership of the Alejandro de Leon November 13 Revolutionary Movement (MR–13).[85] It did not, however, mention a competing revolutionary organization, Fuerzas Armadas de la Revolucion (FAR), led by former army lieutenant Luis Augusto Turcios Lima, which had originally been a part of MR–13 but had broken away to form a separate organization in 1964.[86] The revolutionary program of MR–13 had prompted a good deal of interest, because MR–13 had departed from the customary concept of national democratic revolution and called for an outright socialist movement to be based on an alliance of workers and peasants and to exclude the bourgeoisie. MR–13's attempt to wage a war of national liberation on the basis of an explicitly socialist revolutionary program was hailed by some Marxists[87] but denounced by others, including Fidel Castro, as a Trotskyite heresy.[88]

With regard to Peru, the Chinese press had properly given credit to the Movement of the Revolutionary Left (MIR) and its leader, Luis de la Puente Uceda, as being the initiating force behind the armed struggle being waged in the Peruvian Andes;[89] but Peking also spoke hopefully of the role of the

[85] SCCS, 1965, no. 21, pp. 18–19.

[86] The fact that the pro-Moscow Guatemalan Communist Party (PGT) had joined forces with the FAR during 1965 may help to explain why the Chinese press ignored the FAR. See Régis Debray, "Revolution in the Revolution?" pp. 37–41; and NYT, March 18, 1966, p. 17. Turcios Lima, head of the FAR, was subsequently killed in an automobile accident and was succeeded in command by Cesar Montes. NYT, October 4, 1966, p. 18.

[87] See the editorial in MR, May 1965, and Adolfo Gilly, "The Guerrilla Movement in Guatemala," MR, May and June 1965.

[88] Ernst Halperin, "Peking and the Latin American Communists," p. 149.

[89] For the MIR's program, see Luis F. de la Puente Uceda, "The Peruvian Revolution: Concepts and Perspectives," MR, November 1965, pp. 12–28. For background articles on the revolution, see also CSM, January 28, 1966, p. 9; San Francisco Chronicle, April 25, 1965, p. 11S; and Arnold Payne, "Peru's Guerrilla Politics," New Leader, October 11, 1965, pp. 11–14.

pro-Peking Peruvian Communist Party and an organization called the Revolutionary Students Front.[90] However, in October 1965, the guerrilla movement was destroyed and de la Puente Uceda killed by government forces.[91]

Finally, in discussing the armed struggle in Venezuela, Peking described the relationships among the various revolutionary organizations as follows:

The general name of the Venezuelan people's armed forces is the National Liberation Army [FALN]. It was organized from the workers, peasants, students, free professional people, and the patriotic army, the best sons and daughters of the Venezuelan people. Under the leadership of the National Liberation Front [FLN], which was organized with the Communist Party of Venezuela [PCV] and the Movement of the Revolutionary Left [MIR] as the principal powers, the National Liberation Army has gone from have-not to have, from little to big, continually developing and enlarging.[92]

The organizations mentioned in the Chinese analysis were indeed the principal parties active in the Venezuelan revolutionary situation; but contrary to Peking's interpretation, the PCV, the MIR, and the FALN all appear at times to have operated quite independently, and none seems to have had "principal power" over any of the others. Moreover, it is not entirely clear whether the political arm of the FALN, the FLN which was apparently established in 1965, ever assumed the political functions for which it was intended.[93] Characteristic of Chinese commentaries on revolutionary situations in Latin America, Peking's analyst implied a greater degree of unity within the revolutionary movement, and attributed a

[90] See, for example, *JMJP*, June 22, 1965, p. 5; *JMJP*, August 8, 1965, p. 4; and *Evergreen*, 1966, No. 2, pp. 30–31.

[91] Norman Gall, "Peru's Misfired Guerrilla Campaign," *Reporter*, January 26, 1967, pp. 36–38.

[92] *SCCS*, 1965, no. 1, p. 12.

[93] James D. Cockcroft and Eduardo Vicente, "Venezuela and the FALN Since Leoni," *MR*, November 1965, pp. 29–40. For a more extensive discussion of Venezuelan revolutionary organizations, especially their international relations, see D. Bruce Jackson, *Castro, the Kremlin, and Communism in Latin America* (Baltimore: John Hopkins Press, 1969), particularly chapters 5 and 7.

more influential political role to the communist party, than actually existed.

In addition to the five armed struggles already discussed, Peking endorsed revolutions in seven other Latin American countries during the year: in Brazil, Bolivia, and Haiti where there had been some violence but no sustained revolutionary activity, and in Argentina, Honduras, Nicaragua, and Paraguay where there had apparently been some sporadic guerrilla action. Yet, the Chinese themselves were not consistent in their endorsement of revolutions in Latin America. In May 1965, in the aftermath of the Dominican intervention, they endorsed a total of twelve armed struggles in the hemisphere; but by the end of the year, the Chinese spoke of only eight (Argentina, Bolivia, Brazil, and Haiti had been dropped).

6
SELECTION OF TARGETS
FOR REVOLUTION

Thus far, Part II of this study has sought to answer two major questions with regard to Chinese foreign relations during 1965. First, which revolutions did Peking endorse and which did they not? Second, what was the nature of the Chinese relationship with the revolutionary movements operating in the endorsed countries? In this chapter, we come to a final question, and perhaps the most important one in terms of explaining the ultimate function of support for foreign revolutions in the overall picture of Chinese foreign policy: What criteria seemed to determine the choice of countries as targets for revolution (hereafter TR's) during 1965?

Let us first turn to the Maoist ideology of the national liberation struggle, as described in Part I, and from this ideology construct an ideological answer to the question. To test this theoretical view, we will then look at the TR's endorsed by Peking during 1965 to see if the priorities stated in Chinese ideology actually provide answers to the question why certain countries were endorsed as TR's and others were not. Following this, an alternative explanation will be introduced, which might be described as the state policy thesis.

THE MAOIST EXPLANATION

The national liberation struggle according to Mao Tse-tung and Lin Piao is directed primarily against two enemies, one domestic and one foreign: "feudalism" at home and "imperialism" from abroad. By feudalism, the Chinese seem to mean societies in which power is largely in the hands of traditional landowning elites and in which agriculture is organized on the basis of a system of tenant farming. Imperialism, of course, refers to foreign domination or control and, in the Maoist view, has always meant control by Western capitalist countries.[1]

Let us for the moment accept the Maoist view that Peking's support for overseas revolutions during 1965 was directed toward the primary objectives of freeing the various countries of the developing world from feudal oppression at home and imperialist domination from abroad, and then let us use the Chinese argument as a working hypothesis in an effort to determine to what extent these two considerations actually did influence Chinese policy during 1965.

Unfortunately, feudalism as used by the Chinese Communists is a very difficult concept to operationalize and apply on a worldwide scale. Reliable data capable of systematic evaluation for all the countries of Asia, Africa, and Latin America for the purpose of measuring such relevant factors as relative land ownership by the various social classes in a given society, relative influence on the political process, disparity of wealth in the society, and so forth simply do not exist. Although the concept cannot be systematically applied, some rather more impressionistic kinds of analyses with regard to specific comparative examples can be made.

For example, among the twenty-three countries endorsed as TR's by Peking in 1965, many showed evidence of high degrees of land tenancy and apparent oligarchic control of the

[1] Since the Great Proletarian Cultural Revolution, the Maoists have also begun to accuse the Soviet Union of imperialism. See, for example, the comment on "social-imperialism" in *PR*, 1968, no. 36, p. 12.

political process by traditional elites, which would appear to confirm the Maoist argument that China supports revolutions against feudalism. However, the list of twenty-three also includes such countries as Malaysia and the Philippines, nations that have developed two of the more representative political systems in the Third World. Moreover, among many of the countries *not* endorsed by Peking as TR's in 1965 and which, on the contrary, enjoyed very good relations with Peking, there existed as great if not greater degrees of economic disparity and political oligarchy. For example, two of China's Asian neighbors, Nepal and Afghanistan, countries with which Peking had had friendly diplomatic relations for over a decade, provide two of the best examples of "feudal" economic and political systems that can be found in Asia.

Thus, although the findings are not systematically conclusive because of the lack of necessary comparative data, from an analysis of several cases it does appear that the existence of a feudal social and political system in a particular country did not constitute a major determining factor in Peking's decision whether or not to support a war of national liberation in that country.[2]

Turning to the second part of the Maoist explanation, the concept of imperialism as defined by Peking provides a more readily analyzed argument, and in addition appears to be by far the more important of the two concepts to the Chinese. The revolutions are after all said to be struggles for *national* liberation, and it is the foreign enemy who is indicated as the primary opponent rather than his domestic "lackeys."

[2] For some comparative data on countries endorsed as TR's as compared with countries friendly to China, see Bruce M. Russett et al., *World Handbook of Political and Social Indicators* (New Haven: Yale University Press, 1964). See especially Table 44, Gross National Product per Capita; Table 50, Percentage of Labor Force Employed in Agriculture; Table 69, Distribution of Agricultural Land; Table 70, Farms on Rented Land as a Percentage of Total Farms; and Table 71, Income Distribution Before Taxes. Although most of these measures only peripherally relate to the Chinese concept of feudalism and unfortunately many of the relevant countries do not appear on the most applicable tables, generally, the findings fail to discriminate between countries endorsed as TR's on the one hand, and countries with which Peking maintained friendly relations on the other.

Imperialism is alleged to take many forms. Let us begin with the most obvious one, colonialism. To determine whether or not a certain country is a colony or possession of a foreign power is not a difficult task. Some de facto colonies, such as the Portuguese territories in Africa, are called something else by their foreign masters, but there seems to be little dispute among the nations of the world over what constitutes independent as opposed to colonial status. Here, we will use membership in the United Nations to distinguish independent from nonindependent countries in Asia, Africa, and Latin America.[3]

If we then turn to the twenty-three TR's and divide them according to whether or not they were independent, self-governing states during 1965, we find that only five of the twenty-three were colonies or foreign-controlled territories, which means that eighteen of the twenty-three were recognized by the world community of nations as independent states not directly dominated by foreign powers. Hence, colonialism does not appear to have been a determining factor in Communist China's selection of TR's, because according to the UN membership measure, 75 percent of the twenty-three TR countries had either never been colonized by the West (as in the case of Thailand) or had by 1965 already won their independence.

In this regard, let us look at those colonial territories that were *not* included among the TR's in 1965. Many obviously foreign-controlled countries in Asia, Africa, and Latin America (such as French and Dutch Guiana, Spanish Africa, Portuguese Timor and Macao) were not endorsed as TR's even, as

[3] The use of this measure raises the problem of how to deal with South Vietnam, a country which was generally acknowledged to be independent but which was excluded from the United Nations as were both parts of all the countries which had been divided or partitioned since the end of World War II: East and West Germany, North and South Korea, and North and South Vietnam. Although Saigon was not a member of the United Nations, it did participate in several of the intergovernmental agencies of the United Nations, and the government of South Vietnam maintained diplomatic missions in forty-eight foreign countries. Hence, in this one case, we make an exception and deal with South Vietnam as an independent country although it was not a United Nations member.

in the case of French Somaliland discussed in chapter 4, when armed struggle was actually being carried on within their borders. An interesting area in this regard is Central America, where independent Guatemala, Nicaragua, and Honduras were designated TR's, but colonial British Honduras was not.

The best single case of China's not only tolerating but also contributing to the prosperity of a colonial regime in blatant contradiction to its expressed hostility to foreign colonial domination was Hong Kong, a British crown colony bordering on China's Kwangtung Province, nestling like a veritable imperialist navel in the belly of the communist Chinese mainland. Hong Kong was not just a colony in which 98 percent of the population are Chinese, but also a thriving center of capitalist enterprise and a British military base as well, where on almost any given day during 1965 one could see riding at anchor in Hong Kong's splendid harbor either warships of the British Navy or visiting dreadnoughts from the American Seventh Fleet on "rest and recreation" from the war in Vietnam. Peking's influence on Hong Kong was great. Procommunist labor unions and a chamber of commerce for Hong Kong's businessmen had been organized by Peking; and China virtually dominated the colony's economy by its control of food and drinking water imports from the mainland, by its influence on the colony's labor force, and through the large part played by the official Bank of China and subsidiary pro-Peking banks in Hong Kong's financial affairs. Forty years before, leftist-organized Chinese strikers had brought Hong Kong to a standstill for fifteen months; but from the rise to power of the Chinese Communist Party on the mainland through 1965, there had been few political demonstrations in the colony. On the contrary, Hong Kong during 1965 was politically one of the most quiet spots in Asia; if anything, Peking seemed to be working to control political militance in the colony rather than to foster it. Even "reactionary" India used force to take back the Portuguese colony of Goa, but communist China did nothing about Hong Kong. Peking called for revolution in neighboring independent countries, and demanded that plans for a joint US-British base complex in the faraway Indian Ocean be discontinued, but the Chinese said nothing about British warships or colonial exploitation during the year in Hong Kong.[4]

The answer to why this profoundly paradoxical situation existed seems obvious: one need only look at mainland–Hong Kong trade statistics to find at least a partial answer.[5] But the situation does provide hard and undeniable evidence that, in at least one case, priorities other than those stated in Chinese ideological pronouncements had clearly predominated over those of "national liberation." The Hong Kong case, in turn, raises the question of whether alternative priorities may also have been influential in determining the choice or rejection of other potential targets for revolution.

Before moving on to a consideration of alternative explanations, let us look further at the Maoist conception of imperialism. After all, colonialism is not the only possible manifestation of imperialism. Lenin, it will be recalled, defined imperialism in terms of the export of investment capital from the industrialized countries of the West to the less developed areas of the world; and during the middle 1960s the Chinese themselves tended to define the imperialist enemy more in terms of indirect "neo-colonialism" and "economic imperialism" than direct political control. In fact, if the concept of imperialism means anything in Marxism-Leninism, it relates primarily to economic relations between the indus-

[4] In the latter part of 1965, however, Peking did protest American use of Hong Kong as a support base for the Vietnam War, but the Chinese still did not criticize continued British use of the colony as a military facility. See *PR*, 1965, no. 36, p. 7; and *PR*, 1965, no. 41, p. 13.

[5] For example, Communist China's trade with Hong Kong in 1965 totaled $406.31 million in exports (by far the largest to any country during that year) and only $12.56 million in imports, thus providing Peking with a favorable balance of trade in hard currency of $393.75 million. It was this trade margin that enabled China to purchase much needed food imports from Canada, Argentina, and Australia as well as industrial goods from other suppliers. (Hong Kong trade figures from Far Eastern Economic Review's *China Trade Report*, October 1966, p. 2.) For a discussion of the strategic importance of the Hong Kong trade for the People's Republic of China, see Alexander Eckstein, *Communist China's Economic Growth and Foreign Trade* (New York: McGraw-Hill, 1966), pp. 100–103.

trialized West and the less developed countries of Asia, Africa, and Latin America.

It is extremely difficult to obtain a complete picture of the entire web of economic relations between the West and the Third World, but let us look at a very significant aspect of that relationship: official investment or foreign aid. Government-administered economic aid is particularly important because it is most directly related to government policy-making with respect to both the donor and recipient governments, and it would seem that economic aid could most readily be used to exert political influence over recipient countries. In fact, the Chinese have accused the West of attempting to do just that. Nan Han-chen, speaking in February 1965, said, "The so-called 'economic aid' provided by the imperialists, particularly by the US imperialists, is a typical instrument through which the neo-colonialists attempt to extend their control and exploitation, even to interfere in the internal affairs of or to subvert the recipient countries."[6]

In an attempt to measure the influence of Western aid as a factor in the Chinese decision whether to endorse a given country as a proper target for revolution, let us begin with the United Nations figures for total official investment or aid (grants and loans) from all of the major industrialized countries of the West, plus most of the major aid-giving international organizations, to the countries of Asia, Africa, and Latin America during the four years 1962–1965. In analyzing the United Nations data, if we combine the total of Western governmental aid for each recipient country during all of the four years and then rate the countries in order of total government aid received, we find among the top twenty countries

---

6 *PR*, 1965, no. 10, p. 19. Kuo Wen, in his essay "Imperialist Plunder— Biggest Obstacle to the Economic Growth of 'Underdeveloped' Countries," is more specific: "The imperialists, especially the US imperialists, are doing all they can to use 'aid' as a means to buy over influential politicians, support reactionary regimes, foster financial dependence, maintain and supply satellite troops, 'rent' military bases and try to suppress the people's revolution, etc., in the 'aid' recipient countries. One of the main aims in doing this is to maintain colonialist political control and influence in these countries." *PR*, 1965, no. 26, p. 20.

five of the eighteen independent countries endorsed as TR's by Peking during 1965. However, also among the top twenty aid-recipient countries, we find three (India, Indonesia, and Kenya) of the four independent countries in which armed struggles were going on during 1965 but which were *not* endorsed by the Chinese as TR's. Moreover, among the top twenty aid-recipient countries, there was also a total of eight countries that maintained diplomatic relations with Peking, as well as two others, Chile and Mexico, which, although they had not established official ties with Communist China, maintained the most friendly semiofficial relations with Peking of any of the non-communist countries in the American hemisphere.[7]

More specifically, if we look just at United States economic assistance to the countries of the underdeveloped world (now considering the entire decade through 1965, that is, 1956–1965), we find a similar pattern. Once again ranking recipient countries in terms of total aid received during the decade, we find among the top twenty aid-recipient countries six of the eighteen independent nations endorsed as TR's during 1965, but also two of the four countries in which armed struggles were going on but which were not endorsed by Peking, plus a total of five countries having diplomatic relations with China, as well as, once again, Chile and Mexico.[8]

---

[7] The top twenty aid-recipient countries are listed below with the total Western governmental aid received during the four years 1962–1965, in millions of US dollars:

1.	India	$4,180	11.	Morocco	397
2.	Pakistan	1,938	12.	Indonesia	377
3.	Algeria	1,053	13.	Colombia	343
4.	South Vietnam	962	14.	Tunisia	320
5.	South Korea	891	15.	Jordan	309
6.	Brazil	834	16.	Republic of China	274
7.	United Arab Republic	757	17.	Philippines	258
8.	Chile	540	18.	Mexico	245
9.	Israel	500	19.	Kenya	235
10.	Congo (Leopoldville)	490	20.	Nigeria	193

Figures were compiled from data in Statistical Office of the United Nations Department of Economic and Social Affairs, *Statistical Yearbook, 1967* (New York: United Nations, 1968), pp. 692–695.

[8] The top twenty US economic aid recipient countries are listed below in

What these findings indicate is that whereas five or six of
the eighteen independent countries endorsed as TR's during
1965 had been major recipients of aid from the West, others
had not been. Moreover, and perhaps more significant, other
major recipients of Western foreign aid were some of the very
countries which China claimed to be its best friends (Indonesia, Algeria, Pakistan, and the United Arab Republic). This
is not to deny that there was substantial Western investment,
both official and private, in many of the countries endorsed as
TR's during 1965; there was. Moreover, there is little doubt
that this investment often allowed Western governments, including the United States, to exert a significant influence on
the governments of the recipient countries. However, the
inescapable inference to be drawn from these findings is that
the Chinese concept of imperialism, like the feudalism concept, fails to distinguish between the countries endorsed as
TR's on the one hand and those not endorsed on the other.

---

order of total aid received in millions of US dollars for the decade 1956–1965;
total per capita aid (based on 1965 population estimates) and rank order (in
parentheses) on the basis of per capita aid are listed in the second column:

		Total	Per capita
1.	India	$5,011	$ 10.29 (19)
2.	Pakistan	2,504	24.34 (13)
3.	South Korea	2,473	87.22 (6)
4.	South Vietnam	2,085	129.31 (4)
5.	Brazil	1,746	21.23 (16)
6.	Turkey	1,417	45.14 (9)
7.	Egypt (UAR)	1,041	35.17 (10)
8.	Republic of China	888	71.45 (7)
9.	Chile	797	93.03 (5)
10.	Israel	640	249.71 (1)
11.	Colombia	571	31.60 (12)
12.	Iran	568	24.24 (14)
13.	Indonesia	547	5.23 (20)
14.	Mexico	529	12.39 (17)
15.	Argentina	511	22.86 (15)
16.	Jordan	452	228.74 (2)
17.	Morocco	435	32.65 (11)
18.	Greece	424	49.58 (8)
19.	Laos	396	198.00 (3)
20.	Philippines	373	11.53 (18)

Kenneth M. Kauffman and Helena Stalson, "US Assistance to Less Developed
Countries, 1956–1965," *Foreign Affairs*, July 1967, p. 721. © Council on Foreign
Relations, Inc., New York.

In other words, if, as Peking claimed, Chinese policy toward the Third World was founded on opposition to imperialism and feudalism, and if Peking's support for foreign revolutions was primarily intended to help other peoples to defeat these two enemies, we should then expect to have seen the Chinese adopt a firm, antigovernment position across the board, in support of all people in countries which were suffering under so-called imperialism and feudalism. But this was not the case. The governments of some of these countries were indeed endorsed as targets for revolution, but the governments of others were received by the Chinese as dear friends. Imperialism and feudalism per se simply did not distinguish China's friends from its enemies.

AN ALTERNATIVE APPROACH: THE STATE POLICY THESIS

If the Maoist concepts of feudalism and imperialism do not explain why Peking chose certain countries as TR's and rejected others, what does? What alternative explanation can be made?

At the outset, two points should be made clear. The first is that we cannot assume that China can start a revolution wherever it wants to in the developing world, although in many cases it may try very hard to do just that. For analytical purposes, we must deal only with those areas where armed struggles were actually going on, and try to determine the factors that influenced Peking's attitude toward these struggles. Peking's statement of its own position on this question is perhaps somewhat too modest. The following excerpt from Lin Piao provides a good example of the Maoist line:

Of course, every revolution in a country stems from the demands of its own people. Only when the people in a country are awakened, mobilized, organized and armed can they overthrow the reactionary rule of imperialism and its lackeys through struggle; their role cannot be replaced or taken over by any people from outside. In this sense, revolution cannot be imported. But this does not exclude mutual sympathy and support on the part of revolutionary peoples in their struggles against the imperialists and their lackeys. Our support and aid to other revolutionary peoples serves precisely to help their self-reliant struggle.[9]

The reality of the situation is probably not too far from Peking's view of it. The days of the centrally-controlled, well-disciplined Communist International are over, and today neither Peking nor Moscow appears to be able to wield the kind of authority or impose the sort of discipline on foreign communists and revolutionary movements that Stalin did in his heyday.[10] Today, local communist parties more often tend to devise their own strategy and tactics based on an assessment of the best interests of and opportunities for their particular organization, rather than obediently take orders from either Moscow or Peking. In addition, in order to initiate and sustain a revolution in a foreign country, Peking would have, first, to find or create a revolutionary organization in that country; second, to convince that organization's leadership that it should risk the organization and the lives of its members to wage war against a vastly more powerful governmental military force; and third, presumably to demonstrate to the revolutionary organization Chinese willingness and capacity to significantly support the revolutionary effort. Moreover, most students of contemporary revolutions in the developing areas agree that ultimately the success or failure of a revolution hinges on the movement's success in winning popular support;[11] and China (or any other foreign power) is relatively limited in its capacity to help a revolution win popular support—in fact, too great an involvement in the local effort

9 *PR*, 1965, no. 36, p. 28.

10 For example, a student of Soviet relations with Latin American communist parties has written: "the extent of Moscow's control over individual party policies is limited, based more on suggestion and persuasion than on any formal sanctions. Even under conditions relatively propitious for popular front tactics, local Communists might choose for their own reasons to support guerrilla warfare or urban terrorism, leaving Moscow with little choice but to go along." D. Bruce Jackson, "Whose Men in Havana?" *Problems of Communism*, May–June, 1966, p. 8.

11 See, for example, Chalmers Johnson's early article on the subject, "Civilian Loyalties and Guerrilla Conflict," *World Politics*, July 1962, pp. 646–661.

by Peking, or even local Chinese, would tend to diminish the nationalist appeal of the revolutionary movement (as it did in Malaya) and ultimately weaken rather than strengthen it.

That is not to say that Peking cannot or does not effectively encourage and support revolutionary efforts; on the contrary, many wars of national liberation appear to receive substantial Chinese backing. The point is, rather, that we cannot assume that Peking has the capacity to start a revolution anywhere in the world anytime it wants to. Therefore, if a revolution does not occur, it does not mean necessarily that the Chinese Communists wouldn't want one to occur.

Thus, dealing with only those countries in which armed struggles were actually going on during 1965, we pose the problem as follows: When a revolution occurs, what factors are most influential in determining Peking's decision whether to support it?

The second point that must be made preparatory to discussing the state policy thesis is that, if a sustained anticolonial armed struggle actually occurs in a nonindependent or colonial area, Peking actually has little option but to endorse it because of the clear-cut nature of the struggle in terms of the ideology which the Chinese Communists profess to support. When "oppressed" colonial people take up arms against "imperialist exploitation," the Maoist Chinese are confronted with an unequivocally legitimate national liberation struggle which they can hardly help but endorse. Moreover, Soviet leaders are on constant lookout for discrepancies between Chinese theory and practice to use as ammunition in their battle with Peking (the Soviets have often, for example, pointed to the inconsistencies in Chinese policy with regard to Peking's benevolent treatment of colonial Macao and Hong Kong); and if a revolution were actually to occur in a colonial area, Soviet pressures, as well as those exerted on China by former colonial countries in the immediate area (as in militantly anticolonial Africa, for example), would greatly increase the probability that Peking would be forced to endorse the revolution, even if it did not want to. (With regard to the one exception to this rule during 1965—Peking's failure to endorse French Somaliland as a TR—the level of violence in that French colony had apparently not reached the point at which the Chinese felt it imperative to endorse the revolution contrary to their obvious desire to court the colonial power, France.) There is, therefore, little difficulty in explaining Chinese endorsement of wars of national liberation in the five colonial territories during 1965. The revolutions in Aden, Oman, and the Portuguese territories of Guinea, Angola, and Mozambique were all clear-cut national struggles against colonial authority. The ultimate question, then, involves the *independent* countries of the Third World and may be posed as follows: What factors were most influential in determining Peking's decision whether to support ongoing revolutionary armed struggles in the independent countries of Asia, Africa, and Latin America?

The answer to this question seems to be relatively simple. In contrast to arguments derived from the basic concepts of Maoist ideology, the argument presented here is that the primary factor in Peking's decision is the nature of the policy pursued by the government of a particular country with respect to the People's Republic of China. The likelihood of the country's being endorsed as a TR varies according to important aspects of its government's relative official friendliness or hostility toward Peking.

Both official friendliness and hostility may be seen in positive as well as negative terms. For example, a government's decision not to discourage trade with China may appear to Peking as important an indication of official friendliness as a vote cast for China's admission to the United Nations; contrariwise, the positive decision of a government to establish diplomatic relations with the Republic of China on Taiwan may be seen in Peking as an even more hostile act than a vote cast against the admission of Communist China to the UN.

To attempt to verify this thesis, I have constructed two measures: one, official friendliness toward Peking, and the other, official hostility toward Peking, each of which combines

three factors. The official friendliness measure includes:
1. Diplomatic relations with Peking
2. Vote cast in favor of the admission of Peking to the United Nations in 1965
3. Trade with Communist China in either 1964 or 1965 totaling more than $75 million

No attempt has been made to rate the various factors in terms of relative importance. The diplomatic relations factor was chosen to indicate a government's fundamental position vis-à-vis Communist China. A government's decision to recognize Peking is particularly significant given persistent efforts by the United States to dissuade governments from taking such action. The second factor, the United Nations General Assembly vote, was selected to provide an explicit indication of official policy on an important issue that divides Communist China and the United States (the US being the principal defender of the position of Chiang Kai-shek's Republic of China in the United Nations). Voting results from 1964 would probably have been more appropriate, but because of a financial crisis that year, no vote was taken on the question of seating China.[12] The final factor, trade relations, was chosen to indicate economic as opposed to political policy toward Peking and to provide a rough measure of the political significance to China of beneficial economic relations with foreign countries. This measure is particularly important for distinguishing among those countries that do not have diplomatic relations with Peking. A more sophisticated measure would indicate the balance of trade between the two countries and evaluate the content of Chinese imports with regard to Chinese needs, but this rough measure appears to be sufficient for the purpose of this analysis.

[12] Voting on the question of seating China during 1963 was very similar to that in 1965 insofar as it affects this analysis. The only differences in votes cast by the eighteen countries considered here were that Congo (Leopoldville) and Laos, both of which did not vote in 1965, respectively cast votes against and for the seating of the Peking government in 1963. *Far Eastern Economic Review*, January 21, 1965, p. 100.

The second measure, official hostility toward Peking, also includes three factors:

1. Diplomatic relations with the Republic of China on Taiwan
2. Vote cast against the admission of Peking to the United Nations in 1965
3. Signatory to a defense treaty with the West

The first factor, diplomatic relations with the Republic of China, would seem to be a clear indicator of official hostility toward Peking. Recognition of the Chiang Kai-shek government as the government of China unequivocally denies the legitimacy of the Peking regime and endorses the claims of the Taiwan government to be the rightful authority over all of China, both Taiwan and the mainland. Moreover, such recognition could also be interpreted by Peking as an attempt to interfere in Chinese internal affairs by supporting a rump regime in virtual exile from its own country. The second factor, again, was selected to indicate recent official policy—in this case, a position sharply opposed to Peking. And the third and final factor, defense alliance with the West, is designed to indicate the more long-term orientation of a country's foreign policy with regard to its political commitments and self-identification in the world (for example, more or less pro-West, nonaligned, or pro-communist) and, more specifically, a country's relations with China's imperialist enemies.

The next step is to apply these measures, official friendliness and official hostility, to the eighteen independent countries endorsed by Peking as TR's during 1965 to see if indeed the measures can help explain why those particular countries were selected as targets for revolution. Tables 5 and 6 demonstrate the findings.

When the eighteen countries were analyzed with regard to the first measure, official friendliness toward Peking, fifteen out of the eighteen returned a zero rating, while the remaining three indicated a rating of only one out of a possible three points. With regard to the specific factors, only one country,

Laos, was found to maintain diplomatic relations with Communist China; none of the eighteen countries voted in favor of Peking's admission to the UN in 1965; and only two of the eighteen carried on trade with the mainland totaling more than $75 million during the year.

Turning to Table 6 and the second measure, official hostility toward Peking, we find almost the exact opposite result;

TABLE 5

INDEPENDENT COUNTRIES ENDORSED AS TR'S IN 1965,
OFFICIAL FRIENDLINESS TOWARD PEKING

Country	Diplomatic Relations with Peking[a]	UN Vote Yes 1965[b]	Trade with Communist China over $75 million[c]	Friendliness Rating (Scale of 3)
Asia				
Laos	x	(not voting)		1
Malaysia			x	1
Philippines				0
Thailand				0
South Vietnam		(not UN member)		0
Africa				
Congo (Leopoldville)		(not voting)		0
Latin America				
Argentina			x	1
Bolivia				0
Brazil				0
Colombia				0
Dominican Republic				0
Guatemala				0
Haiti				0
Honduras				0
Nicaragua				0
Paraguay				0
Peru				0
Venezuela				0

[a] *Jen-min shou-ts'e*, 1965, pp. 225–226.
[b] *NYT*, November 18, 1965, pp. 1, 2.
[c] *China Trade Report*, October 1966, p. 2.

TABLE 6

INDEPENDENT COUNTRIES ENDORSED AS TR'S IN 1965,
OFFICIAL HOSTILITY TOWARD PEKING

Country	Diplomatic Relations with Republic of China[a]	UN Vote No 1965[b]	Defense Treaty with West[c]	Hostility Rating (Scale of 3)
Asia				
Laos		(not voting)		0
Malaysia		x	x	2
Philippines	x	x	x	3
Thailand	x	x	x	3
South Vietnam	x	(not UN member)	x	2
Africa				
Congo (Leopoldville)	x	(not voting)		1
Latin America				
Argentina	x	x	x	3
Bolivia	x	x	x	3
Brazil	x	x	x	3
Colombia	x	x	x	3
Dominican Republic	x	x	x	3
Guatemala	x	x	x	3
Haiti	x	x	x	3
Honduras	x	x	x	3
Nicaragua	x	x	x	3
Paraguay	x	x	x	3
Peru	x	x	x	3
Venezuela	x	x	x	3

[a] Personal letter from the Permanent Mission of the Republic of China to the United Nations.

[b] *NYT*, November 18, 1965, pp. 1, 2.

[c] Malaysia: defense arrangement with the United Kingdom. Philippines and Thailand: members of the Southeast Asia Treaty Organization. South Vietnam: bilateral defense agreement with the United States (the US military commitment to Vietnam is also sometimes justified in terms of a general commitment to defend Southeast Asia against aggression under the SEATO agreement; see, for example, President Johnson's State of the Union address in the *NYT*, January 11, 1967, p. 16). The Latin American countries: defense agreement with the United States under the provisions of the Organization of American States.

all of the eighteen countries except two rate high. Fourteen of the eighteen returned a score of three, or 100 percent, on the three factors; and two others, Malaysia and Vietnam, scored two out of the possible three. Only two countries scored less than two: they were Laos and the Congo (Leopoldville), neither of which voted on the UN issue. Again, with regard to the three specific factors, we find that all of the countries but two (Laos and Malaysia) maintained diplomatic relations with the Chiang Kai-shek government on Taiwan; all either voted no, abstained, or were not members of the UN when the vote was taken on the admission of Peking; and, finally, all but one country (Laos again) were party to some kind of defense agreement with the West.

A question that might very naturally be asked with regard to these findings is which came first, Chinese endorsement of revolution in the eighteen countries or their official hostility toward Peking? If TR endorsement came first, a strong implication would be that the foreign governments' official hostility toward Peking was prompted by Chinese support for revolutionary movements attempting to overthrow them. Historically, for example, it could be argued that in the initial period of the foreign relations of the People's Republic of China (1949–1952) when Peking almost universally supported insurrections against non-communist governments, the Chinese provoked attitudes of official hostility among many of the independent non-communist countries of the developing world. It could also be argued, however, that in the period subsequent to 1952, and especially during the mid-1950s, Peking, in implementing its peaceful coexistence policy, offered virtually all governments of the Third World the opportunity to establish relatively conventional and peaceable relations with China if they chose to do so.

Ultimately, it is probably impossible to establish the chain of causality in all of these relationships. In the period from the middle 1950s through 1965, however, it was general Chinese practice in dealing with the new nations of the Third World to offer diplomatic recognition to virtually all the countries of Africa, Asia, and Latin America as they became independent. Generally, only if they refused to establish relations and rebuffed China's overtures did the question of TR endorsement arise. Also, during this period, it appears that in no instance did Peking endorse a war of national liberation against any government with which it had established diplomatic relations (except in the case of Laos which will be discussed below), nor had Peking ever unilaterally broken diplomatic relations with any country once they had been established.

Moreover, Peking sought official diplomatic relations with countries of the developing areas regardless of their political and social systems or initial foreign policy orientation. The case of Guyana (formerly British Guiana, a Latin American colony), which became independent on May 26, 1966, provides a good example. Writing in the *World Marxist Review* several months before Guyana's independence, Cheddi Jagan, head of the People's Progressive Party ("vanguard of the national liberation movement") and former head of government of British Guiana under a system of limited self-rule, denounced the government which would lead Guyana to independence as "pro-imperialist and anti-working-class" and completely "subservient to US imperialism." In the future, Jagan said, the government "will resort to the Hitlerite fascist weapons of terror, anti-communism and racism" and "will move to establish a Latin American fascist-type dictatorship."[13] Yet despite this evaluation by Guyana's leading leftist, when the "puppet government" actually won independence from Britain, Chinese Premier Chou En-lai cabled the new Guyanan Prime Minister Forbes Burnham to convey China's congratulations, and the Chinese press hailed the independence of Guyana as a great achievement in the Guyanese people's "heroic struggle" against British colonialism.[14] Al-

[13] Cheddi Jagan, "Guiana's Struggle against Reaction and Racism for Democracy and Independence," *World Marxist Review*, August 1965, pp. 30–31.
[14] See discussion in "China Greets Guyana's Independence," *PR*, 1966, no. 23, p. 3.

though it was not publicized, the Chinese congratulations were undoubtedly part of an attempt to win diplomatic recognition by the new government, even though that government was considered a tool of imperialism by local leftists. The Chinese attempt was unsuccessful—Burnham did not recognize either Chinese government—but the whole episode does provide an interesting example of the Chinese method of dealing with newly independent countries, and how little Chinese policy may coincide with the interests of local "progressives."

The establishment of diplomatic relations with the countries of Asia, Africa, and Latin America clearly seems to have held high priority in Peking's relations with the Third World in the period through 1965. But if recognition was refused, what then? There remained the inducements of trade and semiofficial contacts with China, which Peking sometimes used in an effort to keep a country from slipping into the enemy camp. But if a foreign government ultimately decided to ally itself with the imperialist enemy against China, Peking apparently felt that it had little to lose by supporting a revolution to overthrow that government. John K. Cooley, *Christian Science Monitor* correspondent for Africa and the Middle East, has described how quickly Chinese policy toward a country can change once the government has rejected Peking's inducements. He reported how Hastings Banda, prime minister of Malawi, refused Peking's offer of official relations (sweetened with a side offer of substantial economic aid) only to be almost immediately assaulted by waves of Chinese hostility accompanied by attempts to influence his own government against him.[15]

If, on the other hand, governments do respond to Peking's overtures and demonstrate an official friendliness toward Communist China, the Chinese then have a stake in preserving these friendly relationships and the governments that support them. During 1965, this policy extended to the point of Peking's not endorsing those countries as TR's even when the

[15] John K. Cooley, *East Wind over Africa* (New York: Walker, 1965), pp. 96–98.

revolutionary efforts aimed at toppling the governments were, as in Burma, led by pro-Peking communists. Table 7 shows the results obtained when those independent countries in which armed struggles were actually being carried out in 1965 but which were not endorsed by Peking as TR's are analyzed according to the same measures, official friendliness and official hostility, as were the eighteen TR's. In contrast to the findings with regard to the TR's, all of these countries return high scores on friendliness (two out of a possible three points) and zero scores on hostility, thus strongly encouraging the inference that it was their state policy toward Peking that made Peking refrain from endorsing them as TR's; whereas the Chinese apparently had no qualms about endorsing as TR's other countries which maintained state policies of official hostility toward Peking.[16]

A few words remain to be said about those countries which were endorsed as TR's during 1965 but which, in the findings reported in tables 5 and 6, did not rate 100 percent on official hostility and zero on official friendliness as did the great majority of the other TR's (thirteen out of the eighteen).

To return to tables 5 and 6 for a moment, it will be recalled that the five countries departing in any way from the general pattern were Laos, Malaysia, South Vietnam, Congo (Leopoldville), and Argentina. However, actually only one country, Laos, failed to adhere to the general trend of the findings characteristic of all the TR's, which was to score high on hostility and low (if at all) on friendliness. The four other exceptions (Malaysia, South Vietnam, Congo, and Argentina) simply departed from the characteristic pattern to some degree, but did not reverse it as did Laos.

Laos is indeed a very special case. It is a country of great

---

[16] The Portuguese government apparently discerned this pattern in Chinese foreign policy. John Cooley reports that in early 1965 in spite of China's active support for the revolutionary movements operating in Portugal's African territories, the Portuguese government was seriously considering the establishment of diplomatic relations with Peking, for, as the Portuguese foreign minister was quoted as saying, "There are no serious reasons for not recognizing Peking, and *many reasons for doing so*" (emphasis added). *Ibid.*, p. 123.

TABLE 7

INDEPENDENT COUNTRIES, SITES OF ARMED STRUGGLE IN 1965 BUT *NOT* ENDORSED AS TR'S, OFFICIAL FRIENDLINESS AND OFFICIAL HOSTILITY TOWARD PEKING

Country	Official Friendliness				Official Hostility			
	Relations with Peking	UN Vote Yes	Trade over $75 million	Friendliness Rating	Relations with Republic of China	UN Vote No	Defense Treaty with West	Hostility Rating
Asia								
Burma	x	x		2				0
India (Kashmir)	x	x		2				0
Indonesia[a]	x	(not active UN member)	x	2	(not active UN member)			0
Africa								
Kenya	x	x		2				0
Latin America								
—								

[a] Indonesia withdrew from the United Nations in March 1965 but returned in September 1966.

SOURCES. Same as for Table 5, p. 172.

strategic importance, bordering as it does on China as well as North and South Vietnam, Thailand, Burma, and Cambodia; it has often been pointed to as the geopolitical key to Southeast Asia. In recent years, Peking has, contrary to its usual practice, maintained official contacts with both the established government in Vientiane and the revolutionary Neo Lao Haksat alternative to it (see pp. 135–136), arguing that the reason for such a paradoxical policy was that the three-faction coalition government set up under the 1962 Geneva agreement had broken apart, and until it was suitably reconstituted, Peking would defend the demands of the left faction even to the point of supporting a revolution against the Vientiane government. Thus, during 1965, there existed the anomalous situation in which a supposedly neutralist Laotian government continued to maintain diplomatic relations with a Chinese government which supported a communist-led revolutionary movement which in turn called for the government's overthrow. Actually, the war in Laos was relatively quiet during the year, the various parties to the action seeming to await the outcome of the Vietnam struggle rather than seeking to broaden the conflict and involve themselves in a Southeast Asian general war.

As for the other exceptions, Malaysia, Vietnam, Congo, and Argentina, these countries demonstrated the same pattern of attitudes toward Peking as did the majority of TR's—high on hostility and low or nil on friendliness—but to a lesser degree than the majority. Malaysia carried on some trade with the mainland and refrained from recognizing the Chiang Kai-shek government; but the Kuala Lumpur government also refrained from recognizing Peking, voted against Peking on the UN representation issue, and maintained a defense alliance with Britain. Vietnam was even more clearly anti-Peking; the country's lower score (two out of the possible three points) on official hostility was simply a matter of Saigon's not being a member of the United Nations. And as for the Congo, the government of that war-torn country had established no formal defense alliance with any of the Western powers and chose not to vote on the China issue in the General Assembly, but it did maintain diplomatic relations with Taiwan and otherwise offered little indication of friendliness to Peking.

Finally, the case of Argentina provides the single exception to the clear-cut 100 percent on hostility and zero on friendliness indicated by all of the Latin American TR's. Argentina scored three on hostility, as did the others, but also scored one on friendliness as the result of a developing trade relationship with China. The Argentine case is particularly interesting, I think, because, rather than detracting from the thesis presented here, it may actually lend more weight to it. It will be remembered from chapter 4 that there was some inconsistency in Peking's endorsement of TR's in Latin America during the year. On a Chinese map published in May 1965, all twelve countries were indicated as TR's; but another map, published after the end of the year and reputing to show TR's for all of 1965, failed to include four of the original twelve, one of which was Argentina. There are obviously many factors that could have determined Peking's decision to drop the four countries from its list of Latin American TR's, and the level of violence sustained by the various armed struggles is probably the most important one. However, with regard to the specific case of Argentina, in the several months between the publication of the two maps the Argentine government had agreed to sell China a much-needed million and a half tons of wheat, an official act that may have had some not inconsiderable influence on the change in Peking's policy toward that Latin American country.[17]

OTHER IMPORTANT FACTORS

Having analyzed the independent countries Peking endorsed as TR's in 1965 and found a striking correlation between endorsement and the various countries' state policies or official attitudes toward Peking, we may now ask what other factors

17 CSM, December 29, 1965, p. 12. China had purchased wheat from Argentina in previous years, but this was by far the largest order to date.

can be said to significantly influence Peking's selection and support of TR's, particularly with regard to the consistency and intensity of Chinese support. This question could be put another way: why is Peking sufficiently interested in some countries to initiate and sustain a policy of support for revolution, but not so interested in others?

Within the single year of 1965, we do find substantial differences in the consistency and intensity of Chinese policy with respect to the endorsement of TR's. For instance, during the year Peking was markedly inconsistent in endorsing targets for revolution in Latin America, while being quite consistent with respect to Africa and Asia. As for the intensity of Peking's endorsement and support, the three measures introduced in chapter 4 (statement of Mao Tse-tung, other explicit endorsement, and implicit endorsement) provide a rough indication of the degrees of intensity of the Chinese commitment.

During 1965, the consistency and intensity of Chinese support for TR's seemed to vary primarily with regard to three major factors: the geographical proximity of the TR, the degree of US involvement in the struggle, and the perceived likelihood that the revolution would be a success or could at least sustain its armed opposition to the existing government.

With regard to the first factor, geographic proximity, Peking seems to have established several orders of priority: (1) countries of continental Southeast Asia and all countries bordering on the People's Republic of China; (2) other Asian countries; (3) African countries; and, finally, (4) Latin American countries. Clearly, the countries located in those areas closest to China preoccupied Peking to the exclusion of all others. During the year, all those independent countries that either shared borders with China or were situated in continental Southeast Asia either had established diplomatic relations with Peking or were designated by Peking as TR's. For countries in this first geographical priority, there was no in-between option; they had to be either friends or enemies. Moreover, the intensity of Chinese endorsement of TR's in the various geographical areas as indicated by the three types of endorsement discussed in chapter 4 shows that the closer a TR was situated to China, the more likely it was to receive an explicit, as opposed to an implicit, endorsement.

Other indicators also support the argument that Peking generally operated in accord with this system of geographical priorities. The number of China's overseas radio broadcast hours varied according to these priorities (see pp. 115–116), and Peking's relations with foreign revolutionary organizations did as well; the only organizations allowed to set up permanent missions in Peking were from Asia (the continent of highest geographical priority), whereas few revolutionaries from Latin America even traveled to Peking during the year (see Tables 2, 3, and 4 on pp. 134, 140, and 148) .

This is not to say, however, that Peking was not interested in countries far distant from China. The difference was one of degree. Thus, Peking's policy toward Latin America indicated little sense of being able to influence developments there either by peaceful or revolutionary means; even if it could, Peking appeared unable to allocate much in the way of resources to support Latin American policy initiatives. As a result, China's Latin American policy demonstrated the least consistency and intensity of support for TR's of any of the geographical areas of the Third World. With the exception of the Dominican Republic, the Chinese press paid little attention to Latin America during the year; and, whereas Peking endorsed a total of twelve TR's in Latin America in May 1965, by the end of the year this figure had dropped to only eight. The single exception of the Dominican Republic points to what was one of the most important advantages for Peking in endorsing and supporting TR's in Latin America, the likelihood of US involvement, second of the factors cited above as major considerations determining the consistency and intensity of Chinese support for TR's.

The best indication of the importance to Peking of armed struggles in which the US became involved is the fact that in every so-called war of national liberation from 1963 through

1965 in which the US took a major part, China stated its support for the other side of that battle with the strongest kind of public endorsement Peking could muster, a public statement by Chairman Mao Tse-tung himself. Of the six major foreign policy statements made by Mao in the period 1963–1965, three were in support of revolutions (in Vietnam, the Congo, and the Dominican Republic), and three were made to support essentially nonviolent mass demonstrations (in the United States, Japan, and Panama). In every case, however, the struggle involved explicit and forceful opposition to US policy.[18] Moreover, other struggles that for different reasons would seem to have prompted the strongest kind of Chinese support, such as the situation in Rhodesia where black Africans were fighting against a white-supremacist minority government for their independence and self-determination, actually failed to receive a personal endorsement by Mao Tse-tung, apparently because the United States was not directly involved. Other Chinese sources tend to confirm this view of the importance of US involvement for Peking. For example, an article on the national liberation struggle in the Congo appearing in the English-language *Evergreen* hailed the war in the Congo as the "first battlefield on the African continent where the people are *in direct conflict with US neo-colonialism.*"[19]

Finally, the third important factor determining the consistency and intensity of Chinese support for a war of national liberation was an obvious one—the likelihood that a revolution would be successful. The degree of enthusiasm seen in the Chinese press for a particular revolution usually could be charted according to the level of violence and the likelihood that the revolutionary movement might prevail. One of the reasons that the Vietnam war, for example, took on such great significance for Peking was not only because of Vietnam's geographical location and the increasing degree of US in-

[18] Five of Mao's six statements appear in the pamphlet *Ch'uan shih-chieh jen-min t'uan-chieh-ch'i-lai ta-pai mei-kuo ch'in-lueh-che chi ch'i yi-ch'ieh tsou-kou* (Peking: People's Press, 1964); and the one on the Dominican Republic was published in *JMJP*, May 13, 1965, p. 1.

[19] *Evergreen*, 1966, no. 2 (emphasis added).

volvement, but also because it seemed likely that the NFL would win. Because of the character of the American government's self-proclaimed commitment in the world—a commitment to defend virtually the entire so-called Free World against "the spread of communism" anywhere—any victory by a communist-led revolutionary movement in any country would be a significant strategic defeat for the United States, and hence a victory for the Chinese.

It remains to be emphasized that the analysis presented here cannot claim to have isolated all of the factors that may have been influential in determining Chinese policy decisions with regard to wars of national liberation—a mere list of possibly relevant variables would take up several pages. However, I have attempted to point up those factors that seemed to be most significant in this area of Chinese foreign policy and to defend the choice of these factors by presenting the findings of relevant empirical research.

7
SUPPORT FOR WARS
OF NATIONAL LIBERATION

There are some striking parallels between Stalin's foreign policy during the long years of the Chinese Revolution and Chinese foreign policy in the years immediately prior to the cultural revolution. Concerning Stalin's policy with regard to foreign revolutions, Milovan Djilas, the Yugoslav Communist, has written:

Because Moscow abstained, always in decisive moments, from supporting the Chinese, Spanish, and in many ways even the Yugoslav revolutions, the view prevailed, not without reason, that Stalin was generally against revolutions. This is, however, not entirely correct. He was opposed only conditionally, that is, to the degree to which the revolution went beyond the interests of the Soviet state.[1]

What Djilas wrote about Stalin and the relationship between Russia's support for revolution and Soviet state interests is applicable to Mao Tse-tung and Chinese foreign policy before the cultural revolution[2]—but in a positive rather than

[1] Milovan Djilas, *Conversations with Stalin* (New York: Harcourt, Brace and World, 1962), p. 132.
[2] This analysis assumes that Mao Tse-tung was in predominant control of Chinese foreign policy during the 1960–1965 period. This proposition is defended in the subsequent discussion in chapter 8.

negative sense. An appropriate paraphrase of Djilas' comment might read:

Because Peking supported revolutions in many places throughout the world—in Vietnam, the Congo, the Dominican Republic—the view prevailed that Mao Tse-tung was unequivocally in favor of revolutions everywhere. This is, however, not entirely correct. Mao supported revolutions only conditionally, that is, to the degree to which the revolution served the interests of the Chinese state.

Djilas, discussing Stalin and his view of revolution, goes on to explain that what Stalin feared was the creation of competing revolutionary centers of Marxist-Leninist orthodoxy which might challenge Moscow's predominance in, and control of, the international communist movement. Hence, Stalin supported only those revolutions he could control.

Mao, on the other hand, did not seem to share this fear. Having won power with little assistance from the Soviet Union, the Chinese Communists were now challenging Moscow's authority within the international communist movement precisely as Stalin feared independent revolutionaries would; but Peking had as yet gained so little effective control of the movement that the Chinese had little to lose by continuing to support revolutions, even if they could not ultimately control their outcome. On the contrary, Peking perhaps had much to gain by maintaining a revolutionary posture, especially at a time when traditional communist parties were being pushed by Moscow in the other direction, toward policies of "peaceful transition." Appealing to the young radicals both inside and outside the communist movement, Peking could apply the double-edged-sword technique: support revolutions against pro-US established governments on the one hand, while on the other push the revolutionary Chinese party line in an attempt to discredit the traditional pro-Soviet parties and to win over their membership to the Chinese philosophy.

However, Communist China had developed at least a limited stake in the existing system, and it was this stake in the status quo that tempered Chinese support for foreign revolutions. In effect, what the official friendliness scale used in chapter 6 actually measured was Peking's stake in preserving good relations with each of the particular countries analyzed; that is, it demonstrated what Peking stood to lose (in diplomatic recognition, support for Chinese foreign policy, and important trade ties) if it supported a revolutionary effort to unseat the government of that particular country. Especially in the period 1960–1965, as Peking pressed its attack simultaneously on the United States and the Soviet Union, Chinese dependence on non-communist states for international support drastically increased. Keenly aware of the danger of China's becoming isolated as Peking faced off against the world's two greatest powers, Mao Tse-tung apparently realized the fundamental importance of maintaining and expanding China's base of support in other areas of the world, both to obtain the imports so crucial to economic development and to broaden the base of its diplomatic support within the world community of nations. The findings of this study document how support for revolutions during 1965 was tailored to avoid endangering China's state relations where they were beneficial to Peking, while supporting those revolutionary efforts that attacked officially hostile governments. Thus, Mao's revolutionary strategy, in a different way, was as closely related to state interests as was Stalin's.

The similarity does not end there. A popular notion for many years among some analysts of Chinese foreign policy has been that what concerned the Chinese Communists most with regard to their support of foreign revolutions was the question of Maoist orthodoxy and the development of foreign revolutions in accord with the Maoist revolutionary model. In other words, proponents of this view argued that the determining factor in Chinese support for revolutions was whether or not the revolutionary organization leading the struggle demonstrated a commitment to the basic requirements of the Chinese revolutionary model, which, above all, insisted on leadership by a revolutionary communist party.[3] But here

3 Recall Lin Piao's unequivocal statement on this point cited earlier: "This

again, the Chinese proved to be no less willing than Stalin to subordinate Marxist-Leninist ideology and the interests of local communist parties to the attainment of objectives beneficial to state policy. Peking's endorsement of the Algerian Revolution as the revolutionary model for Africa is perhaps the best case in point; for the leadership of the Algerian Revolution was not only non-communist, but it also systematically suppressed the local communist movement.

Hence, it is important to distinguish clearly between the interests of the Chinese Communist Party and those of foreign communist parties. It has been argued, for example, that when Stalin forced the CCP into the so-called "bloc within," an alliance with the Kuomintang in 1924 that left the CCP virtually at the mercy of the KMT, and when in 1927 the KMT almost wiped out the CCP as a result, the Chinese Communists learned a lesson they would never forget: a communist party should never allow the Comintern to force it into a position domestically that blatantly violated the party's own interests and might even endanger its very existence.

It is true that the CCP did indeed learn this lesson, and after 1927 the party never again allowed Moscow to lead it into any sort of an alliance with the Kuomintang in which it could not militarily defend its independence; however, this did *not* mean that Peking might not attempt to use foreign communist parties, as Moscow had used the CCP, to serve Chinese interests. The lesson of 1927 was that they, the Chinese Communists, should never let themselves be placed in a position in which they might be slaughtered by a competing political organization; it did *not* mean that the Chinese would not attempt to put another communist party in a similar situation, if by so doing Chinese interests might be advanced. It should be remembered that the CCP disaster in 1927 did not teach Moscow any lesson; Stalin went blithely on his way sacrificing foreign communist parties to the demands of Soviet

---

means that the revolution can only be, nay must be, led by the proletariat and the genuinely revolutionary party armed with Marxism-Leninism, and by no other class or party." *PR*, 1965, no. 36, p. 24.

foreign policy. It was not the Chinese Communists that concerned Stalin, but, as Djilas says, the Russian state.

The essential point is simply that Chinese Communist Party interests cannot be equated with those of foreign communist parties which may be trying to do what the Chinese Communists did in China. The CCP has won power and runs a government which necessarily incorporates definite state interests. For example, a foreign communist party bent on revolution may be trying to do precisely what Peking does not want to see happen (overthrow a friendly government, for instance); or, on the other hand, the traditional communist party (as in Algeria) may not be seen by the Chinese to constitute the most effective leadership to bring about a revolution which Peking does favor. It is one thing to demand communist party leadership of a revolution when you are that communist party; but it is quite a different thing to require it when you are not that country's communist party and when the communist party may be a considerably less effective instrument to guide the revolution you seek to promote than an alternative revolutionary organization.

If Peking was not primarily concerned with helping bring foreign communist parties to power or with seeing the Chinese revolutionary model replicated in the developing world, what was the major Chinese concern? The findings of this study lead to the conclusion that the primary concern of Chinese foreign policy in the period prior to the cultural revolution, either in supporting wars of national liberation or establishing friendly official or semiofficial relations with other countries, was the desire to win adherents to the Chinese program for radical change in the international system. In this regard, the most important factor determining Chinese policy toward any individual country was not the objective class character of the society in question or the proclaimed ideology of the party in power, but the foreign policy being pursued by the country's government.[4]

4 J. D. B. Miller has put it this way: "Clearly, both the Soviet Union and China fête those leaders [of countries in Asia, Africa, and Latin America] who

There is a domestic analogy to this method employed by the CCP to distinguish its friends from its enemies. In domestic Chinese politics since 1949, the question whether an individual would belong to the favored category of "the people" or to the category of "enemies of the people" in terms of the CCP's view of the society has generally been decided primarily in terms of the individual's support or opposition to the official party line, rather than on the basis of objective criteria drawn from Marxist-Leninist ideology, such as an individual's class origin. In other words, if a Chinese mainlander vigorously supported current party policy, he could be pretty well assured of remaining one of "the people"; but if he opposed party policy in spite of the fact that he might come from the most pristine proletarian origins, there was a good chance that he might end up as an "enemy of the people." In domestic policy as well as foreign, epithets of a class character (such as "feudal" and "bourgeois") were often applied to party enemies, but the crucial criterion seemed to be opposition to party policy rather than any abstract class designation.

It is in this sense that the Chinese categorization of foreign countries becomes meaningful. Whether a foreign non-communist country was seen to be "peace-loving" or ruled by "reactionaries," or whether a communist party state was viewed in Peking as "socialist" or denounced as "revisionist," largely depended on the extent to which that country's foreign policy coincided with China's own. For example, the Chinese charge of neo-colonialism didn't necessarily say anything about the domestic politics of the indicted country; that is, there may or may not have been a significant degree of foreign control over the society. However, it did say a great deal about the foreign policy being pursued by the country's government. Just as in the development of the Sino-Soviet dispute through 1965 (although this would change in the period after 1965), the Chinese did not seem to care so much

---

seem likely to agree with their policies, and attack those who do not; the nature of the regime is a secondary consideration." *The Politics of the Third World* (London: Oxford University Press, 1966), p. 55.

what the Soviets were doing in Russia as they did about Soviet policy with regard to China, the countries of the developing world, and especially the United States.[5]

If, for instance, we look at the major issues raised by the Chinese in the Sino-Soviet dispute through 1965, we find that almost invariably they related to foreign policy. Perhaps the most important issue of all to the Chinese was the question of the developing detente in Moscow's relations with Washington and increased US-Soviet cooperation in world affairs—one of the most striking cases in point being concurrent US and Soviet aid to India in 1962 when that country was under attack by China. Other important issues relating to foreign policy were: Soviet focus on peaceful cooperation with the West in general rather than on a militant anti-imperialist policy; Soviet reluctance to give full support to revolutions in the developing areas; Soviet overemphasis (as the Chinese saw it) on the destructiveness of nuclear weapons to the point of falling victim to "nuclear blackmail"; and so forth.

From the Chinese point of view, not only was the Soviet Union's foreign policy profoundly wrong in making accommodations with the enemy, the United States, but also because of what that enemy stood for—active defense of the status quo. In terms of its own ambitions, China was still a have-not country in spite of its developing industry and nuclear weapons capability. The bitterness of the national humiliation of the nineteenth and early twentieth centuries, as has often been pointed out, still burned deep in the Chinese mind; and a determination to "show" the Western world was clearly evident in Chinese international behavior. Western assaults on Chi-

5 This is not to say that Peking was not concerned at all about Soviet domestic policy. Clearly, the post-Stalin political and economic reforms in the Soviet Union had disturbed the Chinese greatly, particularly with regard to the precedent these reforms presented as a model for the development of all socialist countries including China. However, if at the same time Moscow was liberalizing at home the Soviets had continued to support Chinese foreign policy initiatives abroad, and especially had maintained the Cold War confrontation with the United States, it seems that the Sino-Soviet dispute would hardly have reached the proportions that it had by 1965. I am simply arguing that to the Chinese, Soviet foreign policy was decidedly more important than its domestic policy in the period up to 1965.

nese dignity, combined with a traditional sense of China's greatness and cultural importance, appeared to be motivating Peking to search for a much larger role in the world. To attain their much-sought-after place of world respect and power, the Chinese realized that they would have to bring about radical changes in the international status quo. Thus, those who supported radical change and the establishment of new relationships among states beneficial to China were Peking's friends. Those who opposed these changes, even if they were communists, were China's enemies.

Hence, Chinese foreign policy during the early 1960s can best be seen as a militant, nondogmatic assault on the status quo, one which welcomed as allies any groups or individuals willing to commit themselves to policies involving some degree of change in what Peking saw to be the right direction. The international united front that Peking attempted to build took the form of a broad continuum of opposition to the status quo, varying in degree of radicalism and the application of strategy and tactics, in which revolution or wars of national liberation played only a part. As has often been written,[6] the Chinese supported a politically heterogeneous lot throughout the world: from tribal monarchs in the depth of Africa and Gaullist capitalists in France to communist rebels in the jungles of South Vietnam. The only common denominator among this dissimilar array was a favorable attitude toward Peking or a firm commitment to change.

Insofar as they were willing to adopt policies acceptable to Peking, potential members of China's proposed international united front comprised a wide variety of countries, often including both governments and peoples. The political activities engaged in by acceptable members of the united front also varied widely, including: revolution (either communist- or non-communist-led), coup d'etat, street demonstrations, mobilization and organization of the mass population, political education and the development of radical political attitudes,

[6] See, for example, Michel Oksenberg, "China: Forcing the Revolution to a New Stage," *Asian Survey*, January 1967, pp. 2–3.

and even parliamentary agitation for government policy changes to positions more favorable to Peking or less favorable to Peking's enemies. The method, per se, was not so important; whether to support peaceful parliamentary attempts to influence official policy or to opt for a revolutionary assault on the established government became a question of tactics rather than strategy. If the strategy represented a nondogmatic attempt to radically alter the status quo, the tactics employed to attain the strategic goal became secondary, be they votes or violence.

Within the united front, however, revolution played a special role. Revolution was not only the most violent method employed (as well as being the one that most closely fit the Maoist view of the necessary historical development of states by the violent seizure of state power), but it also performed the function of what might be called the "cutting edge" of the united front. The option of being able to choose to support revolutions against established governments provided Peking with substantial leverage in its dealings with foreign governments. China's dichotomous, two-pronged policy toward the developing nations—"peaceful coexistence" or "armed struggle"—created a tension in which foreign governments were constantly kept aware of the possibility that official government hostility toward Peking might be reciprocated by Chinese support for local revolutionaries. The tension was greatest on what might be called the outer edge of the united front, with respect to those countries only minimally qualified in terms of their support for Chinese policy for inclusion in the united front. Peking's policy was continually changing as were the policies of foreign governments and China's enemies might become friends or friends become enemies. The threat of revolutionary sanctions remained an important consideration for any government that might contemplate opposition to Peking.[7]

---

[7] This tension and threat implicit in Chinese foreign policy, of course, could and did operate to Peking's disadvantage as well, by in effect pushing some governments into the arms of China's enemies. Feeling threatened by the

Another important function of revolution in Chinese foreign policy was educational. Apart from any message that Chinese support for a revolution might convey to neighboring governments with regard to the seriousness with which Peking was prepared to pursue its foreign policy objectives, the Chinese appeared convinced that a continuing war of national liberation—especially one in which the US became involved—served as the best possible kind of lesson or example in developing the political consciousness of the masses throughout the world. Each revolution was seen as a further step in mass political education and the mobilization of popular opinion against China's enemies, serving ultimately, the Chinese hoped, to break down the foundation of US popular support both at home and abroad and to isolate and weaken the US government. American intervention in the war in Vietnam, for instance, provided a propaganda issue of great importance to the Chinese. No single issue since the end of World War II had been used more effectively to mobilize and organize world public opinion against the US government.

An obvious third function of support for wars of national liberation for Chinese foreign policy was that if successful, a revolutionary armed struggle would as a result overturn a government hostile to China and replace it with what would very likely be a radical, if not necessarily pro-Chinese, successor regime. Also, if the revolutionary movement adhered to the basic tenets of the Maoist revolutionary model and was ultimately successful in its effort to win power, this would help support Mao's claim to have devised revolutionary theory with a broader potential application than just China. However, this last consideration, the replication of the Maoist model, appeared to have an extremely low priority in Chinese policy during 1965.

For all the importance of revolutionary armed struggle in Maoist ideology, Peking made no dogmatic commitment to the revolutionary approach. Rather, Chinese policy was sur-

---

Chinese, some governments chose to ally themselves with Western powers rather than come to terms with Peking.

prisingly flexible in its use of a variety of tactics. For example, leftist non-communist nationalist states often seemed to play a more important role in Peking's conception of the international united front than did communist parties or communist states. There were, no doubt, several reasons for this. Many non-communist governments in Asia and Africa were relatively insecure in their power and susceptible to Chinese pressure to adopt policies more in accord with those put forth by Peking. Moreover, some non-communist leaders at times have welcomed Chinese policy initiatives when they coincided with their own state interests, particularly for the purpose of balancing the influences of East against West. Also, Peking has enhanced the credibility of certain Chinese policy initiatives by joining with non-communist states on certain issues and encouraging the non-communists, who clearly enjoyed much greater credibility throughout the world than did the Chinese, to promote the common position publicly. The Chinese themselves, for example, could not have put their position more clearly than did the Cambodian delegation to the Tricontinental Peoples' Solidarity Conference held in Havana in January 1966, where that delegation is reported to have called on "all countries which love justice and peace to refuse to cooperate, in political, diplomatic, economic and cultural fields, with the US Government and all governments which energetically support its policy of aggression against Indo-China."[8]

Peking apparently also had held even fonder hopes for certain nationalist leaders, particularly presidents Sukarno and Ben Bella and perhaps even Burma's General Ne Win.[9] There were strong indications, both in terms of local political developments and Chinese foreign policy, that Peking was encouraging and saw some hope that certain nationalist heads of state might take the Castro road to Marxism-Leninism and bring their countries into the international communist move-

8 *PR*, 1966, no. 4, p. 24.
9 See the Burmese Communist Party statement in *Peking Review*, 1967, No. 36, p. 20.

ment through a conversion to communism by the national president. Aside from the resounding defeat that such a development would have meant for US policy, the Chinese would have been particularly eager to see such changes in Indonesia and Algeria—in Algeria because of the endorsement and support given to the Algerian Revolution by the Chinese as the model for Africa and because of the obvious importance of that country in African politics; and in Indonesia because of that country's size, geographical location, and general significance in Asian politics. However, Chinese hopes were rather severely dashed by events during 1965—particularly Algerian Defense Minister Boumedienne's successful coup against President Ben Bella in June and Sukarno's decline in stature and influence following the abortive September 30 Movement in Indonesia. By the end of the year, the conversion route to communism seemed to have been at least temporarily closed.

Perhaps the best way to characterize the foreign policy of Communist China during the early 1960s is to say that it was dominated by the interests of the Chinese state, a state committed to both the enhancement of China as a nation and the propagation of the thought of Mao Tse-tung as the interpretation of Marxism-Leninism most suited to modern-day conditions, especially in Asia, Africa, and Latin America. Thus, to discuss Chinese foreign policy in terms of a dichotomy between national interests and those derived from Marxism-Leninism, it seems to me, is relatively fruitless. Many aspects of Chinese foreign policy combined both. I personally tend to agree with those people who feel that to argue about the extent to which Communist China is either "Communist" or "Chinese" is simply not very productive, primarily because the reality of present-day China so inextricably blends the two that the threads of both are lost in the synthesis. Communist China is a radical nationalist state in which the thought of Mao Tse-tung is the national ideology; and like most communist party-ruled states, China tended to be predominantly socialistic at home and nationalistic in foreign affairs. But ultimately, both in domestic and foreign policy, there was a compromising of values and priorities, some of which were complementary and others of which were not. For instance, we can say that Peking showed little concern for advancing the Maoist revolutionary model or even for requiring communist party leadership of revolutions, and that Peking primarily sought to promote revolution in the developing areas in the hope that every move to the left would mean another step in the undermining of support in those areas for China's national enemy, the United States. Yet, on the other hand, we must also admit that change in a leftward direction—revolutionary or otherwise—also implied progression toward the ideological goal of world communism. In any case, Chinese foreign policy, like the foreign policy of many states, was first and foremost concerned with the preservation and security of the state and the development of its power and prestige, be it for national or ideological reasons, or for both.

PART III
THE GREAT PROLETARIAN
CULTURAL REVOLUTION
AND CHINESE FOREIGN
POLICY

At a press conference held in Phnom Penh on the morning of September 18, 1967, Cambodia's Prince Norodom Sihanouk, always sensitive to shifts in the Peking policy line, spoke out against what he saw to be a sharp change in Chinese policy toward Cambodia in violation of the five principles of peaceful coexistence on which the relations between the two countries were supposedly based. He denounced Chinese intervention in his country's internal affairs, and he spoke of the new Chinese policy as having begun in 1966 with the beginning of the Great Proletarian Cultural Revolution.[1]

Sihanouk was not alone in his perception of a drastic change in Chinese foreign policy begun with the cultural revolution. The effects of the new Chinese attitude toward foreign affairs had swept over the countries beyond China's borders in a series of ever-rising waves, from the beginning of the mass movement of the cultural revolution in June 1966, to the crest of that tide of Maoist militance in August 1967, one which left in its wake chaos and violence and a trail of strained, broken, and battered foreign relationships. One by one, in outbursts

[1] For a text of excerpts from Sihanouk's press conference, see *Foreign Broadcast Information Service*, September 21 and 22, 1967.

of ideological zeal, the Chinese press had transformed carefully cultivated foreign friends into rabid enemies and "tools"
of hostile foreign powers, while both at home and abroad militant young Chinese activists had terrorized local communities,
proclaiming their right to proselytize the world for Chairman
Mao. Violent mass demonstrations against foreign diplomatic
missions in China and personal assaults on individual diplomatic representatives had become commonplace, reaching a
high point with the sacking and burning of the British mission in Peking in August 1967. The Chinese seemed to be
striking out at foreigners indiscriminately; and, as some commentators saw it, the violence of the domestic cultural revolution appeared to be spilling over into Chinese foreign affairs.

Characteristic of the new Chinese approach to foreign affairs
was the opening paragraph of a diplomatic note sent by the
Chinese Embassy in Rangoon on July 11, 1967, to the Burmese Foreign Ministry protesting recent anti-Chinese incidents which had occurred in the country: "Chairman Mao is
the very red sun that shines most brightly in our hearts and
Mao Tse-tung's thought is our lifeline. We must warn you
that we will fight to the end against anyone who dares to oppose Chairman Mao and Mao Tse-tung's thought. Anyone
who dares to oppose Chairman Mao and Mao Tse-tung's
thought is hitting his head against a brick wall and inviting
his own destruction."[2] A good example of this kind of attitude
in operation was the incident a month later involving the
Soviet freighter *Svirsk* which had put into the Manchurian
port of Darien to take on cargo. At issue was the unwillingness
of the ship's captain to hand over to Chinese militants a Soviet
seaman who was accused of insulting Chairman Mao by re-
fusing to wear a Mao Tse-tung badge which had been offered
him by Chinese Red Guards. The captain and three crew
members were subsequently jailed by Chinese authorities,
and the ship and its crew were besieged by Red Guards, thereby plunging Sino-Soviet relations to a new low point. The

[2] *PR*, 1967, no. 30, p. 39.

crew was finally released and the ship permitted to sail only after Soviet Premier Kosygin threatened to cut off Sino-Soviet trade if the situation was not quickly resolved.[3]

Although most analysts would probably date the beginning of China's cultural revolution back to autumn 1965, or even earlier to the 1959 Lushan party conference and to the differences arising among CCP leaders over the failure of the Great Leap, incidents of the sort that directly affected Chinese foreign relations did not begin to occur until after the launching of the mass movement of the cultural revolution in mid-1966. Only when the Chinese masses, and especially Chinese youth, were organized to take direct action against Mao's enemies in the party and the government did foreign affairs become directly involved. Although the mass movement is officially said to have begun on June 1, 1966, the full momentum of mass agitation did not break forth until after the Central Committee meeting in August and the publication of its guidelines for the cultural revolution. Then, the Red Guards appeared, and after being received at huge mass rallies by Chairman Mao and his new successor-designate, Lin Piao, they swept forth over the country in search of any sign of "the four olds," "bourgeois reactionaries," or "power-holders taking the capitalist road." Not long afterward, mass attacks against foreign missions in Shanghai and Peking, and political agitation by Chinese militants abroad, caused sharp international repercussions.

Events in the Portuguese colony of Macao in November –December 1966 signaled the beginning of a series of international incidents stemming directly from the cultural revolution. A dispute originally involving a simple matter of obtaining Portuguese permission for school construction on Taipa Island, one of two islands included within the jurisdiction of the colony, resulted in mass demonstrations and riots led by local Maoists in which eight people were killed. Ultimately, the Chinese government became formally involved, and it and local Chinese leftists made specific demands on the

[3] See especially *NYT*, August 12, 13, and 14, 1967.

Portuguese authorities which they were finally forced to accept. On January 29, 1967, the Portuguese governor of Macao signed agreements with both parties, agreeing among other things to pay an indemnity to injured parties and to return to the mainland any refugees who might seek haven in Macao (formerly as many as 200 Chinese a month escaped to the colony). The political significance of the agreements was that the Portuguese all but formally abdicated their authority in the Chinese enclave, and real political power was taken over by local leftists.[4]

Meanwhile, in Peking, Red Guards demonstrated before diplomatic offices and compounds, and insulted the representatives of foreign governments, while Chinese students abroad, recalled to China to take part in the cultural revolution, provoked incidents in several countries on their way home. A clash between Chinese students and Russians in Moscow's Red Square on January 25, 1967, for instance, led to eighteen days of continuous demonstrations against the Soviet embassy in Peking. The Soviet and Chinese press each called for the overthrow of the other government, and for a time it appeared that the tenuous official tie between the two communist powers would finally be snapped. The Chinese siege of the Russian mission was ultimately lifted on February 12, but incidents along the border between China and the Soviet Union and a mutual feeling of extreme enmity continued.

The year 1967 began with yet another upsurge of revolutionary fervor as seen in the so-called January Revolution against party and government authority, during which Red Guard units, usually with the help of the army, began to seize power from provincial party organizations and replace them with new power structures to be called "revolutionary committees." After a brief pause in February, Ch'i Pen-yu, an editor of *Hung-ch'i*, opened the first specific assault on the two men who were said to be leading the opposition to Chairman

[4] The best sources I have found on the Macao incident are the letters written to the Institute of Current World Affairs by Anthony R. Dicks, an institute fellow living in Hong Kong at the time. See letters dated March 18 and July 20, 1967.

Mao, the Chinese head of state Liu Shao-ch'i (called by the Maoists "the top Party person in authority taking the capitalist road" or "China's Khrushchev") and CCP General Secretary Teng Hsiao-p'ing.[5]

The major foreign incident during the spring of 1967 was the erupting of demonstrations, riots, and later strikes and terrorist attacks in Hong Kong. But there, the history of the earlier Macao incident was not repeated, as British authorities took firm measures to contain the spread of the cultural revolution into the colony.

During the worst of the cultural revolution, communist as well as Western countries were made the subjects of brutal and sustained demonstrations. In a common resistance to Maoist onslaughts among diplomats in Peking, Mongolian, Russian, and Yugoslav "revisionists" joined together with British and French "imperialists" to suffer the insults and even physical brutality of shouting Red Guards. Nor were China's non-communist Asian neighbors free from attack.

By mid-summer 1967, Peking appeared to be literally at odds with the world. An incident of one kind or another had strained China's relations with virtually every government in the communist world, except ever-loyal Albania, and with many of the non-communist countries with which Peking had established diplomatic relations as well. Particularly significant was the friction that the cultural revolution had caused in relations with Peking's former friends in Asia (like Nepal, Ceylon, and Cambodia), and the outright viciousness that came to characterize China's policy toward Indonesia, India, and even Burma. A good example of the state of Chinese foreign affairs in the summer of 1967 is the fact that a single issue of the official *Peking Review*, published on July 14, included reports of disputes with eight different countries (Burma, Indonesia, India, Nepal, Ivory Coast, the United Kingdom, the US and the USSR) as well as the United Nations.

The peak of the year's violent activities came in August. After that, the militance of the Great Proletarian Cultural

5 Translated in *PR*, 1967, no. 15, pp. 5–15.

Revolution in terms of its influence on Chinese foreign relations began to subside. As early as September, for example, an
Indian diplomat arriving in Hong Kong reported that the
Red Guard attacks against foreign diplomatic missions had
abated, and that demonstrations were being conducted in a
restrained and "civilized" manner.[6] The cultural revolution
continued and new incidents occurred, but the summer of
1967 was the high point of the influence of the cultural revolution on Chinese international relations, and it was this
year—proclaimed "the year that the great proletarian cultural
revolution won its decisive victory"[7]—in which new patterns
of Chinese foreign policy became most evident.

[6] *South China Morning Post* (Hong Kong), September 19, 1967.
[7] *PR*, 1968, no. 1, p. 43.

8

THE CULTURAL REVOLUTION

By August 1967, the pattern of Chinese support for wars of national liberation described in Part II had been sharply altered. New considerations were being made, and new priorities had been established with respect to Peking's view of the countries of Asia, Africa, and Latin America. For example, the Ne Win government of Burma, a classic case before the cultural revolution of the Chinese pragmatic willingness to put government-to-government concerns before ideological interests, almost overnight in that long, hot summer of 1967 was transformed by the Chinese media from a long-standing friend to an "arch-criminal" composed of "the biggest traitors in Burma" who were committing "fascist atrocities" against their own people and had clearly, therefore, become a legitimate target for attack by Burmese insurrectionists. What had happened? What had changed?

Perhaps it is best to begin with the Maoists' own view of the cultural revolution, its concerns and objectives.

THE CULTURAL REVOLUTION IN THEORETICAL PERSPECTIVE

With the advent of the cultural revolution, the theoretical focus of Chinese policy statements changed abruptly. Through the end of 1965 and before the appearance of the major public manifestations of the cultural revolution in the spring of 1966, Chinese theoretical proclamations regarding foreign policy had been preoccupied with the problem of how revolutionary movements should seek to gain power in the colonial and semicolonial areas of the world, and Mao's contribution to Marxism-Leninism was defined primarily in these terms. In 1966, however, Maoist concerns turned to problems of postrevolutionary development, and how the "dictatorship of the proletariat" should maintain itself in power in a communist party-ruled state and successfully defend itself from attack by "revisionism." Previously concerned primarily with revolutionary strategy abroad, the Maoists by 1966 were looking inward at China, focusing their attention on laying out the proper program for Chinese socialist development to communism.

To illustrate the earlier theoretical focus, let us return to Lin Piao, who, following the Eleventh Central Committee Plenum in August 1966, was elevated to the number two position in the CCP, replacing Liu Shao-ch'i as Mao's successor-designate. Recall that in his essay "Long Live the Victory of People's War!" published as late as September 3, 1965, when the subterranean beginnings of the cultural revolution were already under way, Lin Piao was primarily concerned with foreign wars of national liberation; in the article, he explicitly stated and described the elements of the Maoist revolutionary model. Lin Piao founded his argument on the proposition that the "principal contradiction" in the contemporary world political situation was that existing between the peoples of the countries of Asia, Africa, and Latin America, on the one hand, and "the imperialists headed by the United States," on the other. In terms of this analysis, the United States was designated as the primary enemy of the world revolution and, hence, the principal target for attack. The Soviets were denounced as a secondary enemy, essentially for their lack of support for the revolution and as "betrayers of people's war." "The Khrushchev revisionists," Lin Piao wrote, "fearing people's war like the plague, are heaping abuse on it." "The two [the US and the USSR] are colluding to prevent and sabotage people's war."[1]

In the period before the outbreak of the cultural revolution, then, Mao's primary contribution to Marxism-Leninism was seen to be as that of revolutionary strategist pointing the way for Asian, African, and Latin American guerrillas to gain power. As Lin Piao put it:

Comrade Mao Tse-tung's theory of people's war is not only a product of the Chinese revolution, but has also the characteristics of our epoch. The new experience gained in the people's revolutionary struggles in various countries since World War II has provided continuous evidence that Mao Tse-tung's thought is a common asset of the revolutionary people of the whole world. This is the great international significance of the thought of Mao Tse-tung.[2]

With the beginning of the cultural revolution, however, the theoretical orientation changed. Maoist writers became concerned with a different kind of problem: how to sustain and protect a successful communist party revolution, especially their own, rather than how to make revolution and take over state power in the first place. From a theoretical point of view, the cultural revolution focused on the future development of China, and it involved a debate within the CCP leadership over the priorities to be established to direct that development (political reliability *vs* professional competence in the selection of leaders; moral *vs* material work incentives; continual remobilization of the population *vs* the creation of functionally specialized bureaucratic structures; periodic "great leaps" into the future *vs* cautious and gradual developmental planning; and so forth). Insofar as Mao's ideas relative to the cultural revolution claimed applicability outside of China, they related to the paths that other communist parties might choose to take after they had already won power.

In his attack on the moderates in the CCP leadership who

1 *PR*, 1965, no. 36, p. 10.
2 *Ibid.*, p. 25.

had frustrated his attempt to press China on to a more radical course of domestic development, Mao argued that, from the perspective of Marxist-Leninist theory, class struggle continues after a communist party has won and consolidated power, and even after the party has successfully collectivized the means of production and reorganized the agricultural and industrial labor force. The threat of bourgeois counterrevolution is ever present as the party attempts to build socialism; and if the bourgeoisie (represented by CP moderates or "revisionists") is not completely defeated, that class may regain power and return the country to capitalism as, the Maoists argued, has been done in the Soviet Union.

On May 18, 1967, *Jen-min jih-pao* published an essay attributed to the editorial departments of *Hung-ch'i* and *Jen-min jih-pao* which stated Mao's view of the cultural revolution quite succinctly:

Chairman Mao tells us that the main targets of the revolution under the dictatorship of the proletariat are the representatives of the bourgeoisie who have wormed their way into the apparatus of the proletarian dictatorship, the handful of Party people in authority taking the capitalist road. The contradiction between the handful of Party people in authority taking the capitalist road on the one hand, and the masses of workers, peasants, and soldiers and revolutionary cadres and intellectuals on the other, is the principal contradiction and is an antagonistic one. The struggle to resolve this contradiction is a concentrated manifestation of the struggle between two classes—the proletariat and the bourgeoisie—and two roads, socialism and capitalism. To expose the handful of Party people in authority taking the capitalist road, put before the public and thoroughly criticize and repudiate their revisionist wares, completely refute, discredit and overthrow them—this is the main task that the great proletarian cultural revolution has to accomplish. This is the general orientation of the struggle and we must hold firmly to it.[3]

A later *Jen-min jih-pao* article, a commentary by the authoritative "Observer," made it clear that Mao's view of the cultural revolution applied not only to China but to all CP-ruled

---

[3] Translated in *PR*, 1967, no. 21, p. 11.

states, and that it was a major theoretical contribution to Marxism-Leninism:

In a word, through this great revolution, all revolutionaries have acquired a clearer understanding of the laws of the development of socialist society, the laws of the class struggle in socialist society and the laws of the revolution under the dictatorship of the proletariat. All this is the great result of the fact that our great leader Chairman Mao has penetratingly summed up the historical experience of the international proletarian revolution and the dictatorship of the proletariat, drawing particularly on the historical lessons of the restoration of capitalism in the Soviet Union, and has analysed the contradictions in socialist society, and creatively developed Marxism-Leninism. . . .

Chairman Mao has . . . solved the theoretical and practical questions of carrying on the revolution and preventing the restoration of capitalism under the dictatorship of the proletariat. This is a great leap forward in the revolutionary theory of Marxism-Leninism. It indicates that Marxism-Leninism has developed into a completely new stage, the stage of Mao Tse-tung's thought.[4]

In the period of the cultural revolution, then, Mao Tse-tung's claim to having creatively advanced Marxism-Leninism was made on the basis of his theorizing about postrevolutionary conditions in socialist countries, rather than because of his contribution to communist strategy for gaining power.[5] This did not mean that Mao as revolutionary strategist and military tactician was forgotten or disparaged, but that the Maoist concern with the cultural revolution and the problems it sought to resolve, plus the struggle for power within the CCP leadership, had led to an overriding preoccupation with domestic politics and internal development.

The shift in Maoist theoretical focus had a profound impact on Chinese foreign relations. Among other things, it called for a Chinese reappraisal of the Soviet Union. In the earlier peri-

[4] Translated in *PR*, 1967, no. 24, p. 15.

[5] "Comrade Mao Tse-tung's *greatest* contribution to the international communist movement is his systematic summing up of the historical experience of the dictatorship of the proletariat in China and of the dictatorship of the proletariat in the world since the October Revolution" (emphasis added). "Advance Along the Road Opened up by the October Socialist Revolution," *PR*, 1967, no. 46, p. 11.

od, when making revolution abroad and upsetting the world
political power structure were China's primary foreign policy
concerns, the United States as main support of the world status
quo was designated China's principal opponent, whereas the
Soviet Union was condemned largely to the extent to which
it failed to support Chinese revolutionary objectives or sided
with the United States. With the advent of the cultural revolution, as the Maoists turned their attention inward to problems of their own domestic development, they began to place
a different emphasis on their differences with the Soviet Union. The Soviets were no longer attacked primarily for their
foreign policy shortcomings, but for what the Chinese said
the "traitorous" CPSU leadership had done in the post-Stalin
period with respect to *domestic* policy. Soviet revisionism was
specified largely in terms of decidedly wrong domestic priorities and policies, and the Soviet Union was set up as the negative example of a communist party-ruled state that had sold
out the October Revolution, turned around on the road to
communism, and was working its way back to capitalism. The
Soviet experience stood as a model of what all socialist states
should beware of and avoid.

In pressing forward the cultural revolution, Mao Tse-tung
focused his energy on both theorizing about and bringing to
reality a competing, Chinese model, one that defined what a
truly revolutionary communist party state should look like
and how it should move through the stage of socialism toward
the final communist ideal. In Maoist theoretical terms, the
principal international contradiction was still that between
the United States (increasingly supported by the Soviet Union)[6] and the people of Asia, Africa, and Latin America; but
in the present period, a Chinese domestic contradiction, that
between the representatives of the proletariat and the bourgeoisie within the CCP leadership, had supplanted all inter-

6 For an example of how the Chinese described the Soviet Union as actually
having become a partner in a worldwide counterrevolutionary effort cooperating with the US against China, see "US Imperialism and Soviet Revisionism
Are Backstage Managers of Anti-China Farce," *PR*, 1967, no. 35, pp. 17–18.

national problems in the minds of China's Maoist leaders.[7] Given the Maoist view of the Soviet Union as the prototype of successful bourgeois counterrevolution in a socialist society, an additional and crucially important dimension was added to Chinese hostility toward the Soviet Union as Maoists sought to resolve their domestic contradiction. No longer was the Soviet Union seen simply as an accessory to American imperialist crimes, but now the very nature of the Soviet political and economic system was perceived by the Maoists as presenting a mortal challenge to the future of China. As a result, the USSR replaced the United States as China's Public Enemy Number One, and revisionism superseded imperialism as the primary issue around which both Chinese domestic and foreign policies revolved. The earlier pragmatism characteristic of Chinese foreign relations gave way to a new emphasis on ideology as Maoists, struggling to establish their claims to theoretical orthodoxy, focused their hostility at home and abroad on the Marxist heresy of revisionism.

CHANGING PATTERNS AND PRIORITIES IN CHINESE SUPPORT FOR WARS OF NATIONAL LIBERATION

Although the cultural revolution had begun to make an impact on Chinese foreign policy during the last half of 1966, major changes in the Chinese view of wars of national liberation were not fully evident until 1967. From the beginning of 1966, Peking had seemed to be pressing its anti-imperialist line in the Third World even harder than during 1965. Relations with foreign non-communist governments were still carefully cultivated, as evidenced by official visits during March and April by Liu Shao-ch'i and Ch'en Yi to Pakistan, Afghanistan, and Burma; but the Chinese appeared to be drawing the line between friends and enemies ever more

[7] For example, Lin Piao, in a speech commemorating the fiftieth anniversary of the October Revolution, spoke of Mao's contribution to resolving the question of how to consolidate the dictatorship of the proletariat and prevent the restoration of capitalism as *"the most important question of our time"* (emphasis added). *PR*, 1967, no. 46, p. 6.

sharply. Four countries in Asia and Africa were designated by the Chinese as new targets for revolution during 1966 (see Table 8); but they were all essentially colonies, and their endorsement by Peking did not break with established Chinese practice. Bahrein is an island protectorate in the Persian Gulf under British suzerainty. The white minority government of Rhodesia had long been an object of Chinese contempt; the only reason it had not qualified as a TR during 1965 was a lack of guerrilla activity. And Southwest Africa (controlled by the Union of South Africa) and Spanish Guinea were both unquestionably colonial territories deserving of liberation.[8]

TABLE 8

CHINESE ENDORSEMENT OF NEW TARGETS
FOR REVOLUTION, 1966

Continent	Country
Asia	Bahrein
Africa	Rhodesia
	Southwest Africa
	Spanish Guinea
Latin America	—

SOURCES. Bahrein: *JMJP*, June 20, 1966, p. 6. Rhodesia: *JMJP*, May 5, 1966, p. 6. Southwest Africa: *JMJP*, Dec. 29, 1966, p. 6. Spanish Guinea: *JMJP*, Feb. 18, 1966, p. 4.

However, the new TR's were endorsed with no particular enthusiasm or consistency, in part because of the limited scale of the various armed struggles, and perhaps because China's major imperialist adversary, the United States, was not directly involved in any of the four countries. The thrust of Chinese policy toward the developing world was still firmly anti-US, and Peking seemed to be hoping that one or another of the wars of national liberation might expand to the point of drawing American troops away from Vietnam.

By August 1966, there were signs of change. The directives

[8] Spanish Guinea became independent Equatorial Guinea in October 1968, and in November, that country became the 126th member of the United Nations. *NYT*, November 13, 1968, p. 3.

decided on by the CCP Central Committee at its meeting in the beginning of that month clearly focused Chinese attention on revisionism to the exclusion of imperialism; and earlier calls for a "broadest possible" international front against imperialism had already been somewhat modified. For example, on August 8, at a mass meeting assembled to celebrate the third anniversary of Mao Tse-tung's statement in support of the American Negroes, a prominent slogan displayed at a meeting urged: "People of the whole world, unite to form the broadest *most genuine* united front to overthrow US imperialism."[9] Addressing the same rally, Kuo Mo-jo explained:

It is our primary task at present to form the broadest and most genuine international united front against US imperialism. This front includes the broad masses of the American Negroes and the American people, all the oppressed peoples and oppressed nations of the world, and all the countries and peoples subjected to US imperialist aggression, control, intervention or bullying, *but it absolutely must not include the flunkeys and accomplices of US imperialism.*

He went on to say that these "flunkeys" were

the modern revisionist leading clique of the Soviet Union [which] is vainly attempting to undermine this genuine anti-US united front in a thousand and one ways under the signboard of so-called "united action."[10]

Kuo Mo-jo's comments in part were a reply to urgings by other communist parties that China join with the Soviet Union and the rest of the communist world to take united action in support of Hanoi and the NFL against the US in Vietnam, but his speech also marked the deepening divisions between Peking and Moscow which were to grow progressively wider through the following summer.

Red Guards, surging forth over the Chinese countryside in the autumn and winter of 1966 calling for revolution in the name of Chairman Mao, were matched in militance and energy by their Chinese counterparts abroad. Chinese diplomats

9 *PR*, 1966, no. 33, p. 19 (emphasis added).
10 *Ibid.*, p. 23 (emphasis added).

posted in foreign countries, returning Chinese students recalled from their studies abroad to participate in the revolution, and even local overseas Chinese demanded the right to propagate Mao Tse-tung's thought. Their activities often resulted in mass demonstrations in foreign countries (especially in "revisionist" communist countries and those Asian countries having large overseas Chinese populations), and often riots ensued. It is as yet unclear in every case whether this Maoist missionary activity had been initiated by official instructions from Peking, or whether it resulted from local or individual commitments to Maoism or perhaps from competition among individuals within Chinese organizations abroad who, fearful for their future careers, were each trying to be more Maoist than the next.[11] In any case, once incidents had been provoked, the Chinese government responded vocally in defense of the local Chinese militants, thus prompting a confrontation between Peking and the local government, often with dire consequences for China's foreign relations. In this regard, Chinese reaction to British attempts to quell the riots in Hong Kong were characteristic of the Chinese position during late 1966 and 1967. Hsieh Fu-chih, chairman of the Peking Municipal Revolutionary Committee, speaking at a rally to support Maoist demonstrators in Hong Kong and to protest

[11] C. P. Fitzgerald has interpreted the motivation behind the actions of the Chinese Embassy staff in London as follows: "Chinese diplomats abroad were placed in a very difficult situation by the Cultural Revolution. They learned that at home people like themselves were under attack, denunciation, and sometimes physical assault. Even to ride in an official car had provoked Red Guard rage and violence. In foreign, above all Western capitals, the Chinese staff, although having few contacts among their colleagues or the general population, still certainly lived like diplomats. They dressed in foreign clothes, rode in cars, dwelt in good houses. They mixed, to some extent with 'bourgeois' people, even if only in the course of duty. All this was highly dangerous. At any moment some zealous employee might (and some did) denounce his ambassador as a revisionist, a bourgeois, a secret supporter of Liu Shao-chi. It became essential to make some clear and public demonstration of the purity of their Maoist thinking, and the most obvious way to get this message across, by means of the world press, was a brawl with the London police, the representatives of the bourgeois imperialist regime. A few broken heads and bruised limbs were a small price to pay for demonstrating true revolutionary zeal and complete adherence to the Cultural Revolution." "A Revolutionary Hiatus," *Bulletin of the Atomic Scientists*, February 1969, p. 58.

"fascist atrocities and brutal attacks on Chinese compatriots" by British authorities, declared, "All activities carried out by our compatriots in Hongkong in studying, propagating, applying and defending Mao Tse-tung's thought are their absolute, sacred and inviolable right. There is no ground whatsoever for the British authorities in Hongkong to interfere."[12]

This was also the Chinese position with respect to incidents provoked in Moscow, Macao, Burma, and other countries where Maoist activists sought to convince others, by persuasion or force if necessary, that the philosophy of Chairman Mao was one of universal and immediate significance. Underlining the importance of ideology in China's international relations, *Jen-min jih-pao*'s "Commentator" pointed to the propagation of Mao's thought as the main concern of Chinese foreign policy:

The rapid and extensive dissemination of the great, all-conquering thought of Mao Tse-tung is the most important feature of the excellent international situation today. The world has entered upon a new era which has Mao-Tse-tung's thought as its great banner. The study and application of Mao Tse-tung's thought has become a mass movement on a global scale, of a magnitude and with a far-reaching influence never before witnessed in the history of the development of Marxism-Leninism.[13]

Given this emphasis, the cultural revolution, gaining in intensity through the spring and summer of 1967, brought several important changes in the Chinese view of wars of national liberation. Some changes, such as the endorsement as TR's of formerly friendly governments, were shockingly obvious; others of equal importance were less apparent.

Table 9 lists the six new TR's endorsed by Peking during 1967. In contrast with the new TR's endorsed in 1966, all of these are independent countries rather than colonies. Three countries (Israel, Cameroon, and Ecuador) fall within the earlier pattern of TR selection determined in large part on the basis of a government's official friendliness or hostility

12 *PR*, 1967, no. 22, pp. 51–52.
13 Translated in *PR*, 1967, no. 43, pp. 26–28.

TABLE 9

CHINESE ENDORSEMENT OF NEW TARGETS
FOR REVOLUTION, 1967

Continent	Country
Asia	Burma
	India
	Indonesia
	Israel
Africa	Cameroon
Latin America	Ecuador

SOURCES. Burma: *JMJP*, July 4, 5, and 6, 1967. India: *JMJP*, July 5, 1967, p. 5. Indonesia: *JMJP*, Aug. 18, 1967, p. 5. Israel: *JMJP*, June 6, 1967, p. 1, and *PR*, 1967, no. 26, pp. 55–56. Cameroon: *JMJP*, Jan. 14, 1967, p. 5. Ecuador: *JMJP*, Jan. 14, 1967, p. 5.

toward Peking as described in chapter 6. The endorsement of the three others (Burma, India, and Indonesia) breaks sharply with that pattern. Moreover, during 1965 all three of the countries in this second group were sites of antigovernment armed struggle, but were not endorsed by the Chinese as TR's (see Table 7, p. 178). If we apply updated scales of official hostility and official friendliness to all six of the new TR's (using 1966 trade statistics and United Nations voting returns, and changes in government-to-government relations through the end of September 1967), the differences between the two groups of countries become clearly evident. As Table 10 indicates, Burma, India, and Indonesia rate high on official friendliness and zero on official hostility, whereas Israel, Cameroon, and Ecuador rate zero on official friendliness and between one and three on official hostility.

Let us take the second group (Israel, Cameroon, and Ecuador) first. The Chinese press demonstrated little enthusiasm in endorsing these three countries as targets for revolution except in the case of Israel. For several years, Israel had been the subject of a good deal of Chinese attention; and the Palestine Liberation Organization, which had been actively seeking to organize Palestine refugees and gain the support of the Arab states to mount an attack on the Israeli government, was

TABLE 10

INDEPENDENT COUNTRIES ENDORSED AS NEW TR'S IN 1967, OFFICIAL FRIENDLINESS AND OFFICIAL HOSTILITY TOWARD PEKING

Country	Official Friendliness				Official Hostility			
	Relations with Peking	1966 UN Vote Yes[a]	1966 Trade $75 million[b]	Friendliness Rating	Relations with Republic of China	1966 UN Vote No[a]	Defense Treaty with West[c]	Hostility Rating
Asia								
Burma	x	x		2				0
India	x	x		2				0
Indonesia	x	x		2				0
Israel				0		x		1
Africa								
Cameroon		(abstained)		0	x	(abstained)	x	2
Latin America								
Ecuador				0	x	x	x	3

a *NYT*, Dec. 1, 1966, p. 12.
b *China Trade Report*, December 1967, p. 2.
c Cameroon, defense arrangement with France: *NYT*, Nov. 17, 1967, p. 1, and *CSM*, Apr. 5, 1968, p. 11. Ecuador, defense agreement with the US under the provisions of the Organization of American States.

received with honor in Peking and permitted to establish a diplomatic mission there. Speaking in Peking three weeks before the outbreak of the Arab-Israeli war in June 1967, S. Gerbou, head of the PLO's mission in China, acknowledged both moral and material support from Peking and spoke of his conviction that armed struggle was the only way to liberate Palestine.[14] When the Arab-Israeli conflict actually began, the initial Chinese response was to label it a war of aggression forced upon the Arab people by the United States and its "lackey" Israel.[15] In subsequent statements, the Chinese focused on several points: the US as the source of the war; the USSR as a false friend of the Arabs who failed to intervene when they were being defeated and who ultimately compromised with the enemy, the US, at their expense; and China as the Arabs' only true and reliable ally. The Chinese clearly sought to use the war to win the Arabs away from both the US and the USSR. Later, Chinese statements on Israel began to focus on guerrilla activities against the Israeli occupying forces and to view the confrontation as an armed struggle by the Arabs to liberate themselves from the Jews.[16]

With regard to the other two countries endorsed as TR's in this group, Cameroon had been endorsed by the Chinese as a TR in the past as recently as 1963;[17] but whereas pro-Chinese Afro-Asian groups had occasionally called for the national liberation of Cameroon by armed struggle during the period 1964–1966,[18] the Chinese had not. Only in 1967 did Cameroon return to the list of Chinese-endorsed TR's, and then only briefly; by the end of 1967 it had once again been dropped.[19] It appears that Cameroon was a borderline case as a TR, prob-

14 *PR*, 1967, no. 21, p. 30.

15 *PR*, 1967, no. 24, pp. 10, 11, 39.

16 For a more recent Chinese evaluation, see the *JMJP* "Commentator" article, "Persistence in Armed Struggle Means Victory," translated in *PR*, 1968, no. 21, pp. 33–34.

17 See, for example, the map on p. 14 of *SCCS*, 1963, no. 2.

18 For example, see the resolution with regard to Cameroon passed by the Afro-Asian Writers' Emergency Meeting on July 9, 1966, reported in *PR*, no. 29, p. 39.

19 *JMJP*, December 28, 1967, p. 6.

ably both because of the lack of continuous and widespread armed struggle against the government, and because of the somewhat ambiguous attitude of the Cameroon government toward Peking. For example, on the question of admitting Peking to the United Nations, from 1961 through 1963 Cameroon voted against admission; in 1965 and 1966 (there was no vote in 1964) Cameroon abstained; and in 1967, Cameroon returned to a position of opposing Peking's admission.[20] With regard to Ecuador, however, there had been little ambiguity in its policy toward Peking in recent years. As Table 10 indicates, Ecuador's rating on the official hostility measure was 100 percent and on official friendliness zero. The only apparent reason for Ecuador's not being designated a TR in 1965 and 1966 was the lack of continuing antigovernment armed struggle. However, when the question of admitting Peking to the United Nations was considered in November 1967, after the Chinese had endorsed Ecuador as a TR in January of that year, the government of Ecuador altered a fifteen-year pattern of voting against the admission of Peking to the UN; it broke with its Latin American colleagues on that issue and abstained from voting on all three proposals concerning Peking's admission (the "important matter" question, the resolution to seat Peking, and the proposal to form a committee to study the matter).[21]

The more interesting group of new TR's endorsed by the Chinese during 1967 is the one that includes those countries (Indonesia, India, and Burma) which had earlier been close friends of China and through 1966 continued to rate high on the official friendliness scale and zero on official hostility. Peking's endorsing these countries as TR's in the summer of 1967 clearly broke with the pattern of Chinese policy with regard to wars of national liberation demonstrated in 1965 and 1966. Analyzing changes in Chinese policy toward these

---

20 Lung-chu Chen and Harold D. Lasswell, *Formosa, China, and the United Nations* (New York: St. Martin's Press, 1967), pp. 404–405; and *NYT*, November 29, 1967, p. 4.

21 *NYT*, November 29, 1967, p. 4.

countries serves to highlight and clarify the shifts in policy which have become evident in the period of the cultural revolution. However, each case involves a different sort of relationship with Peking; and given a strict analytical interpretation of all three relationships, probably only Burma could be properly said to be solely a product of the cultural revolution.

Sino-Indonesian relations had been badly strained by the coup attempt of October 1965, and the relationship worsened as the Indonesian Army progressively moved to undermine the power of Peking's two major friends in Indonesia, President Sukarno and the PKI. The army's violent suppression of the PKI and its drive to topple the president, which finally succeeded in March 1967 when Sukarno was formally removed from office and General Suharto put in his place as acting president, coincided with a series of anti-Chinese incidents involving both official Chinese representatives accredited to Djakarta and overseas Chinese residents in the country. Peking vehemently protested these incidents, and relations between the countries were strained to the breaking point. The developing pro-Western orientation of the new government's foreign policy did nothing to lessen the tension. After the fall of Sukarno, the Chinese press described the successor government as a "naked fascist dictatorship," a reactionary kingdom built on top of a volcano of popular hostility;[22] and in July, the *Peking Review* printed excerpts from PKI Central Committee statements, denouncing the earlier "peaceful transition" policy line as revisionism and calling for armed struggle against the Indonesian government.[23] Not surprisingly, the Chinese greeted the outbreak of guerrilla activity in Indonesia in August with enthusiasm, thus qualifying that country as a new TR. In October 1967, official relations were finally suspended when the Indonesian government withdrew its representatives from Peking and the Chinese theirs from Djakarta.

22 *PR*, 1967, no. 13, pp. 30–31.
23 *PR*, 1967, no. 29, pp. 18–22; and no. 30, pp. 13–22.

The case of India was similar in that it involved the deterioration of a former friendly government-to-government relationship, for both India and Indonesia had maintained official diplomatic relations with Peking since 1950. However, the process of disaffection was a slower one in Sino-Indian relations, and it centered on a gradual broadening of differences in their foreign policies beginning in 1957–1958, rather than on a drastic change in government as in the case of Indonesia. Over the years, Peking became increasingly at odds with New Delhi on a variety of important issues: Tibet and India's granting asylum to fleeing Tibetan refugees, which was an early cause of Sino-Indian friction; the Himalayan border dispute and military engagements along that border between the two countries; improving Indian relations with China's two greatest enemies, the US and the USSR; competition between China and India as leaders of the Third World; and in recent years an important difference of opinion regarding the proper basis for agreement and cooperation among the nations of Asia, Africa and Latin America—that is, Chinese-sponsored anti-imperialism *versus* Indian-backed nonalignment. In spite of these important differences and an extremely strained official relationship since the military conflict of 1962, Peking appeared reluctant to endorse India as a TR. In the spring of 1966, the Chinese had welcomed an armed uprising by a Mizo minority group in Assam, but the Chinese press described it as a nationalities problem rather than a symptom of a national liberation war to come.[24]

After the proclamation of the Great Proletarian Cultural Revolution on the mainland several weeks later, however, China's relations with India, as with so many countries during that period, began to deteriorate markedly. By March 1967, the Chinese, commenting on the outcome of the Indian elections, described Congress Party rule as "a still more reactionary government" and predicted a violent future for India: "The Indian people's opposition to the Congress Party is

24 *PR*, 1966, no. 12, p. 28.

growing stronger and stronger and the crisis in which Indian reactionary rule finds itself is more acute than ever. The whole of India is today littered with dry faggots. It is certain that revolutionary flames will rage throughout the vast territory of India."[25] When, shortly thereafter, an armed peasant struggle against landlords in the strategic Darjeeling area of West Bengal (a narrow triangle of Indian territory almost surrounded by Nepal, Sikkim, and East Pakistan, and only sixty miles from China's Tibet), the Chinese greeted the rebellion with a full page of articles in *Jen-min jih-pao*,[26] proclaiming it as the opening of the Indian revolution, to be led by the revolutionary group of the Indian Communist Party along the road marked by Mao Tse-tung to the ultimate national liberation of India.[27] The rising in West Bengal was short-lived; but, subsequent to the peasant rebellion, the Chinese press began to view all armed struggles in India (including both the Mizo movement and a renewed Naga minority insurrection) as component parts of a broad nationwide struggle for national liberation.[28]

Burma, the final country designated as a new TR in 1967, was a unique case in several respects. The Ne Win government in Rangoon had not only maintained a friendly official

[25] *PR*, 1967, no. 13, pp. 29–30.

[26] *JMJP*, July 5, 1967, p. 5.

[27] A great irony in the appearance of a peasant rebellion in West Bengal at this time is the fact that the government whose authority the rebels were challenging was a United Front Government in which the left wing of the Indian Communist Party was the most powerful force. Hence, the rebellion created a confrontation between revolutionary communists on the one hand and communists enjoying state power on the other. When the West Bengal government eventually took action to put down the uprising, it prompted yet another split in the already divided Indian Communist Party. See *NYT*, July 5, 1967, p. 10, and September 5, 1967, p. 9. The most revolutionary group of Indian Communists have subsequently come to call themselves "Naxalites" after the name of the area in West Bengal where the rebellion occurred, Naxalbari. *NYT*, November 26, 1968, p. 4.

[28] For example, see *PR*, 1967, no. 36, pp. 35–36. Also, *NYT*, May 28, 1968, p. 15, reports Indian intelligence sources as saying that the Chinese have been training some of the Naga insurrectionists and are willing to help them "*if the insurgents link their struggle with other anti-Indian movements* in Assam, Manipur and the Mizo Hills" (emphasis added). For a passionate Indian reaction to the Chinese endorsement of the West Bengal rising, see "China in Naxalbari," *China Report*, August–September, 1967, pp. 1–5.

attitude toward Peking in past years, as had India and Indonesia earlier, but the Burmese policy of friendliness toward Peking had not changed up to the very point of the confrontation with the Chinese in June 1967. Moreover, the Chinese themselves had recognized Rangoon's fidelity and had singled out the Sino-Burmese relationship as a model for China's policy of peaceful coexistence with the governments of noncommunist countries. Burma had, after all, been the first noncommunist country to grant diplomatic recognition to the People's Republic of China; and particularly since the Bandung Conference in 1955, relations between the two countries had been cordial and close. The two governments had agreed on a definition of their common 1,300 mile border in 1960; Peking granted an $84 million aid loan to Rangoon in 1961; and in more recent years Ne Win had been honored in Peking, and Chinese leaders had frequently paid official visits to Rangoon. Yet, in a matter of two weeks at the end of June 1967, the product of eighteen years of careful diplomatic efforts on both sides was, perhaps irreparably, destroyed.

The events in Rangoon that led to the disruption in Sino-Burmese relations followed a pattern characteristic of China's foreign relations during 1967, one which had been seen earlier in Moscow, Macao, Hong Kong, and other countries. The incident involved Chinese demands to be allowed to propagate the thought of Mao Tse-tung abroad, followed by hostile, local reaction to Chinese proselytizing activities. In June Chinese school children in Rangoon had begun wearing Mao badges to class, and the Burmese government had responded by ruling that no such political insignia could be worn. When teachers tried to prevent children from bringing Maoist political material into the schools, they were attacked by the students, as were newsmen who arrived to cover the incident; the activists apparently also tore down the Burmese flag and trampled it. Anti-Chinese riots ensued; ultimately an official Chinese economic aid technician was stabbed to death on the Chinese embassy grounds, and at least one hundred overseas Chinese residents in Burma were killed by enraged Burmese.[29] Official Chinese reaction was rapid and harsh. Peking published a statement on June 29 blaming the Ne Win government for the incident and denouncing its "fascist atrocities" committed against China and Chinese living in Burma.[30] On the same day, demonstrations were organized in Peking against the Burmese embassy, which continued until July 3 when Chinese leaders began to call for the overthrow of the Ne Win government and to proclaim their support for the Burmese Communist Party.[31] Thus, in a period of less than two weeks, Peking had changed from Rangoon's friend of some fifteen years to its mortal enemy, renouncing China's friendship with the Ne Win government and designating Burma the latest in a series of new TR's.

Seeking reasons for this abrupt shift in China's policy toward Burma, analysts have pointed to the fact that prior to June 1967 there had been some indication of a softening of Ne Win's determined nonalignment in world politics and isolation from the West, but nonetheless they have had difficulty finding sufficient cause in Burmese domestic or foreign policy, even from Peking's point of view, to prompt such a violent Chinese response. John H. Badgley, a careful student of Burmese affairs, concludes his analysis of the problem by describing the shift in Chinese policy toward Burma as part of a "global tactic" not unique to Burma, but common to China's recent relations with many of her Asian neighbors. Badgley asserts that "local conditions are of no consideration for the theorists in Peking behind the current strategy." In his view, Rangoon did its utmost to accommodate the Chinese, but ultimately Peking "sacrificed everything in the pursuit of the inner logic surrounding the Cultural Revolution and the Red Guard movement."[32]

If Badgley is right, and I think he is, then the ultimate problem comes down to trying to understand this "inner

29 *NYT*, January 30, 1968, p. 14.
30 *PR*, 1967, no. 28, p. 17.
31 *Ibid.*, pp. 18–21.
32 John H. Badgley, "Burma's China Crisis: The Choices Ahead," *Asian Survey*, November 1967, pp. 757–758.

logic," the reasoning behind the cultural revolution as it relates to Chinese foreign policy. Having already discussed individually the several new TR's endorsed by the Chinese in 1966 and 1967, let us attempt now to generalize about the changes that became evident in Chinese foreign policy with respect to wars of national liberation.

First, as we have seen, especially in the case of Burma, foreign governments which in earlier years had enjoyed relatively normal diplomatic relations with Peking were, during 1967, endorsed as TR's in spite of apparently sincere attempts by these governments to maintain friendly ties with China. This shift in policy implies a changing Chinese definition of acceptable behavior on the part of foreign governments, and seems closely connected to a particular sensitivity on the part of the Chinese to actions taken by foreign governments to prevent the propagation of Maoist ideology. Thus, during the cultural revolution, difficulties in China's foreign relations have been especially prevalent in communist countries and in non-communist countries having large Chinese minorities. This has been the case in large part because the Maoists have apparently placed highest priority in their worldwide missionary efforts on the conversion to Maoism of both overseas Chinese and foreign communists.

Second, there has been a major change in the entire Chinese perspective on wars of national liberation. Before the cultural revolution, wars of national liberation were perceived by the Chinese from a very pragmatic point of view; endorsement of a TR was one of a series of possible tactics to be used to help undermine the pro-Western orientation of world politics. Since the cultural revolution, the Maoists seemed to be concerned primarily with the nature and allegiance of the leadership of foreign revolutionary movements and with the strategy they were employing. In other words, the Maoists seemed to become largely preoccupied with the replication of the Chinese revolutionary model, and they appeared to be extremely eager to see Maoist revolutionary strategy prove to be successful abroad.

And, third, a corollary to the second point, there was also a change in the kinds of revolutionary organizations mentioned in the Chinese press in connection with wars of national liberation. Formerly, Chinese articles dealing with foreign revolutions would include favorable interpretations of revolutionary organizations adhering to a wide variety of political orientations. Peking appeared willing to support almost any revolutionary organization, communist or not, and usually favored those organizations that seemed to be taking the most effective action against the established government. Another important consideration in the earlier Chinese view of revolutionary organizations was to emphasize their nationalist character, particularly when a communist party was involved in the movement. The ideal type organization was one patterned on the South Vietnam NFL, a broad national united front including both communists and non-communists. With the cultural revolution, however, this pattern changed. Being successfully revolutionary was not enough; foreign revolutionary movements had also to proclaim their identification with the strategy and general ideology of Chairman Mao in order to receive much attention from the Chinese press. Moreover, whereas the communist character of national front organizations was earlier played down, during the cultural revolution when national fronts were mentioned at all they were usually explicitly described as being under the leadership of a communist party. Thus, although the Chinese had granted several national front organizations diplomatic status in Peking in 1965–1966, by 1967 these organizations were rarely mentioned. When, for instance, the Malayan National Liberation League was mentioned in early 1967, in connection with its eighteenth anniversary celebration in Peking, the Chinese report quoted the league's representative, P. V. Sarma, as describing the national liberation struggle in Malaya as directed not by his own Malayan Liberation League, but by the Communist Party of Malaya.[33]

[33] *PR*, 1967, no. 7, p. 29. An important exception to the new Chinese em-

Throughout 1967, the Chinese appeared hesitant to endorse enthusiastically any revolutionary effort that was not led by self-proclaimed Maoists. TR's were generally treated in the Chinese press in the period of the cultural revolution from the perspective of promoting Maoism for Maoism's sake. Earlier, the Chinese at least allowed for the theoretical possibility of a communist party coming to power by peaceful means; but after 1966 armed struggle was seen as the only way. Lin Piao's essay in September 1965 provided for the possibility of a non-communist party leading a war of national liberation (as had been the case in Algeria); but during the cultural revolution, the Chinese increasingly demanded not only CP leadership but pro-Chinese CP leadership, and revolutionaries were constantly urged to emulate all aspects of the Maoist revolutionary model.[34]

A good example of the effect Maoism, per se, has had on Chinese policy concerning wars of national liberation is the way in which the Chinese press dealt with the much-publicized Bolivian insurrection of 1967. This was the abortive attempt to overthrow the Barrientos government, begun in March 1967, which was led and organized by Ernesto "Che" Guevara and a group of Cuban cadres. The insurrection was launched prematurely when government forces stumbled upon, or were informed about, the rebels' base camp on a farm near Lagunillas. It ended when Bolivian rangers, trained and advised by American Special Forces, succeeded in capturing Guevara and virtually destroying the guerrilla band seven months later.[35] This was also the movement that led to the arrest of revolutionary theorist Régis Debray, who had spent some time with the guerrillas. The revolution itself was something of a test case of Debray's exegesis of the Cuban revolutionary experi-

phasis on explicit communist leadership of revolutionary movements was Peking's treatment of the South Vietnam NFL which remained as before.

34 See for example, the discussion of armed struggles in Laos, Burma, Thailand, and Indonesia in *PR*, 1968, no. 2, pp. 15–24.

35 The five surviving members of the guerrilla band were reported to have crossed the Bolivian border to sanctuary in Chile on February 22, 1968. *NYT*, February 24, 1968, p. 12.

ence (published in an essay called "Revolution in the Revolution?") and the applicability of the Cuban model to other Latin American social and political environments. In looking at the Chinese reaction to these events, one must recall that Bolivia had been explicity endorsed as a TR in 1965; and Che Guevara had been honored in China when he visited there, and his writings on guerrilla warfare had been reprinted in Chinese periodicals as recently as 1964.[36]

The Bolivian insurrection was headlined in newspapers throughout the world, particularly when it appeared that Guevara was indeed leading the movement. When Guevara was captured and killed, the event received even more publicity, and articles praising or denouncing Guevara appeared in the newspapers of virtually every country in the world—every one, that is, except in China. The amazing thing about the Chinese treatment of the Bolivian insurrection and the martyrdom of one of the world's best-known revolutionary heroes is that the Chinese press said almost nothing about the entire affair. In the spring of 1967, the Chinese mentioned in passing that there was guerrilla activity in Bolivia; but as far as I can tell after having searched the *Jen-min jih-pao*, *Peking Review*, and other Chinese periodicals, the name of Che Guevara was never once mentioned during 1967, before or after he was killed. While much of the rest of the world was eulogizing Che Guevara,[37] the Chinese said nothing. The only way a reader of the Chinese press would have known that the Bolivian insurrection, mentioned once or twice during 1967, had been suppressed was that in listings at year's end of continuing revolutionary efforts the Bolivian affair was simply not mentioned.[38]

36 See Guevara's "Guerrilla Warfare: A Means," reprinted in *PR*, 1964, no. 2, pp. 14–21.
37 See, for example, the Soviet eulogy of Guevara in *New Times*, November 1, 1967, p. 28.
38 Bolivia was mentioned briefly as a TR in the spring of 1967, but no details were given (see, for example, *JMJP*, May 12, 1967, p. 6, and *PR*, 1967, no. 18, p. 38). However, during the summer, the Chinese press focused on student and worker strikes in Bolivia rather than on guerrilla activities (*JMJP*, July 4, 1967, p. 5, and August 26, 1967, p. 6). Finally, less than two weeks after Gue-

The lesson to be drawn from the strange disdain with which the Chinese treated the Bolivian insurrection and their odd rejection of a former revolutionary friend, it seems to me, is that between the period when Guevara and his ideas were welcomed in Peking and the time of his insurrectionary adventures and ultimate death in Bolivia in 1967, the Chinese had become extremely sensitive to questions of ideological orthodoxy. Guevara's approach to making revolution in Latin America involved important departures from the Chinese revolutionary model; and Regis Debray, in proposing general revolutionary theory for Latin America, not only departed from the Chinese experience, but also explicitly challenged the contemporary relevance of many of Mao's ideas. Given the particular Chinese sensitivity to ideological questions during the cultural revolution, this kind of a challenge was hardly welcome.[39]

FUNCTIONS OF CHINESE SUPPORT FOR WARS OF NATIONAL LIBERATION

In an attempt to summarize the changes I have been describing in the Chinese view of foreign revolutions since the cultural revolution, it is useful to try to isolate the functions that support for wars of national liberation, both before and during the cultural revolution, have performed for Chinese foreign relations and then to suggest the way in which these functions have changed over time.

---

vera's death in Bolivia, a PR article (October 20, 1967, pp. 28–31) surveying the "revolutionary situation in Asia, Africa, and Latin America" over the past year, mentioned strikes and demonstrations in Bolivia but made no mention of armed struggle at all or any of the events relating to Guevara's capture and death. However, generalizing about revolution in Latin America, the article concluded that true Latin American revolutionaries had shown that "armed struggle can be victorious *only if it follows the revolutionary line pointed out by Chairman Mao*" (emphasis added).

39 For an extremely harsh critique of Régis Debray's theory of revolution, see the Chinese reprint of an article published by the Marxist-Leninist Communist Party of France, in PR, 1968, no. 30, pp. 11–12. During 1965 Sino-Cuban relations had soured (see Daniel Tretiak, "China and Latin America," Current Scene, March 1, 1966), and this strain in relations continued through 1967, no doubt also contributing to Chinese skepticism concerning the largely Cuban-sponsored revolutionary movement in Bolivia.

It seems to me that Chinese support for wars of national liberation have generally performed four principal functions: first, to punish governments that do not prove amenable to adopting pro-Peking foreign policies and to serve as a threat to those governments that might waver or be undecided in their future foreign policy orientations (it is in this sense that TR endorsement is the "cutting edge" of the anti-imperialist united front); second, to educate and to help mobilize world public opinion by involving the imperialist enemy in situations in which he will show his "true" character through militarily intervening to suppress wars of national liberation, thus providing instructive examples for the development of a more radical world political consciousness; third, to further radical change in the countries of the developing world through the overthrow of existing governments by revolutionary movements; and, finally, fourth, to seek to replicate the Chinese revolutionary experience and to help legitimate Mao Tsetung's claim to having devised a revolutionary strategy suitable to conditions for all of the Third World.

In 1965, these functions were given precedence pretty much in the order in which they are listed: the first appeared to be most important; the second and third were also given a good deal of consideration; but the fourth was given little more than lip service. During that year, the Chinese use of support for wars of national liberation might be best described as an international power politics approach. Peking would support virtually any revolutionary organization, regardless of its leadership, ideology, or strategy, if the Chinese wanted to oppose the government which that organization was seeking to overthrow. On the other hand, Peking would not support pro-Chinese CP-led revolutionary organizations adopting the correct Maoist ideological and strategic policies if the Chinese did not want to oppose the government which that organization was attacking.

With the cultural revolution, and especially during 1967, the Chinese appeared to have reversed the priorities ascribed to the four functions of TR support. The former fourth-place

function became first: during 1967, replication of the Chinese
revolutionary model and the propagation of Mao's thought
were given highest priority even when support for such activities might jeopardize vital Chinese economic and political
relationships abroad (for example, with Hong Kong and Burma). The second and third functions received about the same
priority as before; support for wars of national liberation was
still viewed as an important means of bringing about radical
change and encouraging social and political change in general, although the Chinese position had become so dogmatic
during the cultural revolution that Chinese efforts both to
mobilize world public opinion and to overthrow existing governments probably suffered as a result. The greatest change,
however, occurred with regard to the former first priority
function, use of support for wars of national liberation for the
purpose of positively influencing the policies of foreign governments. This function during 1967 became barely operational at all. As before, TR endorsement during 1967 was
used to punish governments whose policies were viewed by
the Maoists to be unacceptable (the cases of Indonesia, India,
and Burma will all bear this out), but the threat posed by
such endorsement cannot during this period be said to have
been one conducive to the modification of official policies to
coincide with Peking's more closely. The demands the Chinese made of foreign governments had become simply too
extreme to be acceptable to any government. The case of
Burma illustrates quite clearly that the Maoists were insisting
that the Rangoon government allow the Chinese to intervene
in Burmese internal affairs in a manner that could hardly be
tolerated by any government. When the Portuguese colonial
government of Macao was forced to accede to similar Maoist
demands, it in effect surrendered its authority in that colonial
territory.

As a result of this major change in priorities, the earlier
objectives of TR endorsement and support—opposition to
the US and the world status quo and the promotion of radical
change—suffered. In this sense, Chinese policy with respect to

wars of national liberation became in large part dysfunctional. Many aspects of the new Chinese attitude toward foreign affairs were detrimental to the attainment of earlier proclaimed objectives. TR endorsement lost its capability to gain diplomatic leverage, and Peking's focusing on the Maoist credentials of foreign revolutionary movements and publicizing their allegiance to Chairman Mao made for unnecessary difficulties. Emphasizing the pro-Peking communist element in foreign revolutionary movements tended to make for problems of cohesion within the united front, to help legitimate government suppression of the movement, and to diminish the nationalist appeal of the organization. Moreover, requiring that foreign revolutionary organizations declare their allegiance to Maoism at the very time when China had become particularly unpopular throughout the world because of the violence of the cultural revolution, plus encouraging these organizations to publicly support the antigovernment activities of *Chinese* militants (overseas Chinese, Chinese students, or official Peking representatives) in their own countries, could not help further alienating the organizations from local popular support.[40]

AN ASSESSMENT

The remaining question to be answered, of course, is why these changes occurred in Chinese foreign policy. As we have seen, Chinese foreign policy during the cultural revolution evidenced a persistent preoccupation with internal concerns to the detriment of foreign affairs, and it responded vehemently to aspersions cast upon Chairman Mao or his teachings.

[40] Another adverse effect of the cultural revolution on foreign revolutionary movements is best exemplified by reports of the domestic strife that broke out within the Burmese Communist Party. In the process of implementing its own cultural revolution, the BCP apparently went to violent extremes in which some party members were tortured and killed. A *NYT* correspondent in Mandalay reported that among those killed as the result of conflict within the party were three of the eight-member BCP politburo including the party chairman Thakin Than Tun. *NYT*, November 1, 1968, p. 5. A later dispatch from Rangoon indicated that the chairman's body had been recovered by the Burmese government. *NYT*, November 29, 1968, p. 2. Chairman Thakin Than Tun's death is confirmed by *PR*, 1969, no. 13.

Moreover, there was a demonstrated willingness on the part of the Foreign Ministry, if not to initiate in foreign countries proselytizing activities which were very likely to create grave diplomatic incidents, then at least to support firmly the initiators of such activities after an incident had occurred, even when such support might place important national interests in grave jeopardy.

Such a foreign policy orientation, in combination with the other shifts in foreign policy discussed earlier, clearly points to the great importance of the relationship between domestic affairs and foreign policy during the period of cultural revolution. Actually, Chinese foreign policy during 1966–1967 appeared to have become little more than a reflection of domestic events and the struggle going on within China's borders. During this period, Peking seemed to be making foreign policy primarily for the purpose of helping to deal with domestic problems, rather than in an attempt to seek political or economic advantage abroad.

There is little doubt that part of the motivation behind attacks on foreign embassies and ambassadors in Peking and the convening of mass rallies to protest the actions of foreign powers was based on a desire to bolster the Maoist attempt to win popular support, the assumption being that antiforeignism contributes to national unity. Also, charges of treason have been leveled against political opponents, it seems, in large part to mobilize nationalist sentiment against them and for Mao, as well as to undermine foreign alternatives to the Maoist program for Chinese domestic development.

There has probably also been a significant element of frustration in the brutal treatment foreigners received in the Chinese capital, a lashing out at the available foreign target because of the frustrations accumulating from months of "making revolution" without ever really "seizing power." As Charles Mohr, Hong Kong correspondent for the *New York Times,* has pointed out, the Chinese put into practice a double standard on the question of diplomatic immunity: Chinese diplomats abroad must be allowed the right to propagate freely the thought of Mao Tse-tung, but foreign diplomats in Peking might be physically assaulted and their houses burned if the governments they represented did not behave as the Chinese thought they should.[41]

Moreover, to an extent we are not yet fully aware of, foreign policy issues were no doubt injected into the dispute between the rival factions, and the Maoists may have been placed under extreme pressure to live up to their proclaimed revolutionary ideals in the realm of international politics. If this were the case, the question of the continued existence of two foreign colonies on Chinese territory (Macao and Hong Kong) and the previous failure of Peking to support publicly the revolutionary effort of the Communist Party of Burma would have been among the most sensitive issues that could be raised by Mao's opponents, because of their graphic illustration of the great disparity between theory and practice in earlier Chinese foreign policy. If this were true, it would at least partially explain the drastic change in Chinese policy toward these areas.

Perhaps more significant, there is increasing evidence that, during the zenith of cultural revolution activism in the summer of 1967, the foreign policy decision-making process in Peking was not only divided and in dispute, but also the Foreign Ministry had at least partially lost control of both policy-making and policy implementation abroad. Often as not during the summer, the Foreign Ministry seemed to be responding to events initiated by others (whether they were Chinese activists abroad or Red Guard demonstrators in Peking), rather than taking initiatives itself. Also, in the months from May through August 1967, Red Guard militants apparently at times virtually took over the Foreign Ministry and ran it under their direction. Following the violence of August when the cultural revolution began to moderate, Maoists charged that left-wing extremists within the Red Guard movement had misled the revolution and taken actions in both domestic and foreign affairs that went far beyond the objectives of the

41 *NYT*, August 25, 1967, p. 7.

Maoist campaign. The rigidly dogmatic quality of the foreign policies devised and implemented during the summer would lend support to the argument that they were indeed conceived by militant true believers, extreme Maoists who lacked the chairman's pragmatism and who were, as a result, often more consistently and inflexibly Maoist than Mao himself.[42]

Finally, and most important, Chinese foreign policy during 1966 and 1967 can be best understood, it seems to me, as a Maoist attempt to use foreign events and the reaction of people abroad to help legitimate and support Mao Tse-tung's claim to power in China. The principal characteristics of Chinese foreign policy during the period would tend to support this contention: emphasis on the replication of the Maoist revolutionary model abroad at the expense of the interests of the actual revolutionary movements the Chinese claimed to support; unrelenting attacks on Moscow and the extremely heightened Chinese sensitivity to everything that the Soviet Union represented; and attempts by the Chinese press to portray the proselytizing efforts of Chinese abroad as indications of a universal acclaim for the ideas of Chairman Mao. In a sense, what has been reported as the "spilling over" of the cultural revolution into foreign affairs has in part been the result of a conscious effort by the Maoists to use foreign policy to gain domestic advantage.

That is not to say that Mao has purposefully sought to create diplomatic incidents and make enemies of most of the more important governments of the world. This is unlikely. Some attacks on foreign governments—such as that on the Soviet Union—have clearly been intentional; but other international difficulties have resulted from what seem to be unintended, but perhaps unavoidable, effects of the cultural revolution on Chinese foreign affairs. For example, the Maoists, having unleashed a violent mass attack on the status quo at home, could not fail to give at least some encouragement to

[42] For an excellent analysis of the influence of Red Guard rebels on the Foreign Ministry during the cultural revolution, see Melvin Gurtov, "The Foreign Ministry and Foreign Affairs in China's 'Cultural Revolution,'" RAND Corporation Memorandum RM-5934-PR, March 1969.

Maoist adherents making revolution abroad, even when the cultural revolution abroad, as at home, often got out of hand and created difficult problems for the leadership in Peking.

A broader question necessarily involved in attempting to understand the changes in Chinese foreign policy that occurred in 1966–1967 is that of the relationship of foreign policy in general to the cultural revolution. For example, were there important foreign policy issues dividing Mao and his opponents? And, more importantly, who has been in control of Chinese foreign policy in the past? Should the shift in Chinese foreign policy in 1966–1967, for instance, be understood as the result of Mao's taking control of the Foreign Ministry from a more moderate Liu Shao-ch'i, or what?

Here interpretation is most difficult, particularly because there is so little reliable information available concerning the inner operations of the Foreign Ministry and how and by whom foreign policy decisions have been made. To begin with the question of foreign policy issues in the cultural revolution, Donald Zagoria in his book *Vietnam Triangle* argues convincingly that at least three important foreign policy issues divided the CCP leadership in 1965: policy toward the Soviet Union, how to deal with the US in Vietnam, and questions relating to China's national defense strategy.[43] Zagoria sees three factions within the party leadership which he labels "hawks," "doves," and "dawks." The hawks are professional military men like the subsequently purged army chief of staff Lo Jui-ch'ing, who wanted to adopt a harder policy against the US in Vietnam, but at the same time favored softening the dispute with the Soviets for the purpose of cooperating strategically against the US and gaining the military equipment necessary to modernize the Chinese armed forces. The doves were the so-called revisionists, who called for a diminishing of the conflicts with both the US and the USSR, so that China could more effectively occupy itself with problems of implementing "rational" economic development at home. The third faction

[43] Donald S. Zagoria, *Vietnam Triangle* (New York: Pegasus, 1967), chapter 3.

was the Maoists, which Zagoria called "dawks" because they were somewhere in between on the issues. The dawks were not as militant as the hawks on Vietnam—they wanted to maintain an activist anti-US posture but they didn't want to involve China in a war with the US—yet they demanded that China be vigorously antirevisionist at home and abroad, meaning that the Maoists were at odds with both the other factions on the question of better relations with the USSR. The Maoists further opposed the regularization and modernization of the army (they favored a "people's army" on the guerrilla warfare pattern); they were adamantly opposed to the "rationalization" of the economy (they favored social mobilization economics); and they generally argued that China should pursue militantly anti-US and anti-Soviet policies abroad though not take too many chances of involving China in a war with either, depending meanwhile on a people's war defensive strategy for the Chinese homeland rather than one which would rely on modern weapons obtained from the Soviets or developed by the Chinese themselves. Zagoria concludes that the Maoists or dawks ultimately defeated the challenges presented by both factions insofar as they related to foreign policy issues.[44]

Since the publication of Zagoria's book, the Chinese press has made more specific charges against some of Mao's opponents, especially Liu Shao-ch'i, on questions having to do with foreign policy.[45] Liu Shao-ch'i is generally accused of the crimes of revisionism—of being a dove. The Maoists claim that Liu favored the "liquidation of struggle" with both the US and the USSR, was lacking in support of revolutionary efforts in the developing world, and encouraged the Communist Party of Burma to give up its struggle against the Ne Win government.[46] The Chinese have also reprinted more specific and damaging charges against Liu made by foreign revolutionar-

44 *Ibid.*, p. 67.
45 See, for example, the attack made on Lo Jui-ch'ing largely with regard to issues involving the modernizing of the army and China's defensive strategy, in *PR*, 1967, no. 48, pp. 11–16.
46 "Along the Socialist or the Capitalist Road?" *PR*, 1967, no. 34, pp. 10–18.

ies, particularly with regard to policy toward Indonesia and Burma;[47] but the Maoists' own indictments have remained rather general on foreign policy questions. However, it should be emphasized at this point that, all in all, foreign policy issues have played a relatively minor part in accusations made against virtually all of Mao's major opponents.

Implicit in the allegations made against Liu Shao-ch'i— especially those made by the foreign writers—is the proposition that at least some aspects of the earlier pragmatism in Chinese foreign policy were the result of Liu's revisionist influence. The charges imply that Liu successfully opposed Mao's better judgment in at least some areas of foreign policy in the period before the cultural revolution. For example, the Maoists seem to be saying that, had it not been for Liu Shao-ch'i's revisionism, Peking would have supported the Communist Party of Burma throughout its extended attempt to overthrow the Rangoon government, and the CCP would have rejected as revisionism the PKI's earlier "peaceful transition" approach to taking power in Indonesia.

By and large, I think that these implications are false—and perhaps somewhat cynical as well. I think that it is likely that Liu Shao-ch'i and other relative moderates in the CCP leadership generally argued for less militant foreign policies; but in the period since the failure of the Great Leap in 1959, when the men now under attack by the Maoists apparently did have a very substantial influence on Chinese *domestic* policy and were able to prevent the implementation of new Maoist initiatives, the Maoists seem to have maintained their control over Chinese *foreign* policy. It seems to me that the accusations which the Maoists have made against their opponents on foreign policy issues relate, first, to opposition positions taken by these men at various times in the past but successfully defeated by the Maoists and, second, to cynical attempts by the

47 See, for example, Ibrahim Isa, "A Great Victory for the World's Revolutionary People," *PR*, 1967, no. 47, pp. 16–20; and Thakin Ba Thein Tin, "Burmese People's Revolutionary Armed Struggle Is Bound to Triumph," *PR*, 1967, no. 36, pp. 19–24.

Maoists now to blame their opponents for past failures or inconsistencies in *Maoist*-determined foreign policy.

Several points tend to support such an interpretation. First, while Chinese domestic policy in the period 1961–1965 had been quite moderate, providing, for example, for individual private plots and offering material incentives for increased production, Chinese foreign policy grew increasingly radical, thus implying that Mao had remained in control. The Sino-Soviet dispute deepened sharply during the period, and Peking's anti-imperialist line in relations with the countries of the developing world hardened. Moreover, Mao Tse-tung was personally identified with foreign policy during the period, especially from 1963 to 1965, when virtually all of his substantive public statements were directed to foreign policy matters; and the statements which he made articulated the official foreign policy line.[48]

Second, although major aspects of Chinese foreign policy were in dispute during the period, the Maoists successfully defeated their challengers, as Zagoria has shown for the 1965–1966 period. The dispute in foreign policy affairs had essentially been one in which Mao's opponents had challenged his control of policy-making, and failed. Burma is a possible, but unlikely, exception. If the accusations that the Communist Party of Burma makes—and the Maoists print—that pre-1967 Chinese relations with Burma resulted from Liu's anti-Maoist influence on Chinese foreign policy are true, then this interpretation must also be true for the period before 1961. If so, the logical, but very doubtful, inference to be drawn is that Liu Shao-ch'i has been responsible for Sino-Burmese relations virtually since the founding of the People's Republic because, as John Badgley has pointed out, Chinese friendship for the Rangoon government, and avoidance of the Communist Party of Burma, have had a long history.[49]

[48] See the comments concerning past foreign policy in the communique of the Eleventh Plenum adopted on August 12, 1966, in *PR*, 1966, no. 34, pp. 6–8.

[49] John H. Badgley, "Burma and China: Policy of a Small Neighbor," in A. M. Halpern, ed., *Policies Toward China: Views from Six Continents* (New York: McGraw-Hill, 1965), pp. 303–328.

Third, if Mao's opponents had been in charge of China's foreign relations, then the men directly responsible should have been prime targets for attack by Maoist activists and early victims of the cultural revolution. Chou En-lai and Ch'en Yi, the Foreign Minister, were clearly as involved in foreign policy matters as Liu Shao-ch'i, and probably more so. Yet, during 1966 and 1967, although both were sometimes attacked, they did not lose their positions; moreover, they were defended by members of the Cultural Revolution Group itself, such as the group's chairman Ch'en Po-ta.[50] Also, following the Ninth Party Congress of the CCP in April 1969, when ambassadors were once again being posted abroad by the Chinese government, the very first ambassador to be sent out from Peking, to assume the vitally important position in Albania, was Keng Piao, the man directly responsible for Peking's close relationship with Rangoon when he was Chinese ambassador to Burma in the years 1963–1967!

Fourth, if Liu Shao-ch'i really had been implementing a "revisionist" foreign policy prior to the cultural revolution, once the cultural revolution was under way and the revisionists thrown out of office, why wasn't there a more positive and effective change in policy? Taking Burma once again as an example, why didn't Peking's attitude toward Rangoon change in the summer of 1966 instead of delaying until June of 1967? More importantly, why did the final change in Chi-

[50] Additional data support the contention that compared with other areas of the Chinese government, those organizations having specifically to do with foreign relations have come through the cultural revolution relatively well. For instance, in Donald Klein's recent study, "The State Council and the Cultural Revolution" (CQ, July–September 1968, pp. 78–95), we find that the data reported on those four ministries and commissions most involved in international relations in the State Council (Foreign Ministry, Foreign Trade Ministry, Commission for Cultural Relations with Foreign Countries, and Commission for Economic Relations with Foreign Countries) indicate that (1) the heads of all four organizations have either not been criticized at all, or criticized and later rehabilitated during the cultural revolution; (2) all four organizations seem to be currently functioning in the sense that leaders of these organizations had appeared as recently as February 1968 in their organizational roles; and (3) in no case with regard to the four organizations did half or more of the total of minister and vice-ministers become inactive because of cultural revolution generated attacks.

na's Burma policy come only after the Rangoon government had suppressed efforts to propagate the thought of Mao in the country? It seems clear that if the Maoists had actually seized control of a formerly revisionist-dominated Foreign Ministry and chosen to implement new policies designed unequivocally to support revolution against imperialist and reactionary governments everywhere, they certainly could and would have taken earlier and more decisive action than the Chinese Foreign Ministry actually did. For example, rather than waiting for events abroad to demand action by Peking, the Maoists could have given firm support to the Burmese Communists from the outset and, if they chose, could have been rid of the British colonial government in Hong Kong in a matter of weeks.

Finally, events on the mainland since the high point of the cultural revolution in August 1967 tend to indicate at least a temporary return to patterns of precultural revolution foreign policy. There has been an easing of demonstrations against foreign diplomatic missions in Peking, and conflicts with foreign governments have been avoided. More significant, Maoist activists responsible for some of the more extreme incidents of the summer have been denounced, and in some cases their activities have been seen by the Maoist leadership to have been so deviant and unacceptable that they have been purged from positions of power.[51] Also, there has been a renewed emphasis on government-to-government relations in Chinese diplomacy, best exemplified by the new commitment to help construct a railroad link between land-locked Mali and Guinea, the implementation of a similar agreement with Tanzania and Zambia, and even the resumption, in the autumn of 1967, of relatively normal ties with the British colony

---

[51] Particularly prominent among those attacked for their extremist influence on Chinese foreign policy operations were Wang Li, former member of the Central Cultural Revolution Group, and Yao Teng-shan, former charge d'affaires in Indonesia when the Chinese Embassy was under constant attack there, and reputed temporary "Foreign Minister" during the extremist takeover of the Foreign Ministry in August 1967. For an interesting discussion, see Melvin Gurtov, "Foreign Affairs in China's 'Cultural Revolution'."

of Hong Kong. Once again, Peking seems to be concerned
with preserving and improving the very sort of relationship
that characterized Sino-Burmese relations for so many years
before the cultural revolution.

What is perhaps also surprising is the fact that some aspects
of China's foreign relations were not too greatly affected even
by the worst of the events of 1966–1967. Chinese foreign trade
was obstructed by transportation tie-ups in the hinterland
and loading difficulties caused by cultural revolution activities
in China's ports; but throughout the period, China continued
to trade with the capitalist countries of the West, and in some
cases this trade increased.[52] Moreover, during this time, there
were no Chinese-initiated breaks in diplomatic relations with
non-communist or revisionist communist governments as
might have been expected. Five countries did break their official ties with Peking during the two years (Central African
Republic, Dahomey, and Ghana in 1966; and Tunisia and
Indonesia in 1967); but in all cases the ultimate decision to
end or suspend the relationship seems to have come from the
other side, and in every case except Tunisia, these disruptions
of diplomatic relations followed directly from changes of government in the other country. Generally speaking, those areas
of China's foreign relations not appearing to be directly related to the ideological questions around which the dispute
revolved were often ignored by the events of the cultural
revolution.

Also, in spite of all the talk about supporting revolution
and propagating the thought of Mao Tse-tung during 1966
and 1967, Chinese endorsement of and support for wars of
national liberation were carried on within the same instru-
mental framework and for some of the same basic reasons as
before. Even during the cultural revolution, and in spite of
Maoist claims to be seeking the best interests of all peoples of
the world, the Chinese did not support foreign revolutions

---

52 For example, China's imports from West Germany increased sharply during 1966 and 1967, from a total of $79 million in 1965 to $206.5 million in
1967. *China Trade Report*, September 1968, p. 2.

primarily for the purpose of liberating the "oppressed people" of the countries of Asia, Africa, and Latin America as they claimed, but rather to advance objectives based on the perceived needs of the Chinese state. TR endorsement was still determined principally on the basis of a Chinese assessment of a foreign government's official policy with respect to China and China's world objectives. In 1965, the thrust of Chinese foreign policy was anti-imperialist and particularly anti-US, hence the Chinese conception of acceptable foreign government behavior was defined in terms of these concerns. By 1967, the cultural revolution at home had brought ideology to the fore, and antirevisionism and the propagation of Mao's thought had attained highest priority in Maoist considerations. A new definition of acceptable and unacceptable behavior had been adopted, but the means of punishment for noncompliance remained the same. When confronted by proselytizing Maoists, foreign governments that suppressed them became subject to possible punishment by being endorsed as targets of revolution. Burma, again, was the classic example. The title of a front-page *Jen-min jih-pao* editorial, written in response to the Ne Win government's prohibition of Maoist proselytizing, clearly indicates the reason for the endorsement of Burma as a new TR; the editorial is entitled "The Ne Win Reactionary Government Is Courting Doom by Madly Opposing China."[53] Burma was not endorsed as a target for revolution to help further the interests of the Burmese people—or even the interests of the Communist Party of Burma which had been fighting the government for nineteen years by that time—but because Ne Win had opposed China and activities that those people who were in control of the Foreign Ministry at the time deemed vital to their immediate concerns.

When, sometime in the future, the full story of the cultural revolution is told, probably what will be found most characteristic of the violent summer of 1967 will be the fragmenta-

[53] *JMJP*, July 10, 1967, p. 1.

tion of power and the generally anarchic state of both Chinese domestic politics and foreign affairs at the time. "Power seizures" in the Foreign Ministry and actions taken by unauthorized extremists will probably be said to have produced most of the more damaging effects on China's foreign relations.

But Chinese foreign relations were hardly uppermost in Mao Tse-tung's mind during those months as he pressed forward his final great effort to put China firmly on the road toward the fulfillment of his dream. Whether, as most analysts suspect, the Great Proletarian Cultural Revolution will ultimately be viewed as the last gasp of an idealistic old revolutionary having outlived his usefulness in the society he brought into being, or whether, as Mao hopes, it will be seen as the beginning of something new, pointing the way to societies of the future and to progress beyond the so-called "modernized" societies of today, only the future can say.

CONCLUSION

During the cultural revolution, what appeared to be changes in earlier patterns of Chinese foreign policy did not so much represent a new foreign policy as they reflected the precedence of domestic concerns over international interests and the price the People's Republic of China had to pay in international terms for attempting to resolve crucially important domestic problems in the manner Mao Tse-tung chose. In a sense, during this period, the Maoist leadership was trying to withdraw from and shut out international affairs. By autumn 1967, Peking had called home all its ambassadors posted abroad except two; and no major Chinese leader made a trip abroad in the entire two-year period after the Great Proletarian Cultural Revolution actually got under way in the autumn of 1966. Moreover, the chaos that characterized many aspects of China's foreign relations was not so much the result of a conscious effort to radicalize foreign policy as it was the by-product of domestic divisions of power and conflicting policies pursued by a diversity of groups including the Foreign Ministry, Red Guards and militant Chinese students at home and abroad, overseas Chinese radicals, and local Chinese authorities in border provinces.

Given the nature of the cultural revolution, it is not surprising that it had such a profound impact on Chinese foreign relations. The cultural revolution involved a very fundamental dispute within the CCP leadership, not just over policy, but concerning the system itself and the purposes it should be designed to serve. Specifically, there seemed to be a very basic difference between Mao and Liu Shao-ch'i over what the primary task of the social system should be. Liu seemed to be emphasizing economic output; Mao appeared most concerned about the system's human product. This is not to say that Liu cared nothing at all about the cultural ideal of the selfless New Man, but rather that he placed other priorities first (primarily those that would serve to speed the modernization of the Chinese economy). He seemed to be saying that human values and the socialization of the population of China in the Maoist ethic did not so much relate to the social system at large as they did to the schooling of Chinese youth, political "study" or ethics classes, periodic campaigns, and self-cultivation. Mao, on the other hand, seemed to be preoccupied with the causal relationship between social structure and individual behavior, and the behavioral consequences of performing certain kinds of social roles. In effect, he seemed to be saying that what a man is (what he believes, how he thinks, and how he behaves) is not simply determined by what values a child is taught at home and in his school, but, at least equally important, is fundamentally influenced by his everyday experience in the roles he performs in the social system. In other words, Mao seemed convinced that bureaucratization and professionalism would undermine his attempt to inculcate attitudes emphasizing egalitarianism, altruism, and dedication to the community, which he felt should have first priority. Mao seemed to be arguing that China's future and its hopes for greatness rested above all on the successful creation of the New Man, and the social system should be structured primarily for the purpose of insuring that it would help socialize the people of China in this cultural ideal. In Mao's view, to modify the system for the purpose of attaining improved economic performance in the short run, if it should work to the detriment of the long-run socialization function, was to miss the whole point of making revolution in the first place, and was to misunderstand the meaning of true greatness and how it is attained. For Mao, greatness meant not simply an industrialized economy, a high rate of growth in GNP, or major power status in international politics. Rather, it had many dimensions and, most importantly, it had to be founded (as was the revolution to win state power in the first place) on the active support of a mobilized population demonstrating the attitudes and behavior characteristic of the Maoist New Man. Mao seemed deeply worried that the CCP had won the battle (winning state power in 1949) only to lose the war (in laying the foundations for a New China), and he was determined to go to virtually any extreme to put China on the right road to the future.

Hence, the cultural revolution represented a life-and-death struggle for Mao's vision of the good society. Under the traumatic conditions of widespread strife produced by this conflict, it was indeed not surprising that manifestations of the domestic struggle should so greatly disrupt China's foreign relations.

Seen from another perspective, in spite of the Maoist revolution under way within China's borders and the emphasis on revolutionary rhetoric in Chinese statements regarding international affairs, actual Chinese behavior in foreign relations evidenced no greater concern for the welfare of foreign peoples and revolutionary movements than it had in the period before the cultural revolution began. In fact, Chinese agitation abroad during this period probably harmed local revolutionary efforts much more than it helped them. Moreover, Chinese policy even during the cultural revolution continued to focus on the official attitude toward China of foreign governments rather than on domestic conditions within the individual countries.

The reasons for these consistencies in the Chinese approach to international politics even through a period of extensive and profound domestic turmoil are, I think, readily discernible. In spite of the fact that China is the most revolutionary major power on the globe and regardless of Peking's persistent claims to seek and support the liberation of all oppressed peoples throughout the world, Chinese leaders, like the leaders of any state, must establish priorities for political action. In this regard, communist internationalism to the contrary notwithstanding, the CCP's primary constituency—one is tempted to say its only constituency—is the 750 million people of China; and the task of creating, developing, and defending a viable society within the boundaries of the People's Republic is the overriding first priority. Like it or not, Peking must in its foreign relations deal with other countries primarily as states and governments. The Chinese have attempted and continue to attempt to penetrate beyond the state exterior to maintain contacts with different groups within the population of foreign countries by means of communist party contacts and "people's diplomacy." But, by and large, most of the benefits to be derived from international intercourse almost inevitably involve foreign governments (beneficial trade relations, advantageous diplomatic alliances, security arrangements with neighboring countries to protect vulnerable borders, and the like). As a result, Peking probably cares little more, for example, whether Thailand becomes communist than Washington cares if it becomes democratic. In both cases, these concerns are secondary to the primary interest in the foreign policy of the Thai state and what this means for either Chinese or American interests in the immediate area. For both Peking and Washington, the "betterment" of the life of the Thai people through the imposition of either's value system on Thailand is of relatively low priority and is probably in the end sought more for the purpose of helping to legitimate the value system at home than because of any altruistic concern for the livelihood of the Thai people.

It is obvious that entirely different conditions apply in international relations than in domestic politics. The special context of international politics demands a commitment to state self-interest if societies are to survive. To attempt to treat the world as one's primary constituency would be utopian in the extreme and almost inevitably doomed to failure. Moreover, real social revolution can only be carried out and maintained—as the Chinese themselves say—by the people of a given society and not by foreigners (except perhaps as the result of a prolonged foreign occupation, as in the case of the US in Japan after World War II or the Soviets in Eastern Europe, although the outcomes of both experiments now seem to be somewhat in question). Ultimately, it seems that there is really no such thing as a fundamental community of interests between the Chinese Communist Party and the communist party or revolutionary movement of any foreign country, no matter how Maoist it proclaims itself to be. Each revolutionary movement, in China and abroad, must be concerned primarily with its own people, with its own constituency. Foreign revolutionaries looking for assistance from the great centers of revolution in the present era (Moscow, Peking, Hanoi, and even Havana) can safely count on those states to do only that which is in their own self-interest to do and no more. Consolidating and defending a revolution in one country is job enough, and most likely only those revolutionary efforts abroad that have a direct bearing on the interests of the revolutionary state are likely to receive much attention.

By the end of 1969, it was still unclear what new directions Chinese foreign policy might take. Lin Piao, in his report to the Ninth Party Congress in April 1969, perhaps provided some clues of things to come in his assessment of the international situation;[1] and in the latter half of the year, the possibility of an outright war with the Soviet Union loomed large in China's international perspective, in spite of negotiations between the two countries begun in Peking in October. Regarding Peking's relations with the Third World, the countries on the very fringes of the prevailing conception of the international united front—like Burma, Cambodia, and even India and Indonesia—would bear special attention as bell-

[1] See particularly Lin's analysis of major world contradictions. *PR*, 1969, no. 18, p. 31.

wethers of future developments. In theory, the Great Proletarian Cultural Revolution continued, while in practice,
reconsolidation seemed to be the order of the day. The Chinese leadership appeared to be laying the foundations for yet
another new departure in Mao's determined journey into
the future.

REFERENCE MATERIALS

BIBLIOGRAPHICAL NOTE

The general perspective in terms of which this study was conceived owes much to my training at Berkeley and to the influence which my professors at the University of California have had in shaping my perception of contemporary China. Uppermost among their published work, I feel particularly indebted to the late Joseph R. Levenson, *Confucian China and Its Modern Fate*, Volume I (Berkeley and Los Angeles: University of California Press, 1958), for his psychological insights concerning the process of modernization in China and the crucial problem of identity; to Chalmers Johnson, *Peasant Nationalism and Communist Power: The Emergence of Revolutionary China, 1937–1945* (Stanford: Stanford University Press, 1962), for his exploration of the social roots of the communist revolution, the revolution's winning of popular support, and the role which the Japanese invasion played in its ultimate success; and, finally, to Franz Schurmann, *Ideology and Organization in Communist China* (Berkeley and Los Angeles: University of California Press, 1968), for his elucidation of the dynamic of the post-1949 Chinese political system.

Generally speaking, the entire study is based primarily on research in periodical literature from both Chinese and other sources. However, the outline of the history of China's foreign relations which appears in the introduction is drawn largely from secondary sources. In most cases, I depended on the standard works in the field: A. Doak Barnett, *Communist China and Asia: Challenge to American Policy* (New York: Vintage, 1960); V. P. Dutt, *China and the World: An Analysis of Communist China's Foreign Policy* (New York: Praeger, 1966); Allen S. Whiting, *China Crosses the Yalu: The Decision to Enter the Korean War* (New York: Macmillan, 1960); A. M. Halpern (ed.), *Policies Toward China: Views from Six Continents* (New York: McGraw-Hill, 1965); Donald S. Zagoria, *The Sino-Soviet Conflict, 1956–1961* (Princeton: Princeton University Press, 1962); William E. Griffith, *The Sino-Soviet Rift* (Cambridge, Mass.: MIT Press, 1964), and *Sino-Soviet Relations, 1964–1965* (Cambridge, Mass.: MIT Press, 1967); Tang Tsou, *America's Failure in China, 1941–1950* (Chicago: University of Chicago Press, 1963); and Robert Blum, *The United States and China in World Affairs* (New York: McGraw-Hill, 1966). The entire history of Chinese foreign relations from 1949 to the present, however, is currently undergoing a probing reassessment, particularly as regards China's relations with the two superpowers, the United States and the Soviet Union. Two significant contributions to this reevaluation which have already been published are John Gittings, "The Origins of China's Foreign Policy," in David Horowitz (ed.), *Containment and Revolution* (Boston: Beacon Press, 1967); and David Mozingo, "The Maoist Imprint on China's Foreign Policy," in *China Briefing* (Chicago: University of Chicago Press, 1968). Others are forthcoming.

Part I, Revolution in Theory, is based very largely on Mao Tse-tung's published writings: the four volumes of his *Selected Works* (Peking: Foreign Languages Press, 1961–1965) as well as earlier versions of some essays included in that collection, such as *Hsin min-chu chu-yi lun* [On new democracy] (Liberation Association, 1940); his important *On the Correct Handling of Contradictions Among the People* (Peking: Foreign Languages Press, 1960); Mao's major statements on foreign affairs in the years 1963–1964 collected in *Ch'uan shih-chieh jen-min t'uan-chieh-ch'i-lai ta-pai mei-kuo ch'in-lueh-che chi ch'i yi-ch'ieh tsou-kou* [Peoples of the world unite and destroy the American aggressors and all running dogs] (People's Press, 1964); and other works authored by Mao which have appeared in Chinese periodicals.

In analyzing Chinese revolutionary theory, I found it not only imperative to study Chinese theorists—especially Mao and Lin Piao's "Long Live the Victory of People's War!" (*Peking Review*, 1965, no. 36)—but also found it extremely useful to read other contemporary revolutionary theorists. In this connection, I felt that the following were the most instructive: Frantz Fanon, *Studies in a Dying Colonialism* (New York: Monthly Review Press, 1965), and *The Wretched of the Earth* (New York: Grove Press, 1963); Che Guevara, *Guerrilla Warfare* (New York: Monthly Review Press, 1961); Régis Debray, "Revolution in the Revolution?" (*Monthly Review*, July–August 1967); as well as Che's diary of the abortive Bolivian uprising of 1966–1967 which appeared in *Ramparts* (July 27, 1968), and a collection of criticisms of Debray's thesis written in light of the Bolivian revolutionary failure, "Regis Debray and the Latin American Revolution" (*Monthly Review*, July–August 1968). For an extremely perceptive commentary on making revolution in modern, industrialized America, see Free (Abbie Hoffman), *Revolution for the Hell of It* (New York: Dial Press, 1968).

Periodicals formed the main resource base for parts II and III of the study. Of those periodicals published on the Chinese mainland, I relied principally on *Jen-min jih-pao* [People's daily], generally the most authoritative Chinese daily; *Peking Review*, the indispensable English language weekly; and *Shih-chieh chih-shih* [World knowledge], the best single Chinese periodical on foreign affairs, which unfortunately suspended publication in mid-1966 as a result of the cultural revolution. Other mainland periodicals from which materials were drawn are: *Hung-ch'i* [Red Flag] the party theoretical journal; *Hsin-hua yueh-pao* [New China monthly]; *China Pictorial*; *China Reconstructs*; *Evergreen*; *People's China*; and *Kung-tso t'ung-hsun* [Bulletin of activities].

As for periodicals published outside of the People's Republic, many of those published in Hong Kong were extremely useful. These include: the United States Consulate press translation series *Current Background*, *Extracts from China Mainland Magazines*, *Survey of China Mainland Magazines*, and *Survey of the China Mainland Press*; the independent weekly, *Far Eastern Economic Review*, and that magazine's *China Trade Report*; as well as *China News Analysis*, *China Mainland Review* (recently ceased publication), and the *South China Morning Post*.

Finally, with regard to periodicals published in other areas of the world, I relied heavily on two American newspapers, *New York Times* and *Christian Science Monitor* (Boston); and I found other useful material in *China Quarterly* (London), *Monthly Review* (New York), *Peace, Freedom, and Socialism* (Prague), *New Republic* (Washington, D.C.), *New York Review of Books, Journal of Asian Studies* (Ann Arbor), *Atlantic* (Boston), *Foreign Affairs* (New York), *Survey* (London), *Africa Today* (Denver), *San Francisco Chronicle, El Moudjahid* (Algiers), *Pacific Affairs* (Vancouver, Canada), *Ramparts* (San Francisco), *New Leader* (New York), *Problems of Communism* (Washington, D.C.), *World Politics* (Princeton), *Bulletin of the Atomic Scientists* (Chicago), *Asian Survey* (Berkeley), *China Report* (New Delhi), *New Times* (Moscow), *Orbis* (Philadelphia), and *Mozambique Revolution* (Dar es Salaam).

Several mainland documents, published on an annual basis, also provide important data for the student of Chinese foreign relations: *Jen-min shou-ts'e* [People's handbook]; the *Shih-chieh chih-shih nien-chien* [World knowledge yearbook]–*Shih-chieh chih-shih shou-ts'e* [World knowledge handbook] series; *Chung-hua jen-min kung-ho-kuo t'iao-yueh chi* [Collected treaties of the People's Republic of China]; and *Chung-hua jen-min kung-ho-kuo tui-wai kuan-hsi wen-chien chi* [Collected documents on the foreign relations of the People's Republic of China]. A recent publication in the Harvard Studies in East Asian Law series, Douglas M. Johnston and Hungdah Chiu, *Agreements of the People's Republic of China, 1949–1967: A Calendar* (Cambridge: Harvard University Press, 1968), draws upon several of the items listed above, in addition to a wide variety of other sources, for the purpose of compiling a list of all agreements between China and foreign countries during the first eighteen years of the People's Republic. This volume as well should serve as a major aid to students of China's international relations.

Some readers might be interested in further comment on sources consulted for my interpretation of the attempted coup in Indonesia of October 1, 1965. In analyzing the Indonesian question, I used primarily the Chinese press; the *New York Times* and the *Christian Science Monitor; Far Eastern Economic Review*; Tarzie Vittachi, *The Fall of Sukarno* (New York: Praeger, 1967); John Hughes, *Indonesian Upheaval* (New York: David McKay, 1967); and several shorter analyses, such as Daniel S. Lev, "Indonesia 1965: The Year of the Coup" (*Asian Survey*, February 1966, pp. 103–110); Donald Hindley, "Political Power and the October 1965 Coup in Indonesia" (*Journal of Asian Studies*, February 1967, pp. 237–249); Ann Ruth Wilner, "The Communist Phoenix and the Indonesian Garuda: Reflections on Cyclical History" (*World Politics*, April 1967, pp. 500–520); and David Mozingo, "China's Policy Toward Indonesia," in Tang Tsou (ed.), *China in Crisis*, Volume II (Chicago: University of Chicago Press, 1968). Two more recent studies were particularly helpful: Guy J. Pauker, "The Rise and Fall of the Communist Party of Indonesia" (RAND Corporation Memorandum RM-5753-PR, February 1969); and Roger K. Paget, "The Military in Indonesian Politics: The

Burden of Power" (*Pacific Affairs*, Fall and Winter 1968, pp. 294–314).

In conclusion, the sources which I found especially useful in assessing the impact of the Great Proletarian Cultural Revolution on Chinese foreign relations, in addition to the press and press translations, were: Chalmers Johnson, "China: The Cultural Revolution in Structural Perspective" (*Asian Survey*, January 1968, pp. 1–15); the articles by Michel Oksenberg, Carl Riskin, Robert A. Scalapino, and Ezra F. Vogel in *The Cultural Revolution: 1967 in Review* (Ann Arbor, University of Michigan Press, 1968); Chu-yuan Cheng, "The Roots of China's Cultural Revolution: The Feud Between Mao Tse-tung and Liu Shao-ch'i," and Frank N. Trager, "Sino-Burmese Relations: The End of the Pauk Phaw Era," both articles appearing in *Orbis* (Winter 1968); John H. Badgley, "Burma's China Crisis: The Choices Ahead" (*Asian Survey*, November 1967, pp. 753–762); the essays by Uri Ra'anan and Donald Zagoria in Tang Tsou (ed.), *China in Crisis*, Volume II (Chicago: University of Chicago Press, 1968); and, finally, Melvin Gurtov's study, "The Foreign Ministry and Foreign Affairs in China's 'Cultural Revolution'" (RAND Corporation Memorandum RM-5934-PR, March 1969). The most thoughtful and provocative interpretation of the cultural revolution I have seen is a book I came upon only after this study was already in press: Robert Jay Lifton, *Revolutionary Immortality: Mao Tse-tung and the Chinese Cultural Revolution* (New York: Vintage, 1968).

INDEX